FINDING McLUHAN

FINDING McLUHAN

The Mind / The Man / The Message

EDITED BY JAQUELINE McLEOD ROGERS /

TRACY WHALEN / CATHERINE G. TAYLOR

University of Regina Press

Printed and bound in Canada at Friesens.

Cover and text design: Duncan Campbell, University of Regina Press.
Copy edit: Dallas Harrison
Index: Patricia Furdek
Cover photo: Source image by Michael Erard. Mcluhan portrait by Wayne Miller, from Magnum Photos, NYC64776 (W00000/01)

Library and Archives Canada Cataloguing in Publication

Finding McLuhan : the mind, the man, the message / edited by Jaqueline McLeod Rogers, Tracy Whalen, Catherine G. Taylor.

Includes bibliographical references and index.
Issued in print and electronic formats.
ISBN 978-0-88977-374-5 (bound).—ISBN 978-0-88977-375-2 (paperback).—
ISBN 978-0-88977-383-7 (pdf).—ISBN 978-0-88977-385-1 (html).

1. McLuhan, Marshall, 1911-1980--Criticism and interpretation. 2. Mass media criticism. 3. Mass media and culture. I. Rogers, Jaqueline McLeod, 1956-, author, editor II. Whalen, Tracy, 1970-, editor III. Taylor, Catherine, 1954-, editor

P92.5.M3F52 2015   302.23092   C2015-901669-X   C2015-901670-3

10   9   8   7   6   5   4   3   2   1

University of Regina Press, University of Regina
Regina, Saskatchewan, Canada, s4s 0A2
tel: (306) 585-4758 fax: (306) 585-4699
web: www.uofrpress.ca

The University of Regina Press acknowledges the support of the Grants to Publishers program, made possible through funding provided to Creative Saskatchewan by the Government of Saskatchewan through the Ministry of Parks, Culture, and Sport. We acknowledge the financial support of the Government of Canada through the Canada Book Fund for our publishing activities. We acknowledge the support of the Canada Council for the Arts for our publishing program. This publication was made possible through Culture on the Go funding provided to Creative Saskatchewan by the Ministry of Parks, Culture and Sport.

With thanks and love to my family,
Hartley Anne Rogers, Morgan Leigh Rogers,
and Warren Rogers
—JAQUELINE McLEOD ROGERS

For Alec, with love
—TRACY WHALEN

With thanks and love
to my partner, Janice Ristock
—CATHERINE G. TAYLOR

CONTENTS

SECTION 3: SPACE / PLACE / TOOLS

SECTION 4: POLITICS / SEX / RELIGION

SECTION 5: LEGACY / MEMORY / IMAGINATION

ACKNOWLEDGEMENTS

An endeavour such as this warrants many thanks. In 2010, the editors of this volume convened a conference at the University of Winnipeg, Marshall McLuhan in a Post Modern World: Is the Medium Still the Message? We drew a small group of international scholars and invited two keynote speakers, Robert Logan and Douglas Coupland. We were joined in organizing this event by Linda Dietrick from the Department of Languages and Literatures, whose idea it was to build the conference around McLuhan. The conference was generously sponsored by the Languages and Cultures Circles of Manitoba and North Dakota, an association recently disbanded after a fifty-year history of bringing scholars from midwestern Canadian and American universities together to discuss language matters. We also received funding from the Dean's Office at the University of Winnipeg, the Department of Rhetoric, Writing, and Communications, and the Department of Languages and Literatures. The success of the conference encouraged us to put out a call for proposals addressing the question of how McLuhan currently fits into a variety of interdisciplinary scenes.

During the editing of this collection, the University of Winnipeg also provided funding to support several student research assistants who helped with formatting the reference lists and contacting contributors.

We would like to thank the reviewers, who provided detailed feedback, identified sources to explore, and indicated directions to pursue, all of which resulted in better essays. We would also like to thank our contributors, who have been patient over what has been a protracted period of manuscript preparation.

Tracy and Catherine would like to extend special thanks to Jaqueline, who kept the project moving forward not only through her intellectual leadership but also by carrying out the lion's share of organizational work and correspondence.

Jaqueline would like to thank those whom she interviewed for the final section of the book. Michael McLuhan was immensely helpful in sharing a picture of his father at the height of his career as a family man. Eric McLuhan was able to recreate the context of his father's thinking and point to key terms and concepts worth another look. Douglas Coupland was extremely generous in discussing some of the challenges and pleasures of writing a McLuhan biography.

Finally, we would like to thank the University of Regina Press for its support and help. Thanks to Director Bruce Walsh, Senior Editor Donna Grant, and Acquisitions Editor Karen Clark, who was efficient, decisive, and always encouraging in offering suggestions for getting the manuscript to press. Thanks, too, to Dallas Harrison for his careful eye while editing the final copy.

MARSHALL McLUHAN:
TRANSFORMATIONS / ADAPTATIONS

Jaqueline McLeod Rogers and Tracy Whalen

What makes Marshall McLuhan (1911–80) a figure of interest in the twenty-first century? Over the past decade, there have been increasing references to McLuhan and his media theories as scholars in a variety of fields account for the ways in which new communication technology is influencing scholarly identities and practices and altering how knowledge is made and communicated. The figure of McLuhan as a renowned international public intellectual has also been reanimated in the imaginations of many Canadians by Douglas Coupland's biography, published in 2009. McLuhan is an attractive theorist for non-media specialists not only for his prescient observations but also for his ability to provide clear models or patterns. What he tells us about the history of the telegraph, for instance, continues to explain the social history of many communication devices. As an innovation in 1844, the telegraph served no prescribed purpose and was used as a toy, a device for play, yet with rapidity "the instant all-at-onceness and total involvement of the telegraphic form" led to huge social changes, such as the forming of a collective organization for newsgathering in 1848 as the basis of the Associated Press (*Understanding Media* 339–40). It is easy to transfer McLuhan's broader point—that initially we misunderstand and misapply devices that quickly go on to change our identities and lives—to explain recent developments, such as the global adaptation to the cell phone, which has changed for many of us from frivolity to ever-at-hand extension.

Many people recognize phrases such as "the global village" and "the medium is the message," and the concept of "hot" and "cool" media, even if they are not entirely clear about their meanings. But aside from these contributions to the vernacular—which have infiltrated mainstream discourse even if they convey inchoate rather than precise formulations—there is increasing recognition across the academy that the world anticipated and foretold by McLuhan makes sense of the world that we now inhabit. This collection addresses the question of how media and mediation processes have changed in the thirty years since his death, with an eye to how such developments and networks offer extensions of mediated practices that adhere to or depart from his predictions about technological changes and futures. It explores his enduring commitment to questions of adaptation and transformation and responds to his call to actively participate in understanding technologies.

We imagine this collection as appealing to generalists and interdisciplinary scholars, and this sense of readership has guided the shape of the introduction as well as the selections featuring different voices, themes, and refractions of McLuhan's thinking. We want to make McLuhan a salient figure—both as polymath and as intellectual architect—to those encountering him for the first time or re-encountering and re-evaluating him. In naming our audience and establishing rhetorical awareness, we are guided by a goal that responds to his commitment to formal cause, defined in one formulation as "the 'ground' that gives rise" to outcomes (McLuhan and McLuhan, *Media and Formal Cause* 89). Although "formal cause" is something of a vexed and complex term, it is possible to say what it is not—linear, empirically based, deterministic, and singular. Our imagined reader is the formal cause of this collection, running parallel to the motive that inspired McLuhan's own intellectual productivity, according to his son and frequent co-author Eric, who says "that it is the reader, individual and together, that is the formal cause of [any given] book" (McLuhan and Zhang 442). Frequently, McLuhan referred to writing for an audience who needed to become aware of media, to assume agency over technology, as he insisted with characteristic dramatic metaphor: "[I]t seems to me the best way of opposing it is to understand it, and then you know where to turn off the buttons" (*Video McLuhan*). Contemporary readers living in the high-speed, technologized world that he predicted might be more aware than readers of his time of this affliction, and for this reason they stand to benefit from and possibly extend his insights as new forms of media and attendant somnambulisms emerge.

Reading McLuhan today is different from reading him in the 1960s and 1970s, when most of his influential work was published. The world has changed—and changed in many of the ways that he foresaw. The word *prescience* is often invoked by current commentators who have witnessed the cultural shift from print-world individuality to networked "all-at-onceness" that McLuhan predicted; such an assessment is voiced, for instance, in a recent review by architect and editor Nancy Levinson: "Print culture, for so long the indispensible agent of intellectual life, now seems to have been not inevitable and essential but contingent. As the eerily prescient Marshall McLuhan put it in *Understanding Media*: 'It is the framework that changes with each new technology, and not just the picture within the frame'" (156). Apart from the explanatory power of his ideas in contemporary times, readers now have a better vocabulary for understanding the sometimes inchoate patterns that he admitted were difficult to articulate. In *The Global Village: Transformations in World Life and Media in the 21st Century*, published in 1989, his co-author Bruce Powers expresses the candid hope that twenty-first-century readers, with their experiential, conceptual, and linguistic tools, might find McLuhan penetrable where earlier audiences were puzzled:

> He said that the sons and daughters of "the flower chil-
> dren" would transform the world because they would find
> words to translate what had been ineffable to their par-
> ents. The ineffable to McLuhan was what was dimly seen
> at Woodstock and Haight-Ashbury—that the entire world
> was in the grasp of a vast material and psychic shift be-
> tween the values of linear thinking, of visual proportional
> space and that of the values of the multi-sensory life, the
> experience of acoustic space. . . . It needs a completely new
> frame of reference. McLuhan provides one. He presents it
> in a triad of new terms: visual space, acoustic space, and
> the tetrad. (ix)

Although concepts of synchronicity, polyvocality, and interactiv-
ity are the currencies of much theorizing, they were not when Mc-
Luhan was writing, so his task was not only to explore patterns
shaping human experience and expression but also to find words
to capture and represent the concepts that he had in mind.

But on another level, emerging terminologies create roadblocks
to understanding McLuhan. Sometimes the language that he uses
is out of sync with current usage—for example, his "electronic"
or "electric" world is "digital" or "virtual" to us. Apart from language differences, the culture of technology and communication
that he observed has changed in many ways, as he knew it would,
describing the only thing constant as "change itself" (McLuhan
and Nevitt, "Argument" 1). Although he was a prescient thinker, it
often takes work to adapt his ideas to a range of phenomena, many
of which were not in existence during his lifetime, and to make
sense of his always-evolving lexicon, in flux as the words that he
favoured not only accrued layered meanings during his lifetime
but also have since fallen into disuse.

THE MIND

As a rhetorician, McLuhan acknowledged the participatory role
of the addressee in making and extending meaning, which explains his disavowal of dialectics, understood as empirically

driven content indifferent to audience. In the interview included at the end of this collection, Eric McLuhan says that his father was "rhetorical from start to end," a position that he elaborates in an interview elsewhere:

> Those familiar with rhetoric know well that adaptability is the essence of that science. The aim of the doctus orator is to be able to address any audience on any occasion about any subject and to produce any desired effect on that audience. That is the essence of oratory is transformation of the audience. Whereas the aim of dialectic is to change the mind of the hearer, that of rhetoric is to change the hearer himself [sic]. Rhetoric, then, is always fundamental to media study. (McLuhan and Zhang 454)

Understanding McLuhan as a rhetorician sheds light on some of his central yet often misunderstood approaches. He viewed technologies "as rhetorical tropes we use to express and enhance our humanity, and can therefore be read and analyzed for their cognitive, social, and cultural effect" (Morrison n. pag.). He was not simply resisting thoroughness and depth by casting his ideas in the form of aphorisms or by offering them as discontinuous probes and percepts. His methodology followed from viewing knowledge as contingent and transforming, in a world that offers no proof in the arts or sciences but probable foundations—similar to what rhetoricians such as Walter Fisher and Wayne Booth understand as the logic of "good reasons" often narratively understood.

Equally important, McLuhan opposed the fragmentation or disciplining of knowledge into fields, arguing from the medieval trivium that rhetoric and grammar should trump dialectics— philosophical and proof-based reasoning—though such linear and empirically fashioned reasoning came to the fore in Gutenberg's time (Gordon 104). McLuhan made frequent references to his commitment to combining the arts and sciences against the drive for specialization that accompanied the print age, arguing that such a division "becomes increasingly problematic, especially as more people spend more and more time in exclusively human-made environments" (Anton 2). His own academic life was filled with rich partnerships and cross-disciplinary studies: trained and accomplished as a literary scholar, he turned media and cultural analyst by working closely with anthropologists, urban theorists, physicists, and artists, among others. He welcomed interdisciplinarity as a contemporary turn, noting that we have "become integral and inclusive again, after centuries of dissociated sensibilities" (*Understanding Media* 334). Although rhetoric might have been his guiding framework, and though he is often cited as a founding presence in media studies, his themes are thoroughly interdisciplinary and thus appeal to readers with different disciplinary affiliations.

Scholars and students of rhetoric might be especially struck by the ways in which McLuhan's commitment to studying everyday discourse resembles current moves to examine a widening range of private and public rhetorics. McLuhan studied political speeches, forms of popular literature, advertisements, and visual images—going so far as to consider the influence of non-literate everyday technologies such as the lightbulb and fashion—for their power to persuade us and define the discourse through which we live our lives. Those in art history and criticism might recognize the terms "figure" and "ground," which McLuhan adapted to encourage us to reframe and defamiliarize our usual perceptions in order to train ourselves to see and sense more of the world as it is and not merely as we have been habituated to regard it.

Of interest to contemporary linguists is the currency of McLuhan's recognition of the non-transparency of language, one of our earliest communication technologies. Embedded in his aphorism that "the medium is the message" is his belief that underlying the abstractions of language are "percepts" that shape our sense of the world based on sensory perceptions. Listening to poetry, we do not find meaning but look for images and listen for rhythms in an act of sensory perception that engages the whole body. Sociologists might be drawn to his sense of urgency that we understand how experience is mediated by everyday technologies to avoid what McLuhan referred to as "motivated somnambulism" (*Culture Is Our Business* n. pag.). With the unprecedented speed of change, he was particularly concerned that young people might "turn on, tune in, drop out," adopting a "stop the world I want to get off" stance (McLuhan, Hutchon, and McLuhan, *City as Classroom* 165). Theorists of education and those in the field of medicine might also locate points of interest in his oeuvre and our collection. Here Doug Brent traces some of McLuhan's epistemological interests and applications, while Catherine Jenkins applies McLuhan's theories to developments in health-care technology.

Cultural studies scholars might be called to reconsider McLuhan as a valuable theorist of time and spatial relations, in many ways anticipating the spatial and mobilities turn in theorizing orientation and identity. Any such reconsideration must take place against the residual bias created by Raymond Williams, who dismissed what he considered to be McLuhan's "technological determinism"—a frequent if misguided critique of someone now understood as arguing that we are not mere consumers but active producers of media (Cavell 222), captured in McLuhan's own inimical phrasing: "There are no passengers on Spaceship Earth. We are all crew" (quoted in Vallero 367).

Apart from recognizing his cross-disciplinary appeal, some of his themes have interdisciplinary application. For example, his work with the body and the senses prefigures broad-based models, referred to as the "bodily turn" and "sensory revolution" (Howes 11). McLuhan was intensely interested in the effects of media on the senses, conceiving of the senses as ratios among the five-sense sensorium. Whereas oral culture synthesized human sensory perception (e.g., the acoustic, haptic, and visual), alphabetic print culture privileged the visual, a dominance unseated by an electronic age that again invites multisensory experience. McLuhan's insights about the senses touch on contemporary scholarship examining how we know our world through sensation, an interdisciplinary field of study that spans the sciences, social sciences, humanities, and art studies (e.g., Bacci and Melcher; Howes). McLuhan's interest in the sensorium started with embodiment, beginning with the five senses and extending into explorations of the nervous system, bodily sense, and other external networks. These preoccupations make McLuhan relevant within the context of the bodily turn in academic scholarship. Questions of human subjectivity, embodied consciousness, cultural inscription, and performativity have been taken up by feminist scholars, phenomenologists, political scientists, historians, sociologists, biologists, and cultural theorists, among many others. These various traditions are informed by figures such as Maurice Merleau-Ponty, Judith Butler, Michel Foucault, and Gilles Deleuze and Felix Guattari. McLuhan's notion of acoustic space, as James Scott argues in this volume, can be productively understood through the lens of neuroscience, which offers a means of understanding embodied cognition and the dynamic interplay between body and environment, one in which bodies adapt to changing physical environments and are transformed in the process.

Performance, a predominant theme in recent thinking about identity and representation, is yet another framework for understanding McLuhan, self-consciously performative in the sense of being drawn to the dramatic and the playful. Many readers will recall, for instance, the famous cinematic moment in Woody Allen's *Annie Hall* when McLuhan steps out from behind a playbill and tells a pompous Columbia University professor that "You know nothing of my work. . . . How you ever got to teach a course in anything is totally amazing." Will Garrett-Petts, discussing the film in terms of the artist's statement, observes that "few would argue that McLuhan's presence in the scene doesn't make a difference" (65, 66). This *deus ex machina* moment epitomizes the presence of McLuhan as a medium for the many selves that he would perform in his books, letters, lectures, conversations, and even marginalia. As Yoni Van Den Eede points out in this volume, McLuhan was influenced by growing up in a family that prized public speaking. His mother was a teacher of elocution; the dramatic monologue and oral recitation were likely staples of McLuhan's upbringing. Rhetorical performance can be traced in his dramatic voice, particularly the apocryphal tones concerning the technology and the media that might drown the unsuspecting sailor. This dramatic quality was not engendered through emphatic tone or booming voice, however, but through a startling incongruity between his style of delivery and his extreme and at times bizarre proclamations. As Richard Kostelanetz noted, "[h]is phrases are more oracular than his manner; he makes the most extraordinary statements in the driest terms" (Understanding McLuhan").

McLuhan was drawn to the dramatic: aphorism, metaphor, analogy, and popular culture. He studied the dramatic visual style of comic books. He correctly predicted in *Understanding Media: The Extensions of Man* that medical dramas, with their "obsession with bodily welfare," would be hugely popular (328). Like rhetorician Kenneth Burke, he viewed social activity in terms of drama. In *The Medium Is the Massage: An Inventory of Effects*, McLuhan writes that "[s]urvival is not possible if one approaches his environment, the social drama, with a fixed, unchangeable point of view—the witless repetitive response to the unperceived" (McLuhan and Fiore 10).

THE MAN

In this volume, none of the contributors supplies a full biographical treatment of McLuhan. Having some sense of his life will help readers to make sense of the chapters, particularly those in the last section, which deal with politics, sexuality, and religion (issues that arc from his life to his work), and of the final interview section, which touches on many biographical points. Although we offer a sketch of McLuhan's life and accomplishments, we encourage readers to turn to more fully realized biographical studies by Philip Marchand, Terrence Gordon, and even the more fanciful Douglas Coupland.

Marshall McLuhan was born in Edmonton in 1911 to Elsie and Herbert Marshall McLuhan. His younger brother Maurice was born in 1913, and the family moved to Winnipeg in 1915, to a house at 507 Gertrude Street in old Fort Rouge. McLuhan received his early education in Winnipeg and grew up to study literature at the University of Manitoba. Interested in intellectual competition and refinement, he headed to Cambridge University and received another degree studying literature in 1936. There he converted to Roman Catholicism in 1937, a conversion that shocked his Protestant family (Maurice became a Protestant minister) and continued to engage his spirit throughout his life. Although the extent of the influence of faith on McLuhan's thinking and written theorizing is still in dispute—as the chapter by David Beard and

David Gore in this collection demonstrates—the common wisdom is that faith served as the centre of his life if not of his theory. Yet in letters McLuhan spoke of faith as a radiance that infuses a life: "[B]elief in God alters existence . . . making it mystical and converting a leaden and uninspired human into something lyrically super human" (quoted in Gordon 75). These sentiments suggest that his intellectual commitment to pattern recognition and his belief that the world could be understood by those devoted to the effort might have been informed by his powerful faith.

In 1939, McLuhan married American Corinne Lewis, with whom he eventually had six children in a marriage that lasted to the end of his life. He received his PhD from Cambridge University, completing a dissertation on Thomas Nashe in which he made a case for the centrality of humanities-based approaches to all forms of knowing (a dissertation whose influence David Linton traces in this collection). Although McLuhan did not refer frequently to Nashe in his later publications, this study revealed the basis of intellectual affiliation with rhetoric by pointing out the importance of grammar and rhetoric over dialectics. He argued that dialectics is the form of reasoning that has been privileged by alphabet literacy, drowning out more intuitive and exploratory approaches that favour pattern recognition rather than a single airtight truth.

During the 1940s, McLuhan moved between the United States and Canada to take up several different academic teaching appointments. In 1951, he published *The Mechanical Bride: The Folklore of Industrial Man*, a study of advertising and North American culture in which he vented against the effects of mechanization, print, and industrial culture on human individuality and assertiveness. In this early work, he was overtly critical of consumer passivity in the face of aggressive marketing, using a vituperative tone that he later eschewed for a studied neutrality in the role of provocateur. Although the volume has sometimes been criticized for taking a conservative stance opposing media and technology, McLuhan was at the forefront of considering popular culture as the subject of serious study.

In the early 1950s, he moved with his family to Toronto, and at the University of Toronto he established the Culture and

Communications Seminar (1953–55). This graduate seminar was co-directed by cultural anthropologist Edmund Carpenter and included in its membership British urban planner Jaqueline Tyrwhitt, political scientist Thomas Easterbrook, and psychologist D. Carleton Williams. They explored interdisciplinary approaches to develop methodologies and new grammars to understand "environments created by electronic communications technologies." A journal titled *Explorations* "was launched as a means of 'cutting across the arts and social sciences by treating them as a continuum,' placing special emphasis on studying the effects of media on oral, visual, and post-visual cultures" (Darroch n. pag.).

McLuhan's next major work was *The Gutenberg Galaxy: The Making of Typographic Man* (1962), revealing how electronic culture put pressure on print culture, enough to propel humankind to return to oral culture—albeit to a new form of orality, transformed by electric and digital environments. There are values associated with print culture, such as individuality and privacy, whose eclipse McLuhan regrets; this regret is expressed in letters rather than this book, however, for in this publication and future ones he presents his ideas in a neutral tone, hoping to find this stance more productive for provoking readers to think.

In 1964, with *Understanding Media* (co-written with though not co-credited to his colleague Edmund Carpenter), McLuhan reached a mass audience. At this stage, more than a public intellectual, he became a pop culture icon, the magnitude of which James Morrison describes:

> The title of the 1969 *Playboy* interview—"Marshall McLuhan: A Candid Conversation With the High Priest of Popcult and Metaphysician of Media"—over and above the fact that he was chosen to be interviewed at all is emblematic of his "elevation" (unlikely for a tweedy, donnish Professor of English at the University of Toronto) into the pop pantheon peopled by such paragons as Leary and his sidekick Richard Alpert (later to become Baba Ram Dass), the Beatles, the Maharishi Mahesh Yogi, Peter Max, Mary Quant, Twiggy, Roy Liechtenstein, and Andy Warhol. (n. pag.)

McLuhan wrote a number of important books in the years following, many of them co-authored with scholars from non-literary fields. Perhaps the best way to convey his output is to list in chronological order the books referred to most frequently in the chapters that follow that he wrote or co-wrote (for complete bibliographic information about his publications, see Gordon 436–54).

- *The Medium Is the Massage: An Inventory of Effects* (1968)
- *Through the Vanishing Point: Space in Poetry and Painting* (1968)
- *War and Peace in the Global Village: An Inventory of Some of the Current Spastic Situations that Could Be Eliminated by More Feedforward* (1968)
- *Counterblast* (1969)
- *From Cliché to Archetype* (1970)
- *Culture Is Our Business* (1970)
- *City as Classroom: Understanding Language and Media* (1977)
- *Laws of Media: The New Science* (1988)
- *The Global Village: Transformations in World Life and Media in the 21st Century* (1989)

In 1980, after having suffered several strokes and a final period of speech paralysis, McLuhan died. At the time of his death, his public popularity and scholarly reputation had waned. Yet over time his ideas have contributed to shaping media studies and attracted interdisciplinary notice that appears to be on the rise.

THE MESSAGE

The rewards and vexations of examining McLuhan's ideas are highlighted by the chapters in this volume. Those in the first three sections contextualize McLuhan's interest in words, imagery, and materiality and explore the fit of his thinking with contemporary cultural theorizing. The chapters in the fourth section and the interviews in the fifth section present a more personal side of McLuhan—some appreciative, some more critical. Whereas the chapters in the first three sections emphasize his relevance to our world and times, those in the fourth section locate McLuhan in his world. The interviews in the fifth section build on the position that experience and intellect are intertwined, looking at his private life from the perspectives of his now adult sons and his most recent biographer.

The chapters in Section 1 emphasize language, taking up the topic of "Work/Word/Play." Rhetorician Doug Brent explores how to teach McLuhan effectively, offering a template with the portability to shape course work dealing with McLuhan across the humanities and social sciences. He provides suggestions to help students avoid stumbling over these particular obstacles to understanding McLuhan: the misconception that he was a technological determinist and the tendency to feel anxious in the face of inconsistency and humour.

The next two chapters in Section 1 focus on that suggestive word *figure:* McLuhan as an antimodern figure and his favourite figure of speech, metaphor. Elizabeth Birmingham and Kevin Brooks locate McLuhan in the midst of his many titles—poet, (right-wing) postmodernist, modernist-in-style-if-not-philosophy—and to this list add the term "antimodernist." They describe McLuhan as "modernist" in style and technique but antimodernist in belief, entailing a desire for the authentic, essentially a disavowal of modern culture with its scientific rationalism and industrialism. Reconfiguring McLuhan as antimodernist, the authors contend, not only expands a critical vocabulary limited to modernism and postmodernism but also lends insight into his changing attitudes to modernity over his career (e.g., "cranky" in *The Mechanical Bride* and somewhat more positive in late career).

Yoni Van Den Eede's "Exceeding Our Grasp: McLuhan's All-Metaphorical Outlook" engages with one of McLuhan's central figures of speech, metaphor. Van Den Eede first examines what he calls McLuhan's "theoretical" metaphors (e.g., the global village, hot versus cool media, discarnate man) and takes up the question of whether one should understand these metaphors literally or figuratively. He also studies metaphor-as-instrument (what he calls the "meta-theoretical" use of metaphor), specifically McLuhan's metaphor of the probe in terms of media critique, art and humour constituting two methods of destabilizing society's fixed points of view. Metaphor is ubiquitous in McLuhan's works and operates in multiple and sometimes circular and self-referential ways.

Section 2 shifts the emphasis from linguistic to spatial and visual dynamics by examining connections among "Image/Figure/Ground." Given the prominence of McLuhan's metaphor of the figure/ground gestalt in his studies of media, this theme seems to be fitting. James Scott shares insights gleaned from his access to McLuhan's personal library, specifically the books of Sigfried Giedion and Ernst Gombrich, two influences on McLuhan's thinking about space and literacy. In McLuhan's marginalia, Scott traces the value of these contemporary thinkers: they helped McLuhan articulate the gap between spatial theory and language/rhetoric. Giedion shared with him "a concern for the disruptive impact of modernism and of a need to reknit the organic fibres of Western culture," but, more importantly, Giedion's writing about the historical creation of vertical and horizontal space informed McLuhan's thinking about "the linearity of writing and its enclosure with a schematic of up/down, left/right." The work of art historian Gombrich also resonated with McLuhan, his annotations suggesting continual efforts to speak the link between art history and language, for instance the connections between Euclidean space, perspectivist drawing, and typography. Both sources, Scott argues, set the stage for what McLuhan termed "typographic man."

Adam Lauder brings to light the probable influence of Canadian advertising executive, marketing theorist, and multimedia artist Bertram Brooker (1888–1955) on McLuhan's sensibilities. Apart from being a likely influence on McLuhan, Brooker himself emerges in Lauder's portrait as a figure of interest for scholars who study the development of Canadian media theory and practice. By exploring and animating Brooker and his world, this chapter contributes to the project of historicizing the rich media environment in the Toronto area.

Finally, in "Buffalo Tracks and Canoe Codes: Marshall McLuhan and Aboriginal Media's Dissident Genealogy in Canada," Kathleen Buddle insists that McLuhan failed to account for the individuality and particularity of Indigenous culture and media presence. Her chapter joins a long-standing critical conversation about him: as a technological determinist and "mere stylist," he offered broad readings. She claims that this determinism is inadequate to explain the accommodative and inventive ways in which Aboriginal people have shaped new media forms according to traditional communication needs and interests, contending that this culture challenges McLuhan's notion that the medium is the message.

Section 3, "Space/Place/Tools," looks at McLuhan's sense of the value of the "built" world, from the vast built environment of the city to the more confined spaces of the library and surgical operating rooms. Jaqueline McLeod Rogers looks at McLuhan's concern about cities as having outgrown their founding purpose of providing a stable material space for communication and safety. Although McLuhan aptly predicted our move toward becoming citizens in a global village of digital connection and increased human flow and cultural mobility, McLeod Rogers finds evidence that he remained committed to human-scale, community-building values of cultivating green spaces and supporting face-to-face social relationships. He did not so much pronounce the death of the city as its transformation from a fixed form to one more open and mobile.

Focusing on "The Library as Place," Karen Brown and Mary Pat Fallon follow a similar path in noting that the turn to virtual communication has not rendered material places and face-to-face interactions obsolete but defined our need for them. They point out that we now regard the library less as a material archive or repository of books than as a place without physical walls that promotes virtual communication. Yet, as libraries are renovated to reflect the changes wrought by technology, they are deliberately reconstructed as material spaces for civic engagement and public participation.

Catherine Jenkins, examining "The Message in Medical Imaging Media," takes McLuhan at his word as a communications theorist concerned with the modernist Everyman. She tests his predictions of a multisensorial future through technological innovation against one of the countless electronic devices to have emerged in our era of "perpetual reinvention of new technologies":

the "Vscan," an iPodesque ultrasound device that comes complete with a USB cable and docking station.

The last two sections begin to bring McLuhan the man into focus, in each case exploring some aspect of the interaction between his personal life and his intellectual life. Section 4 examines his thoughts on and comments about the controversial and time-sensitive topics of "Politics/Sex/Religion," topics that often reveal a person's character and identity as well as intellectual disposition and bias. Readers who remember being warned to avoid discussing these topics in polite company will find in McLuhan an exemplar of such reticence. Although he wrote in times of sexual revolution and political foment and from deeply held personal religious conviction—converting from Protestantism to Roman Catholicism in 1937—for a voluble writer he was remarkably quiet on these topics, addressing them indirectly or by implication rather than head on. We often get glimpses of the personal, yet they are not enough to enable us to draw a definitive portrait of the man.

Examining McLuhan's stance on our national politics, Allen Mills notes his awareness of and theorizing about the division between francophone and anglophone cultures that was so acute in his time. For McLuhan, culture in Quebec remained tied to tribal and collective principles, whereas English Canadian culture celebrated individualism. Mills speculates that McLuhan's vision of these divergent histories led to his predicting or expecting the inevitable separation of French-speaking Quebec from the rest of the English-speaking nation. He also explores some of McLuhan's correspondence with then Prime Minister Pierre Trudeau, bringing to light a relationship that, according to his son Michael in the interview in this volume, was important enough to have contributed to McLuhan's decision to return to Canada from his post at Fordham University in New York in 1968.

David Linton draws a portrait of McLuhan's archly conservative gender politics. Comparing McLuhan to media capitalist Hugh Hefner, Linton points out that both wrote in the age of religious and political revolt associated with the youth culture movement. Both became influential media figures at about the same time, with the publication of *The Mechanical Bride* in 1951 and *Playboy* in 1953. Yet McLuhan's and Hefner's views about sexuality differed in response to the zeitgeist: "As McLuhan responded to the religious, sexual, social, and media upheaval of his times by becoming ardently orthodox and at times reactionary, Hefner became ardently heterodox at least in social and sexual terms." Linton also traces the conservatism of McLuhan's thinking to the influence of sixteenth-century scholar Thomas Nashe.

David Beard and David Gore argue that McLuhan scholarship has not paid sufficient attention to the influence of Catholicism on McLuhan's thinking; theology informed not only his personal beliefs and practices but also his theorization about the effects of media technologies. They find in Richard Lanham's notion of "toggling" (the vacillation between two equally viable interpretations) a generative method for reading McLuhan's insights in both secular and religious ways. Drawing on the rich philosophical work of Charles Taylor, they contend that secular readings in rhetoric and communications studies "fail to appreciate more generally the impact that theology can play in media criticism and theory." Whereas Linton speculates that McLuhan might have been hiding views that he believed to be unfashionable and rather too conservative to attract public interest, Beard and Gore argue that present-day secularity makes current readers insensitive to statements of faith as they appear in McLuhan's work.

Section 5 includes three interviews, one each with sons Michael and Eric McLuhan and one with recent biographer Douglas Coupland. This section differs from the others in focus and tone, providing the sort of marginalia whose value Scott helps us to recognize in his chapter on McLuhan's marginal notes. The section opens with a brief introduction that establishes the varying circumstances governing each interview as well as what each contributes to our understanding of McLuhan. Interviews with Michael and Eric McLuhan capture a side of their father that helps us to appreciate the man and his times. Eric reflects on his close working relationship with his father and his sense of key patterns and ideas. Michael captures some of his thoughts about the burdens and advantages of having a father who is a famous Canadian and reveals his sense of protectiveness when biographers and scholars represent, critique, and even imagine the life and ideas of his father. Coupland presents his views about the challenges and rewards of writing a biography of McLuhan and about the various forms that biography can take. He discusses as a matter of ethos being drawn to a form of biography that foregrounds connections between author and subject, that explores other and/as self, and he shares the roles of memory and imagination in his writing.

We expect that this collection will be particularly valuable in animating McLuhan—both the mind and the man—not only for first-time readers but also for those returning to him and re-evaluating him for reading our contemporary world. Although his aphorism "the medium is the message" continues to create misunderstanding and even resentment among those who think that it is the creed of technological determinists, reading McLuhan through a rhetorical lens helps us to make sense of this statement and appreciate that at its core it suggests that what one says is always shaped by shifting media environments and changing audiences—a quintessentially rhetorical way of thinking and acting.

WORKS CITED

Anton, Corey. "McLuhan, Formal Cause, and the Future of Technological Mediation." *Review of Communication* 12.4 (2012): 1–14. Web.

Bacci, Francesca, and David Melcher. *Art and the Senses*. Oxford: Oxford UP, 2011. Print.

Cavell, Richard. *McLuhan in Space: A Cultural Geography*. Toronto: U of Toronto P, 2003. Print.

Coupland, Douglas. *Marshall McLuhan*. Toronto: Penguin, 2009. Print.

Darroch, Michael. "Giedion and Explorations: Transatlantic Influences on the Toronto School." www.mediatrans.ca/Michael_Darroch.html. Web.

Garrett-Petts, Will. "Exhibiting Writing: On Viewing Artists' Statements as Art." *Open Letter* 13.4 (2007): 64–78. Print.

Gordon, W. Terrence. *Marshall McLuhan: Escape into Understanding*. Toronto: Stoddart, 1997. Print.

Howes, David. *Empire of the Senses: The Sensual Culture Reader.* New York: Berg, 2005. Print.

Kostelanetz, Richard. "Understanding McLuhan (In Part)." *Books. The New York Times on the Web.* 29 Jan. 1967: n. pag. Web.

Levinson, Nancy. "The Big Picture." *Journal of the Society of Architectural Historians* 68.2 (2009): 155–56. Web.

Marchand, Philip. *Marshall McLuhan: The Medium and the Messenger.* Cambridge, MA: MIT P, 1998. Print.

McLuhan, Eric, and Peter Zhang. "Pivotal Terms in Media Ecology: A Dialogue." *Et Cetera: A Review of General Semantics* 69.3 (2012): 246–76. Web.

McLuhan, Marshall. *Culture Is Our Business.* New York: Ballantine, 1970. Print.

——. *The Gutenberg Galaxy: The Making of Typographic Man.* Toronto: U of Toronto P, 1962. Print.

——. *The Mechanical Bride: Folklore of Industrial Man.* London: Routledge, 1967. Print.

——. *Understanding Media: The Extensions of Man.* New York: Taylor and Francis, 1964. Print.

McLuhan, Marshall, and Quentin Fiore. *The Medium Is the Massage: An Inventory of Effects.* 1967. Toronto: Penguin, 2003. Print.

McLuhan, Marshall, Kathryn Hutchon, and Eric McLuhan. *City as Classroom: Understanding Language and Media.* Agincourt, ON: Book Society of Canada, 1977. Print.

McLuhan, Marshall, and Eric McLuhan. *Media and Formal Cause.* Seattle: NeoPoiesis, 2011. Print.

McLuhan, Marshall, and Barrington Nevitt. "The Argument: Causality in the Electric World." *Technology and Culture* 14.1 (1973): 1–16. Print.

McLuhan, Marshall, and Bruce R. Powers. *The Global Village: Transformations in World Life in the 21st Century.* New York: Oxford UP, 1989. Print.

Morrison, James C. "The Place of Marshall McLuhan in the Learning of His Time." *Counterblast: The E-Journal of Culture and Communication* 1.1 (2001). Web.

The Video McLuhan. Toronto: McLuhan Productions, 1996. VHS.

Vallero, Daniel A. *Paradigms Lost: Learning from Environmental Mistakes, Mishaps, and Misdeeds.* Oxford: Butterworth-Heinemann, 2005. Print.

WORK / WORD / PLAY

CHAPTER 1

TEACHING McLUHAN

Doug Brent

As this volume demonstrates, there is continuing scholarly interest in Marshall McLuhan's work despite continuing mistrust of his iconoclastic style in many quarters. But scholarly interest on its own is not enough to ensure that a figure such as McLuhan continues to have real and lasting influence. We need to be able to pass his legacy on to the next generation—not just to graduate students who might conceivably form the next generation of McLuhan scholars but also to undergraduate students who might well not go on to further academic work in the field but will be in positions to have their ways of seeing productively altered by acquaintance with some of McLuhan's constellation of ideas.

One of the few existing publications on the pedagogical challenges of McLuhan is David Bobbitt's "Teaching McLuhan: Understanding *Understanding Media*." Bobbitt provides a useful overview of what he sees as the basic themes that run through McLuhan's work and offers insights into how these strands of thought might be teased out and made more intelligible to students. In this chapter, I offer some of my own observations on boiling down McLuhan's themes to help students get a grip on them. However, I also want to explore the subject of teaching McLuhan from a somewhat different angle, looking at the most common obstacles that students often experience in trying to comprehend his remarkably confusing intellectual gymnastics.

GOALS

It is important to ask *what is the purpose of teaching McLuhan's work in the first place?* Of course, McLuhan is an important figure in the media studies landscape, and a course in communication studies without McLuhan would be like a course in the history of rhetoric without Aristotle or a survey of English literature without Shakespeare. But inclusiveness alone is thin justification for the inclusion of any figure, important or not. What makes McLuhan particularly important to *students*?

As alluded to earlier, the answer lies in our understanding of the larger goals of a liberal arts education. From Dewey to Boyer (and arguably back to Isocrates), scholars of education have argued that the purpose of a liberal education is not just to equip students with knowledge but also to extend their ability to think critically and see the world in new and more complex ways. Developmental psychologists such as William Perry, and others who trace their lineage to Perry, like to divide this process into identifiable stages of growth from a relatively black-and-white epistemological stance, through increasingly complex (though often confusing) stances, to an ability to achieve warrantable beliefs while still maintaining a relativistic overall epistemology. For these scholars, the key to helping students break out of their dualistic mode is the disequilibrium caused by exposure to new ways of thinking:

> Many institutions of higher learning have succeeded, sometimes through careful planning, sometimes through the sheer accident of their internal diversity, in providing for students' growth beyond dualistic thought into the discovery of disciplined contextual relativism. Many would hope to encourage in their students the values of

Commitment, and to provide in their faculties the requisite models. To meet this promise, we must all learn how to validate for our students a dialectical mode of thought, which at first seems "irrational," and then to assist them in honoring its limits. To do this, we need to teach dialectically—that is, to introduce our students, as our greatest teachers have introduced us, not only to the orderly certainties of our subject, but to its unresolved dilemmas. (Perry 109)

For students studying any form of communication theory, McLuhan's intellectual probes are clearly suited to exposing them "not only to the orderly certainties of our subject, but to its unresolved dilemmas."

My goal in teaching communication history in general, and McLuhan in particular, is that students will never be able to look at a communication technology in the same way again. When they consider the question of intellectual property (as when they download a song or movie from a non-sanctioned source or become frustrated in their search for information by firewalls around online books), I want them to know how recent the invention of copyright really is, how it is tied to the development of particular technologies of reproduction, and how other attitudes to intellectual property have prevailed under other circumstances. I want them to be able to contemplate the latest digital technologies that manufacturers are attempting to sell them in terms that go beyond "How cool is that!" and get at the more problematic changes in thinking that each new extension of our nervous systems brings about. Most of all, I want them to see technological changes as being at the centre of a constellation of intellectual, social, and political changes that goes far beyond the introduction of new practical capabilities.

McLuhan, of course, is not the only prominent thinker who can help students to see their world of communication technologies in new and different ways. It is important to situate McLuhan in the larger landscape both of thinkers with whom he has explicit connection (Ong, Innis, Eisenstein, Postman, Meyrowitz, and others) and of others who share his complex view of the communication landscape without necessarily taking their inspiration directly from his work (Carey, Schudson, Beniger, and others who take a historical-cultural view of media). But without McLuhan's ability to make connections across technologies, global regions, and stretches of time, it would be vastly more difficult to disrupt students' prior understandings of how media function, often unconsciously, in our lives.

It is worth remembering that McLuhan's ideas were developed in the context of education. *Understanding Media: The Extensions of Man* evolved from *Report on Project in Understanding New Media* that McLuhan prepared for the unsuspecting National Association of Educational Broadcasters—a report that James Carey describes as "the damnedest thing I had ever seen" (295). Not surprisingly, the report totally bewildered the association that had commissioned it, and its curricular suggestions were never put into practice. However, the fact that the first audience of what was to become *Understanding Media* was a group of educators—according to Carey "the first receptive audience McLuhan found for his speculations concerning media" (295)—should remind us how deeply McLuhan believed that his ideas were particularly important in educating the young on the effects of the media in which they were immersed. Moreover, they were developed in a pedagogical context during his early years as a junior professor of English. Philip Marchand's biography of McLuhan paints him as an earnest pedagogue whose main mission was to shock his students out of complacency with little regard for curriculum or decorum. Not that all students necessarily appreciated his *laissez-faire* approach to teaching, in which a lecture on Francis Bacon might devolve into a verbal dissertation on Batman that would certainly not help students to pass their exams (Marchand 182). Nonetheless, Marchand notes that McLuhan had a profound if quirky respect for his students, regarding them as collaborators in making meaning out of his oracular pronouncements, much as his cherished New Critical approach to literature sees the reader as a collaborator who creates the poem anew in the act of reading it. That process of wrestling with McLuhan's pronouncements to see which ones trigger important ideas and which ones must be set aside as either incomprehensible or utter rubbish is still an excellent way of inducing students to see things differently, question the obvious, and never be afraid of a new idea.

BLOCKAGES

Before surveying in more detail what I think McLuhan can offer undergraduate students, I would like to address several factors that I think can get badly in the way of a neophyte's ability to appreciate him. I examine these blockages under the headings of "Anxiety of Determinism," "Anxiety of Consistency," and "Anxiety of Humour."

Anxiety of Determinism

Any student who has encountered McLuhan briefly before might well have done so under the banner of "technological determinism." In fact, one of the most commonly used introductory texts, Julia Wood's *Communication Theories in Action: An Introduction*, presents McLuhan in a section headed "Technological Determinism." (Another popular introductory text, Emory Griffin's *A First Look at Communication Theory*, also used to introduce McLuhan under the banner of "technological determinism," but in more recent editions he has vanished altogether—perhaps not a good sign of his popularity in more mainstream communication studies.) In some respects, the description is not completely unfair. As Wood says, "The theory of technological determinism states that technology—specifically, media—decisively shapes how individuals think, feel and act and how societies organize themselves and operate" (229–30). Most readers of McLuhan would accept that this statement is fully accurate, at least as far as it goes. Most of his work is devoted to cajoling the reader into paying far more attention to the influence of media than ever before, and his single-minded focus on this subject can fairly be extrapolated to a conviction that, if media are not the *only* cause of social change, they are certainly the most powerful.

Unfortunately, the "determinism" part of the label suggests that McLuhan saw the effects of media as totally inescapable. A student who has encountered him in this way might well have pigeonholed

5

him as a single-cause thinker who can see no other factors at play and therefore has a simplistic understanding of social change. To describe McLuhan as "simplistic" is to miss the point entirely, of course, but such impressions are not always easy to dislodge. Early critics of his work, such as Raymond Williams, criticize him on precisely these grounds: "If the effect of the medium is the same, whoever controls or uses it, and whatever apparent content he may try to insert, then we can forget ordinary political and cultural argument and let the technology run itself" (131).

It is important, therefore, to locate McLuhan more securely in the context of what he himself thought he was doing. In the introduction to the second edition of *Understanding Media*—an introduction now sadly absent from subsequent editions—McLuhan compares himself to Poe's sailor, who, carried into the maelstrom and seemingly doomed, eventually stops struggling against the water with his body and begins instead to apply his mind. By observing the patterns in the wreckage as it is carried about by the whirlpool, now sinking, now reappearing higher up in the water, he is able to apply these patterns to escape the power of the water and survive. This paints McLuhan in a much less deterministic light, as a pattern watcher who believes that we are helpless against the power of media only if we fail to understand them.

In his writing, McLuhan portrays himself as a neutral observer, determined not to judge, only to describe, media, and only occasionally does he slip into moral judgment. However, in the many recorded interviews with McLuhan that survive, we can occasionally catch a clearer glimpse of his less neutral stance that the purpose of understanding media is, if not to extol or decry them, at least to control them and deflect some of their less desirable effects. In a 1966 interview with CBC's Bob Fulford (available in the six-volume video collection *The Video McLuhan*), McLuhan steps out from behind his cover of neutrality and explains his position on the control of media. The sequence is so revealing that it is worth reproducing here verbatim.

FULFORD: Is there a period in the past or a possible future that you'd rather be in?

McLUHAN: I'd rather be in any period at all as long as people are going to leave it alone for a while.

FULFORD: But they're not going to, are they?

McLUHAN: No. So the only alternative is to understand everything that's going on, and then neutralize it as much as possible, turn off as many buttons as you can, and frustrate them as much as you can. I am resolutely opposed to all innovation, all change, but I am determined to understand what's happening, because I don't choose just to sit and let the juggernaut roll over me. Many people seem to think that, if you talk about something recent, you're in favour of it. The exact opposite is true in my case. Anything I talk about is almost certainly to be something I'm resolutely against, and it seems to me the best way of opposing it is to understand it, and then you know where to turn off the buttons.

It's not possible, of course, to know how much this is another of McLuhan's many thought-provoking poses. But such incidents provide a solid perspective on McLuhan, not just as a closet conservative (see, e.g., Linton, this volume) but also, more importantly, as a person who believed ardently in the power of understanding to provide control, as far from being a true "technological determinist" as it is possible to get. Terms such as Joshua Meyrowitz's "medium theory" and Neil Postman's "media ecology" capture the essence of McLuhan's work much more accurately than "technological determinism."

Anxiety of Consistency
Ironically, the better students are as readers, the more disturbing they are likely to find McLuhan. Less experienced readers typically focus on a few sentences here and there in a source and don't worry much about how they connect with the rest of the text, assuming that they have even read the rest of it (see, e.g., Howard, Serviss, and Rodrigue). As students become better readers, they learn to look for consistent arguments woven through larger

stretches of text. They look for explicit warrants for claims and use their knowledge of argumentative structures such as textual juxtaposition to tell them, for instance, that paragraphs following a major claim are likely to furnish either further warrants for the claim or logical inferences derived from it.

Of course, this is not the way to read McLuhan. In a deliberate attempt to shock his readers out of the numb stance of the technological somnambulist, he seemingly, and often actually, makes leaps from topic to topic, resulting in paragraphs that seem to have little logical connection to each other. We seem to be following a mind determined to pack as many new ideas onto each page as possible without making connections explicit or at times worrying whether they exist at all. His style is cyclic rather than linear, and sometimes an observation will clarify, or at least add depth to, another observation made fifty pages away. On the other hand, it might simply contradict it.

A case in point is McLuhan's analysis of the newspaper in *Understanding Media* as a mosaic medium that emphasizes participation in process rather than a linear point of view. This view articulates well with related claims by writers such as Schudson and Carey on the effects of the union of the telegraph and the newspaper near the end of the nineteenth century and even with Postman's more negative claims that the downfall of extended argument, deepened by television, can be seen as starting with the same confluence of technologies. It places the newspaper usefully as a precursor to the mosaic and involving form of television. Yet it seems in contradiction to McLuhan's observations elsewhere that the critical factor in television is the turn from the eye to the ear and from the hot media of print and paper to the cool, low-definition medium of television. One can explain this by pointing out that it is electricity that promotes modern media's reversal at various break boundaries that might not be synchronous with each other in time and that the newspaper's power stems from its relationship with electronic news distribution beginning with the telegraph. But to make this explanation work, one must also face the fact that McLuhan's distinction between "hot" and "cool" media, presented in Chapter 2 of *Understanding Media* as if it is the road map to understanding all media, is just a probe that works well in some contexts but not in others—certainly not by the time we get to Chapter 21 on the press.

The sooner students realize this, the better off they will be. As long-standing McLuhan scholars, we easily forget the degree to which one must abandon standards of linear argument, and even at times the Aristotelian principle of non-contradiction, to appreciate the freewheeling multiplicity of directions in which McLuhan's agile mind takes us. To appreciate McLuhan, students need to be told, repeatedly and with examples, that, when he comes up with a seemingly contradictory idea, sometimes it's possible to bring it into logical alignment with other ideas, and sometimes it's okay just to say, "Well, I guess McLuhan just had another new idea."

In short, students need to give themselves permission to let go of the very skills that they are learning to apply to other texts. It seems to be a lot to ask students, whose grip on strategies of reading is often uncertain to begin with, to learn to suspend those strategies to appreciate an author who prided himself on breaking out of the linear point of view associated with the typographic age. I find it helpful to point out early in the game that McLuhan clearly recognized his own bizarre non-linear and sometimes contradictory style—at least twenty pages into his chapter on television, for instance, he gives away the game that he has been playing for the first nineteen pages by announcing, "Now that we have considered the subliminal force of the TV image in a redundant scattering of samples . . ." (*Understanding Media* 329).

This ability to get control of one's own expectations and to learn to accept not only strange new ideas but also strange new ways of presenting ideas is essential for reading McLuhan and important as part of the journey to complex understandings of competing propositions that is an important goal of a liberal education. We just need to remind ourselves of what students are up against and not to be too disappointed if they are confused or even resistant. (One student commented at the end of the course that there must be better ways of understanding media than by "divining science from madness." He might have had a point, but there is something to be said for the attempt, even when largely unsuccessful.)

It is also important for students to realize how much against the grain of current communications theory McLuhan was. His diatribes against the then-dominant paradigm of mass media effects research—invariably quantitative studies of the effects of media *content* rather than the media themselves—illustrate how dearly he loved attempting to blow the dominant paradigm out of the water. His cheeky dismissal of Lazarsfeld's entire mode of thinking—"Professor Lazarsfeld's helpless unawareness of the nature and effects of radio is not a personal defect, but a universally shared ineptitude" (*Understanding Media* 298)—illustrates, on the one hand, why McLuhan was disliked or, worse, ignored by most of the contemporary communication studies establishment. On the other, it serves to explain his habit of outrageous overstatement, another stylistic quirk that often disturbs students and makes it hard for them to hear what he is saying. Once they understand the lengths to which McLuhan thought he had to go to shake up the dominant paradigm, which he was convinced was utterly misguided, they are often somewhat more forgiving of his tendency to overstate his case. As McLuhan himself put it in a 1967 interview with Gerald Stern,

> [f]or me any of the little gestures I make are all tentative probes. That's why I feel free to make them sound as outrageous or extreme as possible. Unless you make it extreme, the probe is not very efficient. Probes, to be effective, must have this edge, strength, pressure. Of course they *sound* very dogmatic. That doesn't mean you are committed to them. You may toss them away. ("Marshall McLuhan" 284–85)

Anxiety of Humour
A final roadblock—well, perhaps not the final one, but the last one that I want to take time to discuss—is McLuhan's quirky sense of humour. McLuhan enjoys himself immensely as he weaves double entendres and puns (often bad or obscure or both) into what is overall a deadly serious project. McLuhan scholars tend, on the whole, to have a humanities background and both understand and take in stride his punning allusions to Joyce, Shakespeare, and a

hundred other literary and philosophical figures by which students, not necessarily being of a humanities bent themselves, are simply puzzled.

I don't mean to say that students don't have a sense of humour. They frequently appreciate writers such as Neil Postman and Edward Tufte, who use an acerbic wit in the service of their lamentations over the effects of television and PowerPoint respectively. However, just as students have trouble dealing with McLuhan's Picasso-like ability to present contradictory views of the same subject at once, so too they have trouble with a sense of humour that involves pulling punning allusions seemingly out of thin air to make an argument rather than enlivening an argument that would still hold together without it. The tension between serious purpose and intellectualized humour is one of McLuhan's great attractions once you get used to it, but we can't allow ourselves to forget how much of a roadblock it can be to students struggling to get a better grip on his ideas. Perhaps the best advice to students echoes that of a film critic from the 1980s (whose details have now, alas, vanished into parts of my mind that resist data retrieval), who offered this advice on how to appreciate the film *Airplane:* "If a joke falls flat, don't worry about it. There'll be another one along in a second."

KEY CONCEPTS

In the previous section, I emphasized some of the aspects of reading McLuhan that can hamper students' ability to appreciate what he has to offer. Teaching McLuhan often requires a heavy dose of advice, repeated and demonstrated frequently, on how to read him without becoming hopelessly frustrated. However, there is more to teaching him than removing roadblocks. In this section, I want to highlight the concepts that I believe are most rewarding and go the furthest in helping students to see media in radically new ways.

Hot and Cool
In fact, I find this one of McLuhan's less productive concepts in the long run. The terms lend a false air of rule-governed regularity

to his view of media that in many ways detracts from his more important ideas, and it is interesting to note how the terms tend to move into the background and eventually drop out altogether in his later work. Nonetheless, they set up ways of helping students to see media in entirely new and often counterintuitive ways.

For instance, seeing television as a cool and therefore participatory and involving medium sets up discussions on how this counterintuitive idea applies to a medium traditionally thought of as inducing passivity in its audience. Once students get past their puzzlement over why McLuhan makes so much of the physically low resolution of 1960s television (another of his less productive ideas), they can begin to speculate on the differences between intellectual participation such as we normally associate with reading print and a more emotional, subliminal participation that bypasses conscious cognition but is no less involving for that. McLuhan's description of television as a cool medium becomes less a set of ideas to be taken away wholesale and more a heuristic, a means of thinking about, for instance, how experiencing a television show is different from experiencing a film.

Retribalization and Living Mythically

Most students are already familiar with the concept of the "global village" but only as commonly used in its loose sense to suggest that electronic media have potentially put us in contact with every part of the globe. Of course, McLuhan means much more than that. The idea of the global village is closely tied to the concept of retribalization and living mythically in the age of electronic media. We are a global village in the sense that we live as a gigantic tribe held together by mythic structures, not just as a group of people who can easily talk to each other over a virtual back fence.

The idea of living mythically is another counterintuitive one for students, which makes it particularly productive if the object is to destabilize their felt sense of who they are and how the world works. A discussion of what myth is and how it regulates a culture allows, first, for productive connections with work such as Ong's studies of Homeric poetry. Students easily fall into debate over which aspects of modern life are like or not like those of an oral society, and they become aware of the powerful role of story in our lives. Such a debate also leads to the question of how the age of print might have destabilized the mythic life of oral and early chirographic cultures and replaced them with what McLuhan describes as the fragmented and specialist forms of the industrial age. It is easy to take for granted that we are still a highly specialized culture, but some probing with McLuhan's terms can lead students to question the degree to which we are still specialized in the sense that McLuhan attributes to a typographically oriented industrial age or whether electronic technologies have indeed blended roles as well as reawakened the sense of myth as a major mode of thinking. Whether students agree entirely with him on these matters is largely moot. The exercise of marshalling arguments against his ideas is as productive as finding areas of agreement—perhaps even more so.

Students who find McLuhan's ideas difficult to swallow whole, given his oracular style and his reluctance to offer proof of his assertions, can find comfort in parallel work that not only starts with his basic ideas on the power of media but also pursues it into some analogous places. His ideas on the blending of roles in a retribalized age tie well into work such as that of Meyrowitz, who discusses (in terms somewhat easier to follow than McLuhan's) how television breaks down separate roles created by print—separations between male and female, children and parents, politicians and the public. Here, too, students' familiar notions of social structures are destabilized as the students contemplate how much of the taken-for-granted culture in which they live might be a product of the media that they experience.

Break Boundaries
Like Bobbitt, I find McLuhan's concept of reversal and recapture of older forms one of his most productive. An ambitious teacher might pursue the concept further to introduce the more complex concept of the tetrad with its emphasis on enhancement, obsolescence, retrieval, and reversal. However, I have found that the simpler concept of reversal at a break boundary is enough for students to digest in their first serious encounter with McLuhan and provides more than enough fuel for discussion.

The initial concept can be illustrated by noting the ways in which media speed up or, in McLuhan's terms, heat up through the progression from orality through hieroglyphic, the alphabet in chirographic cultures, and finally print, and then reverse with the advent of television. But the simple concept of a single major break boundary soon devolves into questions of whether there have been other break boundaries that we can identify. Did the union of the newspaper and the telegraph create a new form, not only mosaic in structure but also highly communal in organization, that can be considered the first step in recapturing a more tribal form of social life? What other break boundaries do we note in more recent history? To what extent does the very new represent at least a partial recapture of older forms?

Predictions and Applications

Despite his modest comment that he was always careful not to predict anything that hadn't already happened, it is interesting to see where some of the predictions that McLuhan made have led. His prediction that nationalism will yield to tribalism in the form of a reawakening of ethnic identity, for instance, is borne out not only in the breakup of the USSR and Yugoslavia (events that, we must remind ourselves, occurred before most of our students came to political consciousness or were even born) but also in more recent events, from the separation of South Sudan to the continued aspirations of many Quebecers for sovereignty.

More interesting and provocative than looking at predictions that have been more or less borne out is looking at media that McLuhan did not explicitly predict but that might have been predicted by extrapolation from the trends that he observed. His terms can easily be applied to the personal computer, the Internet, Facebook, text messaging, and a host of other technologies that he clearly would have immensely enjoyed discussing had he lived long enough to witness them. Some of the conversation regarding such technologies can slip easily into the facile—"Is the Internet hot or cool?" is not, in itself, a particularly interesting question. But by applying other ideas, such as retribalization, despecialization, centralization/decentralization, and in-depth participation to twenty-first-century media, students can see the media that they use every day in a much larger historical and cultural context. (Paul Levinson does an expert job of this in *Digital McLuhan: A Guide to the Information Millennium*, but it is a lot more fun to let students make up and justify their own speculations.) Although I don't particularly want to read any more essays on Facebook and text messaging, which seem to be the default topics when students are asked to write on media, class discussions on these media in the light of McLuhan's ideas, or medium theory in general, further the project of defamiliarization of the taken-for-granted that I have been promoting throughout this chapter.

CONCLUSION

McLuhan, I have argued, is particularly suited to the project of furthering students' intellectual growth by questioning and defamiliarizing the taken-for-granted experiences of their lives. However, I hope that in the process of illustrating this argument I have not been guilty of seeming to promote a "right" way to teach McLuhan or of suggesting which of his ideas are more important than others. My examples of both roadblocks and key concepts are intended only to suggest what has seemed to work for me over many years of experimenting with productive ways to work McLuhan into a course on communication history.

I also hope that this recipe swapping illustrates how some larger principles of teaching apply to this particular subject. When teaching anything, it is important to be able to reach below one's knowledge not only of the subject but also of processes—how to read the texts, how to be most productive in applying one's understanding, how to transfer learning from one environment to another, how to construct an argument in ways appropriate to the subject. All of this knowledge long ago became tacit for experts in any field, and it is vital to make it explicit again for students. Throughout this chapter, I have tried to show the degree to which the ability to read McLuhan is an acquired skill. The barriers to understanding are different from the standard problem of understanding complex texts that all students encounter as they work their way into unfamiliar subjects. McLuhan is not only complex but also beset with barriers that result from his refusal to follow traditionally accepted forms of argument. Recognizing such barriers is an important first step in helping students to unpack the richness of his ideas.

It is important to give students permission to accept some of McLuhan's ideas, to adapt others, and to reject still others. It is easy for a McLuhan scholar to project a sense that all of his ideas are productive. This can lead students to think that they have to take McLuhan as a monolithic block. It is much more productive to treat his ideas as he wished them to be treated, as heuristics to be tested against the criterion of how well they help us to think differently about media and the world.

I generally tell students that I think about half of McLuhan is pure genius and the other half is pure bullshit, and that I am never quite sure which half is which. This seems to comfort them immensely.

WORKS CITED

Bobbitt, David. "Teaching McLuhan: Understanding *Understanding Media*." *Enculturation* (Dec. 2011): n. pag. enculturation.net/teaching-mcluhan. Web.

Carey, James. "Marshall McLuhan: Genealogy and Legacy." *Canadian Journal of Communication* 23.3 (1998): 293–306. Print.

Griffin, Emory A., ed. *A First Look at Communication Theory*. 12th ed. New York: McGraw-Hill, 2012. Print.

Howard, Rebecca Moore, Tricia Serviss, and Tanya K. Rodrigue. "Writing from Sources, Writing from Sentences." *Writing and Pedagogy* 2.2 (2010): 177–92. Print.

Levinson, Paul. *Digital McLuhan: A Guide to the Information Millennium*. Florence, KY: Routledge, 2001. Print.

Marchand, Philip. *Marshall McLuhan: The Medium and the Messenger*. Toronto: Vintage, 1989. Print.

McLuhan, Marshall. "Marshall McLuhan and G.E. Stern." *McLuhan Hot and Cool.* Ed. Gerald E. Stern. New York: Dial Press, 1967. 266–302. Print.

———. *Report on Project in Understanding New Media.* Urbana, IL: National Association of Educational Broadcasters, 1960. Print.

———. *Understanding Media: The Extensions of Man.* 2nd ed. Markam, ON: Penguin Canada, 1964. Print.

Perry, William G., Jr. "Cognitive and Ethical Growth: The Making of Meaning." *The Modern American College.* Ed. Arthur Chickering. San Francisco: Jossey Bass, 1981. 76–116. Print.

The Video McLuhan. Toronto: McLuhan Productions, 1996. VHS.

Williams, Raymond. *Television: Technology and Cultural Form.* Florence, KY: Routledge, 1974. Print.

Wood, Julia T. *Communication Theories in Action: An Introduction.* 3rd ed. Boston: Wadsworth, 2004. Print.

CHAPTER 2

MARSHALL McLUHAN
IN AN AGE OF LABELS:
THE DESCRIPTIVE VALUE OF ANTIMODERNISM

Elizabeth Birmingham and Kevin Brooks

S cholars have pinned various and sometimes contradictory labels onto Marshall McLuhan, his work, and
his ideas over the more than fifty years that he has received scholarly attention. Most scholars try to place
his work on a historical, philosophical, and aesthetic
continuum that posits modernism at one end and postmodernism at the other. Such scholarship has led to a host of labels
to describe both his ideas and the man himself: "modernism in reverse," "unthinking modernity," "first postmodernist," "right-wing
postmodernist," and "schizoid." The last label represents Donald
Theall's clever attempt to define McLuhan as this "sophisticated
luddite dedicated to the literacy of the man of letters, who was
still fascinated by the modernist, technocultural 'tradition of the
new' and by the potential post-literate revival through the techno-
culture of a 'new tribalism'" (*Virtual McLuhan* 27). As valuable as
a term such as "schizoid" might be for McLuhan himself, it does
mark him as an intellectual aberration rather than a product and

producer of the persistent transatlantic antimodernist critique of the twentieth and twenty-first centuries. A few scholars have noted his early conservatism as an outgrowth of the antimodernist movement of the late nineteenth century and early twentieth century, but variations on modernism and postmodernism dominate scholarly understandings of McLuhan's work, and his persistent antimodernism remains largely ignored.

We argue that scholarly discourse of the twenty-first century would benefit significantly from using the term "antimodernist" to understand the whole of McLuhan's career as well as a host of other artists, architects, and social movements that have proven difficult to define and interrogate using the modernist-postmodernist continuum. By understanding antimodernism as a lengthy and persistent cultural response to modernity, a response that is alive and well in contemporary culture, we offer a redescription of McLuhan that argues for his continuing importance as part of a long intellectual tradition closely related to a number of twentieth-century and twenty-first-century cultural products and movements. Before we make the case for using "antimodernist" as a label for McLuhan, however, we sort through the prominent labels that have been applied to the man and his work, and then we define the term "antimodernism" more thoroughly.

McLUHAN'S MANY LABELS ON THE MODERN-POSTMODERN CONTINUUM

Prior to the emergence of the modern-postmodern continuum, McLuhan's political conservatism was well established and named. In his influential analysis of Innis and McLuhan from 1967, James Carey effectively critiques McLuhan's anti-liberalism: "The liberal tradition argued that human freedom is solely the result of man's rationality. McLuhan contends, however, that the overemphasis on reason in the liberal tradition has resulted in man's alienation from himself, from other men, and from nature itself" ("Harold Adams Innis" 36). When Carey looks back on that critique in his 1998 article "Marshall McLuhan: Genealogy and Legacy," he is even more pointed, suggesting that, though

McLuhan was "the most important public intellectual in North America" during both the Vietnam War and the Civil Rights movement, his "conservative politics made him indifferent to the outcomes of these two protest movements" (2, 3). Daniel Czitrom's criticism of McLuhan follows his mentor Carey's argument, with something close to the "antimodernist" label: "Through his own literary criticism, McLuhan expressed a personal variant of the Tory, neo-Catholic, antimodern tradition flourishing on both sides of the Atlantic" (167). Although Czitrom uses the term "antimodern," he does so not to label McLuhan or his ideas but to indicate the intellectual milieu from which he emerged. McLuhan is pegged not as an example of that tradition or someone who forwards antimodernist values but as a "personal variant" (167). Historian Daniel Horowitz also follows this line of McLuhan analysis, citing the above sentence from Czitrom and adding to it the claim that "[i]n the 1930s and 1940s McLuhan embraced quite conservative positions, core beliefs from which he never fully moved" (139). Horowitz's claim that McLuhan's "conservative" values remained largely unchanged refers to the values of the "antimodern" tradition that Czitrom notes. This traditional conservatism, and the antimodern tradition from which it developed, became the core of McLuhan's more "forward-looking conservatism," as described by Grant Havers (523), a sort of positive antimodernism that Arthur Versluis labels "prophetic" (129).

Labelling has been difficult for scholars challenged to reconcile McLuhan's literary modernism with his almost postmodern communicative strategies and his core conservative values. McLuhan scholars, while largely in agreement with accounts representing the conservative impulse in McLuhan and his often prophetic work, have generally preferred to invent their own terms to describe the uncomfortable marriage. For example, Judith Stamps's "unthinking modernity" and Glenn Willmott's "modernism in reverse" both appear in titles of books exploring McLuhan's philosophical work. Stamps argues that McLuhan, like Innis, was a critic of modernity and that the two can be productively compared with the left-leaning Frankfurt school. Willmott maintains that McLuhan's theories are animated by a movement between modernist and postmodernist thought and that McLuhan broke with modernism through an idealization of a premodern past. It is in this romanticism of a premodern past that Willmott notes, but does not name, McLuhan's antimodernist tendencies. Certainly both of these phrases, "unthinking modernism" and "modernism in reverse" embrace the notion shared by Versluis's description of antimodernism as "the great refusal," a critique of symptoms of modernism such as "environmental destruction, loss of local and regional culture, the erosion of religious traditions, and other problems" (128).

Other critics, while still recognizing McLuhan's conservatism, employ derivations of the term "postmodern" to label McLuhan. Richard Cavell's *McLuhan in Space: A Cultural Geography* argues that McLuhan's interest in "space" (acoustic and visual) emerged out of the "[m]odernist context" but made a "significant post-modernist contribution" (6). Rather than "unthinking modernity," Cavell argues, McLuhan's project with its "progressivist assumptions . . . is more productively assessed within the context of post-modernism" (7). In terms of sorting out labels, all three critics see roughly the same tendencies and preoccupations in McLuhan, but each offers his or her own label. Havers also reacts to Stamps, Willmott, and other progressivist readings of McLuhan but is worried that these readings overlook the obvious conservative core values identified by Carey, Czitrom, and, since them, Horowitz. Havers holds on to the conservatism by coining the phrase "right-wing postmodernism" to counteract the left-leaning analyses of McLuhan that emerged in the 1990s from scholars such as Stamps and Willmott. Havers sees McLuhan's "forward-looking conservatism" as distinct from traditional conservative critiques of liberal modernism (523). Even Carey, while simultaneously describing McLuhan's conservatism, writes that McLuhan "was, in a certain sense, the first postmodernist" ("Marshall McLuhan" 3), adding further confusion to the mix of labels. Despite this incredible mix, the term "antimodernism" is rarely employed to describe McLuhan specifically or as a conservative critique of modernity generally.

This omission is understandable; antimodernism has not entered scholarly vocabulary in any significant way, as a Google N-gram analysis of the terms "antimodernism," "modernism," and "postmodernism" demonstrates (see Figure 1). A few scholars, however, have convincingly documented the well-defined anti-modernist critique of emerging modernism between 1880 and 1920 (Lears) and ongoing critiques of modernism throughout the twentieth and twenty-first centuries that frequently are, but should not be, labelled "postmodern" (Luke; Versluis).

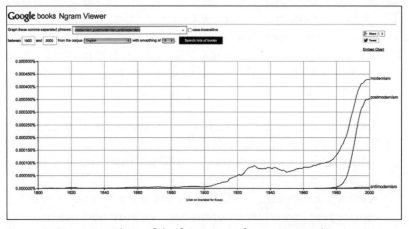

Figure 1: N-gram analysis of the frequency of use: "Antimodernism," "modernism," "postmodernism," 1800-2008. Conducted 30 June 2014.

Our goal in this chapter is to employ the descriptive power of antimodernism to argue three points: (1) that McLuhan is an important mid-century antimodernist figure who has been understandably mislabelled by readers and overlooked by scholars of antimodernism; (2) that McLuhan scholarship would benefit from using the antimodernist label to synthesize existing research and productively connect McLuhan's work to other related cultural movements; and (3) that broad, transdisciplinary adoption of the antimodernist label would effectively expand critical discourse beyond the limiting binary of modernism and postmodernism. Moreover, the term allows us to document the persistence and popularity of antimodern impulses across centuries, as a typical and natural response to what Versluis refers to as the "destructive consequences of modernism," arguing that "Modern industrial society in its very nature calls forth antimodernism in the creative individual" (96).

UNDERSTANDING ANTIMODERNISM

As Figure 1 illustrates, antimodernism has not entered scholarly or popular discourse in any significant way, but modernism and postmodernism have led, since the 1980s, parallel lives. Antimodernism, however, is thoroughly described and documented by T.J. Jackson Lears in *No Place of Grace: Antimodernism and the Transformation of American Culture, 1880–1920*. Antimodernism took, and still takes, many forms, but its historical catalyst, Lears suggests, was a "feeling of overcivilization" by the end of the nineteenth century, a

> transatlantic dissatisfaction with modern culture in all its dimensions: its ethic of self-control and autonomous achievement, its cult of science and technical rationality, its worship of material progress. . . . Haltingly, half-consciously, Europeans and Americans alike began to recognize that the triumph of modern culture had not produced greater autonomy (which was the official claim) but rather had promoted a spreading sense of moral impotence and spiritual sterility—a feeling that life had become not only overcivilized but also curiously unreal. (4–5)

Lears argues that the response to this overcivilization was contemplation of "medieval beliefs and values" (142). They were not necessarily historically situated but those conjured up by the late-Victorian imagination in an effort to recover what Lears calls a "primal irrationality" that the Victorians ascribed to a variety of premodern civilizations (143), including pre-Meiji-era (1857) Japan, of interest to late-Victorian Europeans and Americans alike. The premodern fantasy projected into a possible future created the space for antimodernism, which mushroomed into social movements, such as the Arts and Crafts movement, that hoped to tame the machine as a tool for workers and artists (63).

Particularly important for our chapter is a definitional clarification that Lears makes: "What [literary] critics call modernism and what I call antimodernism share common roots in

fin-de-siècle yearning for authentic experience—physical, emotional, or spiritual" (xix). The only resolution to this "termino-
logical muddle," he says, is to "point out that modernity has one
meaning for historians [like him], a very different meaning for
literary critics" (xix). Lears explains this difference between historical and literary modernism: "In large measure, literary modernism arose as both religious and secular dissent from historical
modernity. Such writers as Adams, Yeats, or Eliot acknowledge[d]
the fragmentation of self and universe but also yearned for a re-
stored sacred center at the heart of the modern spiritual chaos"
(296). Lears's description of literary modernism aligns nicely with
Versluis's claim, cited above, that the condition of modernity
"calls forth antimodernism in the creative individual" (96).

Lears focuses his scholarly efforts on the historical period
1880–1920, but he acknowledges both the antimodernist interest in medieval values and the late-twentieth-century affiliations
with antimodernist values: "[T]he avant-garde preoccupation
with authentic experience, like that of the medievalists and Orientalists, has frequently blended with a sleeker version of modern culture stressing self-fulfillment and immediate gratification.
Superficially at odds, antimodernist, avant-garde, and advertisers
have often been brothers under the skin" (xix). Two articles in a
special issue of *Telos* devoted to *The Limits of Modernity* build on
Lears's work with an emphasis on late-twentieth-century and early-twenty-first-century manifestations of antimodernism. Versluis presents a compelling case for understanding antimodernism
as a long-standing perspective from which to analyze and critique
the limits of modernity. He acknowledges the importance of well-
known nineteenth-century antimodernists such as Henry David
Thoreau, John Ruskin, William Morris, and Orestes Brownson,
followed in antimodernist spirit by literary giants such as Eliot,
Rilke, and Yeats (97). Versluis offers less well-known examples of
early-to-mid-twentieth-century antimodernists in writers such
as traditionalists René Guénon and Martin Lings (98), and Tim
Luke, in his response to Versluis, notes "fringe figure" examples
of late-twentieth-century antimodernism via environmental rad-
icals such as Ted Kaczynski and the Earth Liberation Front. Luke
agrees that the antimodernist critique has circulated throughout

the twentieth and twenty-first centuries, less well identified and separate from the postmodernist critique of modernism, but he calls for more precise sorting of antimodernists, and he calls for attention to more significant twentieth-century antimodernists (141–42). In the next section, we argue that McLuhan is one such example of an important mid-twentieth-century antimodernist whose work brings explanatory power to analyses of the many contemporary social movements that are difficult to interpret as politically left or right and whose critiques of modernism are philosophically difficult to read as postmodern.

McLUHAN'S ANTIMODERNISM

Building on these definitions of antimodernism, we see six ways in which McLuhan connected to the antimodernist movement of the early twentieth century, and all of these connections persisted throughout his career. In other words, antimodernism was neither a historical period that he moved through nor a phase in his thinking and work but an evolving, consistent critique of modernism that transitioned from cranky disillusionment in *The Mechanical Bride: Folklore of Industrial Man* to occasionally optimistic prophesying in his works of the 1960s and 1970s.

McLuhan's Antimodernist Heroes
McLuhan's philosophical, political, and literary roots—his early heroes—are the figures most closely associated with antimodernism. G.K. Chesterton and Hilaire Belloc—the former's influence clearly documented, the latter noted only in passing—were part of the British antimodernist movement that both Lears and Versluis define, a movement that, according to Lears, "sought to create islands of wholeness in a fragmented capitalist society" (64). Stamps argues that McLuhan shared Chesterton's "Catholic form of philosophical organicism" (98), and W. Terrence Gordon's biography documents McLuhan's extensive debt to Chesterton as a Roman Catholic, a rhetorician, and an agrarian (38–60). Although Arthur W. Hunt III argues that McLuhan shrugged off his "agrarian mind" (we would say "antimodern ideology") by the late 1960s,

Havers sees rightly, we think, that "the paradox of McLuhan's right-wing politics is that it is not classically 'conservative.' This is a forward-looking conservatism, anticipating that electric technology will first demolish the liberal individualist print age, then replace it with a retribalized community" (523).

McLuhan as Neo-Medievalist

McLuhan was a medievalist (and classicist) in the antimodern tradition. His criticisms of modernity align with the work of Victorian neo-medievalists such as Ruskin and Morris, who shared his interest in (and concern for) the future of book arts (Jackson and Rothkopf 53), and connect to them through his complex relationship to critics such as Lewis Mumford (Carey, "McLuhan and Mumford" 162–63). From his dissertation on classical education from antiquity to the early modern period, McLuhan was a proponent of the humanist tradition and a critic of the abstract, disengaged philosophers and dialecticians. Theall says in his review of Cavell that "He [Cavell] omits to note that McLuhan considered himself a traditional grammarian who used the resources of the trivium. . . . McLuhan was attached to the classical world, as interpreted in the late Middle Ages and the early Renaissance" ("McLuhan's" 257). Carey offers his highest praise of McLuhan on this topic: "In short, McLuhan taught us to see new relations between the medieval and the modern world and new relations among our apprehensive capacities and their extension in technological form" ("Marshall McLuhan" 4). McLuhan saw in the medieval past resonances with and relationships to his present.

McLuhan's posthumously published and co-authored with Eric McLuhan *Laws of Media: The New Science* offers the tetrad as a multisensory, multidimensional tool for analysis reminiscent of medieval, four-dimensional exegesis (50–51). The McLuhans saw in the early-modern work of Francis Bacon and Giambattista Vico a critique of the Renaissance's "abstract Method" (3), and they saw in the twentieth century visual space being obsolesced, acoustic space retrieved (39). Bacon and Vico are chronologically Renaissance figures, but the McLuhans' reading of them turns them into figures not unlike McLuhan himself: critics of dominant trends in education and society, forward thinkers with one foot deeply planted in the past, in the humanist tradition. Similarly, Francesco Guardiani, in "The New Middle Ages: Medievalism in McLuhan and Vacca," argues that in *The Gutenberg Galaxy: The Making of Typographic Man* McLuhan "reinvented medieval logic," a non-linear logic, through his claim that "electricity is medieval in nature, anti-modern in spirit, and anti-mechanical in practical experience" (5). For McLuhan, the move to electricity in communication technologies was a step into a medieval future.

McLuhan as Orientalist

In addition to the medievalist preoccupations that McLuhan shared with antimodernist thinkers, his antimodernist tendencies showed in his comments on Orientalism, which seem to both celebrate a shift in the traditional hierarchies of power between East and West and reinforce stereotyped notions of the "Oriental" other as pre- or non-literate, tribal, ancient, and mythic. In *The Medium Is the Massage: An Inventory of Effects,* one of McLuhan's Madison Avenue anti-book collaborations with Quentin Fiore, McLuhan asserts that "Electric circuitry is Orientalizing the West. The contained, the distinct, the separate—our Western legacy—are being replaced by the flowing, the unified, the fused" (145). Here McLuhan seems to welcome "Orientalizing the West," though he associates the East with a premodern wholeness and organic spiritual flow. These notions of the "Orient" as a totalizing whole are not much different from those espoused by early-twentieth-century Aesthetic Orientalism. Mari Yoshihara describes this process by which Asia was constructed as the West's "other": the West "typically associated Asia with pre-modern simplicity, naturalness and tradition—in sum, Asia embodied what historian Jackson Lears calls 'antimodernism'" (26). Yoshihara notes the early-twentieth-century association (particularly Japan among Asian countries) with qualities such as simplicity and purity. In "Tribalization of the Global Village: Marshall McLuhan, Orientalism, and Technocultural Panic," Matthew Reilly explains that "McLuhan's Orientalism brazenly adopts metaphors and analogies that most well-educated people today either critique or avoid. . . . McLuhan's discourse reinforces his personal ties to radically primitivist moderns such as Ezra Pound or Wyndham Lewis" (1).

McLuhan's argument that television was specifically "Orient-alizing the West" was a response to the rapid social change that McLuhan attributed to the medium. His discussion of "television child" theorizes the child immersed in a television-saturated environment, taking in information in non-linear pictographs, part of a global flow of information. His focus on constructing Asia's premodern wholeness in contrast to Western "typographic man's" linearity is closely related to that tendency we have already noted in antimodern thought to posit a future built on a fantasy construction of the past—an Asian "wholeness" that never quite existed.

McLuhan as Ad Man

Lears's quick sketch of twentieth-century antimodernists suggests that medievalists, Orientalists, and advertisers are "brothers under the skin," and McLuhan certainly came to take on the persona of an "ad man" through his collaborations with commercial designer Quentin Fiore and his reluctant admiration of the power of advertising. In *Understanding Media: The Extensions of Man*, McLuhan describes advertisements as preliterate icons striving to achieve a premodern kind of "programmed harmony among all human impulses and aspirations and endeavors" (202). "Using handcrafted methods," he continues, "[advertising] stretches out toward the ultimate electronic goal of a collective consciousness" (202). His analyses of the emerging electronic culture consistently invoke the language of antimodernism ("harmony," "handcrafted," "collective consciousness"), though he also notes the need to educate students on the power of images that are "forcefully insidious" (204–05), and he sees the "integrating and interrelating" work of television as anything but innocent (206). What is important to understand is that McLuhan did not envision a continuation of the modernist, literate world dominant at the time, nor did he envision the postmodern world described by the likes of Jean Baudrillard. Douglas Kellner attributes their differences to McLuhan's ecumenical Catholicism in contrast to Baudrillard's puritanical Protestantism, but for our purposes Kellner also illustrates a sharp contrast between antimodernist and postmodernist responses to the intensifying media environment:

McLuhan ... believed that the media could overcome alienation produced by the abstract rationality of book culture which was being replaced by a new synaesthesia and harmonizing of the mind and body, the senses and technologies. Baudrillard by contrast sees the media as external demigods, or idols of the mind—to continue the Protestant metaphor—,which seduce and fascinate the subject and which enter subjectivity to produce a reified consciousness and privatized and fragmented life-style (Sartre's seriality). Thus while McLuhan ascribes a generally benign social destiny to the media, for Baudrillard the function of TV and mass media is to prevent response, to isolate and privatize individuals, and to trap them into a universe of simulacra where it is impossible to distinguish between the spectacle and the real, and where individuals come to prefer spectacle over "reality" (which both loses interest for the masses and its privileged status in philosophy and social theory). (n. pag.)

The McLuhan-Baudrillard contrast is important to think about in McLuhanesque, acoustic terms. Baudrillard's thought is not the logical, sequential, historical development of McLuhan's thought: both views are still in play as we celebrate the antimodernists' global unifying potential of social media via the Arab Spring and lament the postmodernists' spectacle of political campaigns that promise hope and change but deliver the status quo. And both theories are challenged by Kellner, a supporter of neither and a purveyor of a more sustained, rational, modernist account of the political and social power of advertising and media in this and other works.

McLuhan as Literary Modernist

McLuhan's literary modernism is carefully articulated by Elena Lamberti in "Marshall McLuhan and the Modernist Writers' Legacy," and according to Lears, literary modernism, especially in the conservative hands of Eliot, Pound, and Yeats, results in an antimodernist response to modernity. Lamberti notes the "philosophy of composition" that linked them: "In the experimental work of modernist writers, the medium (writing) is somehow the message, as new technical devices are developed to convey a new world vision" (64). Lamberti lists other similarities: the quest for a new aesthetics, new sensibilities, reader involvement, the process as part of the show, the "conscious craftsman" replacing the "omniscient narrator and . . . critic" (70). The "conscious craftsman" description resonates with the Arts and Crafts movement central to the antimodernist spirit of the late nineteenth century and early twentieth century, and Theall's descriptions of McLuhan the artist resonate with both the Maker movement and the Do-It-Yourself culture of the twenty-first century documented in *Handmade Nation: The Rise of DIY, Art, Craft, and Design* (Levine and Heimerl). Theall suggests that McLuhan is a "complex maker of poetic assemblages" (*Virtual McLuhan* 41), and he draws on a provocative line from McLuhan's letters: "The citizen of the electronic era is a do-it-yourself man" (52). Cavell, even in the process of trying to define McLuhan as a postmodern artist, notes that his "intention was to urge us all to take on the condition of artists" (94). McLuhan's craftsmanship can be associated with modernism, as Lamberti has done, and his participatory, egalitarian ideas about artistic production can be associated with postmodernism, as Cavell has done, but both principles of craft and citizen artists are also central to the Arts and Crafts movement, and the contemporary craft, arts, and DIY movements, according to Andrew Wagner, trace their roots to the nineteenth century, not to postmodernism. McLuhan, understood as a literary modernist grounded in antimodernist values, provides a bridge between early-twentieth-century and early-twenty-first-century creative responses to the conditions of both modernity and postmodernity.

McLuhan as Conservative

Havers offers an analysis of McLuhan's conservatism that aligns closely with the argument that we are making, but he comes to the conclusion that McLuhan was a right-wing postmodernist. He does not offer this reading as distinct from an antimodernist reading; rather, he responds to Stamps, Willmott, and the general academic trend through the 1990s to find progressive and left-leaning possibilities in McLuhan's work. Havers notes McLuhan's affiliation with the European (and Southern U.S.) conservative, anti-capitalist, anti-liberal tradition (516), and he draws on the work of Shadia Drury to establish the viability of a right-wing postmodernism. Paraphrasing Drury, he writes that, "whereas the [postmodern] left seeks to expose and deconstruct these myths as masks for power, the [postmodern] right intends to use myths for the purpose of saving or reconstructing conservative types of regimes or political spaces" (518). Like Havers, we do not see any way to argue that McLuhan himself became more progressive or left leaning throughout his career, but we also do not see the need to label him as postmodern when antimodern is more historically and philosophically accurate. His apparent "progressive" turn, as Havers argues, is an example of forward-looking conservatism, but it is part of the prophetic antimodern tradition. Versluis ends his essay with a stirring account of the value of antimodernists, an account that can effortlessly be applied to McLuhan:

> The antimodernists do have important things to tell us. In many respects, they represent the prophetic voice that warns us that if we continue to follow our present course, we may well end in catastrophe. They point out the dark side of modern society, its explosiveness and destructiveness, the ways in which technology and centralization of power leach meaning from life, fragment us, and separate us into ever greater divisions between rich and poor, powerful and powerless, even as they continue to allure us with greater materials prosperity and technological power. The warnings of the antimodernists are often dire, but the best among them also affirm a vision of a better society—a more ethical way of life—and remind us of our spiritual purposes and responsibility. Antimodernists, far from representing a purely negative or pessimistic current, advance a critique of the society in which we live in order to call us toward a better one. Our future quality of life, perhaps even our survival, may depend upon whether we begin to heed their warnings. (129–30)

To sum up this section, we need to ask, and answer succinctly, "What do we get if we understand that McLuhan was an antimodernist?" We can see greater continuity between the cranky McLuhan in *The Mechanical Bride* and the somewhat more optimistic McLuhan who understood the electronic revolution to be offering a retrieval of medieval values, organicism, and a holistic world distinct from the mechanized, specialized, and fragmented modern world. Without antimodernism, his late-career optimism is generally perceived as a form of playful postmodernism even though the fragmentation, celebration of difference, and breaking down of hierarchies generally associated with postmodernism are diametrically opposed to some of his fundamental values. Although we acknowledge that the surface playfulness of McLuhan's later-career anti-books, wordplay, and one-liners share much with postmodernism, the commonality lies in the way in which both antimodernism and postmodernism stand in opposition to the rationalities and mechanization of modernism. Rather than tease apart the many differences in the ideological stances of these two movements, we find it more useful to think about the utility for cultural critics of a term such as "antimodern" to help them understand both McLuhan's work and the twentieth-century preoccupation with what Lears names the quest for the real: a longer, more powerful strand of conservative thought than generally acknowledged, a "diffuse . . . but influential cultural force" (307).

APPLICATION: ANTIMODERNISM THROUGH THE CENTURY, ACROSS FIELDS

Reintroducing and arguing for the relevance of the term "antimodernism" in twenty-first-century critical discourse have value beyond understanding McLuhan. In this final section, we want to illustrate the importance of keeping this term alive in our descriptions of twentieth-century and twenty-first-century art, architecture, and media. The neglect of "antimodernism" as a term and category has left scholars with a truncated critical vocabulary: modernism's only critics are presumably postmodernists and their variations: postcolonialists, posthumanists, poststructuralists, and so on. Reintroducing an overlooked critical term such as "antimodernism" can help scholars to expand the descriptive vocabulary generally used to theorize the twentieth century, a vocabulary frequently limited to that modernism-postmodernism continuum.

Antimodernism can also help critics to make sense of important contemporary cultural artifacts and the ways that they fit into larger movements. For example, the indigenous American architectural movement the Prairie School is regularly slotted by historians into a broader history of international modernism, though its practitioners and their preoccupations are decidedly unmodern. Similarly, understanding McLuhan as antimodern offers a framework to better theorize the acoustic space of Frank Lloyd Wright's architectural work and the tensions between medium and message in contemporary media artifacts, such as science fiction blockbusters like *Star Wars* and *Avatar,* and to contrast those films with the more unabashedly antimodernist works of Japanese animation, such as Hayao Miyazaki's *Ponyo.*

Recognizing contemporary versions of antimodernism and their ongoing cultural appeal can also help us to understand the power of potentially unifying phrases such as the "global village" or simply the concept of ONE, the name of the foremost postideological advocacy group seeking to eliminate global poverty. The concept can help us more readily to see patterns among diffuse cultural movements such as home birth, steampunk subcultures, urban agriculture, cage fighting, Pinterest and DIY culture, religious communitarianism, second amendment separatists, the Occupy movement, and Greenpeace—whose reliance on McLuhanesque strategies has been documented in Stephen Dale's *McLuhan's Children: The Greenpeace Message and the Media.*

Although we draw brief examples of the persistence, popularity, and simultaneity of antimodernism within modern/postmodern movements from architecture and film, a rich variety of contemporary social movements and artifacts would benefit from similar analyses. Although his personal ideology is characterized as conservative, by his late career McLuhan focused especially, and almost apolitically, on issues of the environment and culture. Some scholars tend to read Wright's environmental and anti-corporate preoccupations as leftist, and stylistic features of his work as modernist, but like McLuhan the cultural concerns that Wright shares with antimodernists tend to be conservative.

Wright is an example that highlights this tension between the celebration of the natural and indigenous and a conservative, individualistic cultural agenda. The work produced during his years as part of what is now known as the Prairie School of architecture, in the earliest part of the twentieth century in the Midwestern United States (1907–13), represents his attempt to develop an indigenous American architecture, using local materials, in buildings organically sited to follow the land's curves—or, in the case of prairie houses, rectilinearity. Wright, arguably the most well-known architect in the United States, is most often characterized in modernist histories as an important figure in international modernism. Although the exteriors of his domestic dwellings of the time did bear superficial likenesses to some European modernist projects in their clean lines and attempted break from historical precedents, in most ways his work questioned and contradicted the celebration of the machine age and technologies of mass production typically embedded in modern architecture. In fact, Wright's architecture of the Prairie School era can be read alternatively and productively as antimodern in the medieval handcrafting of its production, the conservative cultural values imbued in its maternal, "hearth-centred" construction of family, and the celebration of its (arguably) organic relation to site, natural materials, and indigenous landscaping.

Architectural historian Sigfried Giedion, an important McLuhan peer, aligns Wright closely not only to McLuhan's preoccupations but also to those of antimodernism, claiming that Wright's work draws on the "Far East" not in terms of using uncreative historical precedents but, "like Matisse with Negro or Persian art, from an inner, sympathetic relationship" (394). Wright was the spirit of the East and of making a future of the fantasy past. According to Giedion, "The secret of Wright's work is that he saw in the tradition of the American house those elements which could be used as a basis for its future" (396). Moreover, Wright houses use space in novel ways, with rooms flaring outward from a central core, with continuous vertical and horizontal interpenetrating space, which "brought life, movement, freedom into the rigid and benumbed body of modern architecture" (403). Although Giedion understands Wright as improving architecture, he does not understand him as reacting to modern architecture, nor, in 1941, can he give voice to a notion such as acoustic space, which might help to interpret both the wholeness that Wright hoped to impart in interiors and his refusal to nod toward the Victorian predilection toward ornamented visual spaces, rooms framed for viewing objects, not opened to both hearth and out of doors, for tactile interaction with "honest" construction materials.

Giedion aligns Wright's preoccupations with the rhetoric of antimodernism without, of course, using the term, suggesting that, "As a prophet, a preacher, and [an] agrarian individualist, he preaches hatred of the city and return to the soil and to productive, self-sufficient community" (421). At the same time, Giedion situates Wright's work on a continuum leading inexorably toward architectural high modernism, under the subheading "Toward Pure Forms" (379). Rather than a stepping stone on the path to modernism, Wright (and others involved in the Prairie School) should be read as embracing antimodernist preoccupations of which, like McLuhan, he never divested himself. Reclaiming the term "antimodernism" offers scholars both the explanatory power to understand architectural artifacts as part of a complex cultural moment and the opportunity to reclaim the intellectual sources of a movement too long subsumed within a narrative of modernist progress.

While reclaiming the term "antimodernism" is useful in understanding and explicating a range of artistic and creative movements of the past two centuries, framing McLuhan as an antimodernist also offers a method of reading media products such as film. The persistence of antimodernist themes in Hollywood film in many ways reflects a persistent cultural anxiety about the modern technological condition. For example, in two landmark science fiction films, *Star Wars* (1977) and *Avatar* (2009), "antimodern" values are clearly expressed (paradoxically by pushing the limits of filmmaking technology). In *Star Wars: A New Hope* (see Lucas), the appeal of "the force" as a mystical life energy, and the "farm boy" rebels who have spawned a rebirth of what Han Solo calls "[h]okey religions and ancient weapons," are antimodern concepts when juxtaposed with the images of modernism and mass production gone wrong: the stark, sterile, and reflective interiors of the Death Star and mass-produced humans—the Clone Troopers. The ultimate powers in the saga are all users of the force, the familial wins out over the corporate, the antimodern trumps the modern, and ultimately, perhaps, the pro-capitalist bureaucracy is undermined. Although the cynical might suggest that the film's mythos has endured for nearly forty years because of George Lucas's ability to market trinkets and manage a global transmedia enterprise, the films and their world have also managed to engage multiple generations of fans with their antimodern longing for a galactic future much like America's agrarian/cowboy past.

James Cameron's *Avatar* enacts an even more complex battle with the antimodern, (tribalized and primitive) Na'vi overcoming the modern military-scientific-industrial complex and offering the "Western" overcivilized hero, Jake Sully, literally numbed by the paralysis of injury, the opportunity to "feel" again through his interaction with primitives and to believe again through the wholeness of religious experience. At the same time that these two blockbuster films offered strong antimodernist images and ideologies, both pushed the envelope of filmmaking, embracing cutting-edge technologies to produce spectacular effects. Although the term "antimodernist" is helpful in understanding the conservative cultural thread running through a variety of contemporary artifacts, it does not necessarily help us to understand the medium or techniques of films.

In contrast, the term "antimodern" strongly resonates with the Japanese animated films of Hayao Miyazaki. Miyazaki's films share an antimodern stance in both content and form—in this case, the medium is the message. The medium—hand-drawn cel animation—harkens back, literally to medieval times, to twelfth-century scroll "animation" (Hu 26–27). Anime uses many of the same compositional and stylistic techniques used in Japan's Edo-period woodblock prints; in fact, the hand-layering of colour in animation compositing is similar to the hand-inking techniques used to tint woodblock prints (Hu 32–33). Through that low-tech process of creation, anime embraces a mode of production that is mechanical, handmade, and decidedly "other" than the production techniques of contemporary film, demonstrating a synchronicity of medium and message. As media ecologist and East Asian scholar Thomas LaMarre puts it, anime, as a medium, "minimizes the narratives of technology" (6), shaping films that question modernism's techniques and teleologies, not simply in content but also in form. The anime films of Miyazaki are well-known artifacts that illustrate this confluence of antimodern rhetoric, technological anxiety, and a medium that both looks different and "looks" differently. As film, it directs viewers' looking, and that gaze is decidedly not cinematic but, as LaMarre calls it, a "primordial form of panoramic perception" (38).

Although much contemporary anime has resorted to employing sweatshop labour in Korea, Taiwan, or China, Miyazaki's studio retains a more "workshop" approach to production, according to Helen McCarthy. LaMarre extends this view: "Indeed, the Ghibli [Miyazaki's production company] combination of artistic hierarchy and cooperation, with energetic youth under the guidance of charismatic leaders in the service of preserving and sustaining a brand of animation and a worldview, calls to mind some of the quasi-feudal communities evoked in Miyazaki's animations" (100). LaMarre names this set of predispositions that Miyazaki critiques the "modern technological condition."

LaMarre asserts that the message of "Miyazaki's animations impl[ies] that modern technology is not just dangerous in its applications but in its effect on human perception and human thought" (91). Sociologist Max Weber used the term "disenchantment" to describe ways in which modernist preoccupations with scientific understanding and rational processes have created a secular and demystified world (Habermas 2). Miyazaki's films mourn the loss of that disenchantment and, at a cultural level, suggest that antidotes might be found in tradition and a reacquaintance with the natural world. One example is Miyazaki's 2008 film *Ponyo*. Although the story is simple enough for children, who always already inhabit a numinous world, Ponyo's magic offers adults the possibility of re-enchantment as an antidote to destruction of the natural world and devaluation of the spiritual world brought about by the values of modernity. *Ponyo* advocates embracing the magic of childhood as a means of revaluing the natural world and inter-vening in the destruction that we humans have brought through our desires to comprehend, control, and subjugate nature, climate, and evolution. The notion of antimodernism helps us to interpret Miyazaki's work as an artifact of a broad intellectual history, one that is not simply "right-wing postmodernism" or "leftist critique of modernism" but forward thinking and, like McLuhan, some-times hopeful.

CONCLUSION

"Antimodernism," we have been arguing, is a valuable term that can enrich critical discourse and clarify values not easily mapped onto a modern-postmodern continuum or a right-left political scale. If the term has not always been available to us, the impulse to critique modernity's symptoms is powerful and persistent. We understand that trying to (re)introduce antimodernism into critical discourse dominated by the modernism-postmodernism binary will take sustained efforts to adjust how scholars talk about values embedded in the work of artists, other scholars, and social movements. We also understand that, in the logic of scholarly dis-course, reintroducing an old term is more difficult than inventing a new one because the scholarly enterprise is largely modernist in nature. Scholars are more inclined to ask "What's after post-modernism?" than to take a "collide-oscopic" inventory of what is going on, as McLuhan labels his own project in *The Medium Is the Massage* (McLuhan and Fiore 10). But if prominent twen-tieth-century intellectual and artistic figures such as McLuhan and Wright come to be understood as "antimodernists," and the ideological values embedded in the globally popular *Star Wars*, *Avatar*, and Studio Ghibli productions come to be understood as "antimodernist," then scholars in a variety of disciplines might take the term more seriously and see its value for describing a per-sistent critique of modernity that relies not on a deconstruction of the metaphysics of presence but on a reunification of values around interests shared by some on the left and right, such as pro-tection of the environment or reduction of global poverty.

WORKS CITED

Cameron, James, dir. *Avatar.* 20th Century Fox. 2009. DVD.

Carey, James W. "Harold Adams Innis and Marshall McLuhan." *Antioch Review* 27.1 (1967): 5–39. Print.

——. "Marshall McLuhan: Genealogy and Legacy." *Canadian Journal of Communication* 23.3 (1998): 1–8. Web.

——. "McLuhan and Mumford: The Roots of Modern Media Analysis." *Journal of Communication* 31.3 (1981): 162–78. Web.

Cavell, Richard. *McLuhan in Space: A Cultural Geography.* Toronto: U of Toronto P, 2002. Print.

Czitrom, Daniel J. *Media and the American Mind: From Morse to McLuhan.* Chapel Hill: U of North Carolina P, 1982. Print.

Dale, Stephen. *McLuhan's Children: The Greenpeace Message and the Media.* Toronto: Between the Lines, 1996. Print.

Giedion, Sigfried. *Space, Time, and Architecture.* 3rd ed. Cambridge, MA: Harvard UP, 1954. Print.

Gordon, W. Terrence. *Marshall McLuhan: Escape into Understanding.* New York: Basic Books, 1997. Print.

Guardiani, Francesco. "The New Middle Ages: Medievalism in McLuhan and Vacca." *McLuhan Studies* 1.6 (n.d.): n. pag. projects.chass.utoronto.ca/mcluhan-studies/v1_iss6/1_6art5.htm. Web.

Habermas, Jürgen. *The Philosophical Discourses of Modernity.* London: Polity, 1985. Print.

Havers, Grant. "The Right-Wing Postmodernism of Marshall McLuhan." *Media, Culture, and Society* 25.4 (2003): 511–25. Print.

Horowitz, Daniel. *Consuming Pleasures: Intellectuals and Popular Culture in the Postwar World.* Philadelphia: U of Pennsylvania P, 2012. Print.

Hu, Tze-Yue G. *Frames of Anime.* Hong Kong: Hong Kong UP, 2010. Print.

Hunt, Arthur W., III. "Media Ecology, Sacred Earth, and the Agrarian Mind." *EME: Explorations in Media Ecology* 8.2 (2009): 115–32. Print.

Jackson, Robert H., and Carol Zeman Rothkopf, eds. *Book Talk: Essays on Books, Booksellers, Collecting, and Special Collections.* New Castle, DE: Oak Knoll, 2006. Print.

Kellner, Douglas. "Baudrillard: A New McLuhan?" *Illuminations: The Critical Theory Project.* N.d. pages.gseis.ucla.edu/faculty/kellner/Illumina%20Folder/kell26.htm. Web.

LaMarre, Thomas. *The Anime Machine: A Media Theory of Animation.* Minneapolis: U of Minnesota P, 2009. Print.

Lamberti, Elena. "Marshall McLuhan and the Modernist Writers' Legacy." *At the Speed of Light There Is Only Illumination: A Reappraisal of Marshall McLuhan.* Ed. John Moss and Linda M. Morra. Ottawa: U of Ottawa P, 2004. 63–84. Print.

Lears, T.J. Jackson. *No Place of Grace: Antimodernism and the Transformation of American Culture, 1880–1920.* Chicago: U of Chicago P, 1994. Print.

Levine, Faythe, and Cortney Heimerl, eds. *Handmade Nation: The Rise of DIY, Art, Craft, and Design.* New York: Princeton Architectural, 2008. Print.

Lucas, George, dir. *Star Wars: A New Hope.* LucasFilm. 1977. DVD.

Luke, Tim. "Alterity or Antimodernism: A Response to Versluis." *Telos* 137 (2006): 131–42. Print.

McCarthy, Helen. *Hayao Miyazaki: Master of Japanese Animation.* Berkeley: Stone Bridge, 2002. Print.

McLuhan, Marshall. *The Mechanical Bride: Folklore of Industrial Man.* 1950. Corte Madera, CA: Ginko, 2002. Print.

———. *Understanding Media: The Extensions of Man* New York: Signet, 1964. Print.

McLuhan, Marshall, and Quentin Fiore. *The Medium Is the Massage: An Inventory of Effects.* 1967. Corte Madera, CA: Ginko, 2001. Print.

McLuhan, Marshall, and Eric McLuhan. *Laws of Media: The New Science.* Toronto: U of Toronto P, 1988. Print.

Miyazaki, Hayao, dir. *Ponyo.* Studio Ghibli. 2009. DVD.

Reilly, Matthew. "Tribalization of the Global Village: Marshall McLuhan, Orientalism, and Technocultural Panic." *Viz.* 2011. viz.dwrl.utexas.edu/content/tribalization-global-village-marshall-mcluhan-orientalism-and-technocultural-panic. Web.

Stamps, Judith. *Unthinking Modernity: Innis, McLuhan, and the Frankfurt School.* Montreal: McGill-Queen's UP, 1995. Print.

Theall, Donald. "McLuhan's Canadian Sense of Space, Time, and Tactility." Review of *McLuhan in Space: A Cultural Geography,* by

Richard Cavell. *Journal of Canadian Studies* 37.3 (2002): 251–59. Print.

——. *The Medium Is the Rear View Mirror: Understanding McLuhan.* Montreal: McGill-Queen's UP, 1971. Print.

——. *The Virtual Marshall McLuhan.* Montreal: McGill-Queen's UP, 2001. Print.

Versluis, Arthur. "Antimodernism." *Telos* 137 (2006): 96–130. Print.

Wagner, Andrew. "Craft: It's What You Make of It." Levine and Heimerl 1–3.

Willmott, Glenn. *McLuhan, or Modernism in Reverse.* Toronto: U of Toronto P, 1996. Print.

Yoshihara, Mari. *Embracing the East: White Women and American Orientalism.* New York: Oxford UP, 2003. Print.

CHAPTER 3

EXCEEDING OUR GRASP:
McLUHAN'S ALL-METAPHORICAL OUTLOOK

Yoni Van Den Eede

Ah, but a man's reach should exceed his grasp,
    Or what's a heaven for?
          —ROBERT BROWNING, "ANDREA DEL SARTO"

Displaying his love for wordplay, Marshall McLuhan used to cite a twist on Robert Browning's well-known inspirational line: "A man's reach must exceed his grasp or what's a metaphor" (*Understanding Media* 64). McLuhan was a man of the word in more than one sense. He grew up in a Protestant family steeped in public speaking, converted to Catholicism during his twenties, and became a professor of English—eventually devoting his attention wholly to the workings of media. He was also a man of many words. He wrote or co-wrote an admirable number of books, papers, and letters. But his true forte was the spoken word: McLuhan never got tired of conversing, whether in small or in large company, either to the delight or to the frustration of that company, as biographers W. Terrence Gordon and Philip Marchand both note. Even his written works mostly read like oral improvisations, stirring mixed emotions much as his verbal speech did.

McLuhan gradually started dedicating more of his time to the study of communications and media during the 1950s, and it should come as no surprise that "the word" began to take central stage in this work. But "the word" was now spoken by popular culture: advertisements, television, radio, newspapers. What is more, in his first major work on media, *The Gutenberg Galaxy: The Making of Typographic Man,* McLuhan analyzes the influence of the phonetic alphabet and the movable type printing press on overall culture. This discovery, namely that a certain configuration of "the word" or words (the uniform, repeatable order brought about by the alphabet or printing process) speaks its own cultural language, having observable effects on our society, cultural mindset, and worldview, eventually led to the famous phrase "the medium is the message." The word speaks a word, so to speak.

That is not to say that McLuhan was a linguist or structuralist. His approach was consciously piecemeal, aphoristic, sometimes even somewhat incoherent. Yet throughout his probings, the concept of metaphor stands out, and McLuhan equips it in several ways and many places. Metaphor was already a guiding light in his doctoral dissertation on the trivium and the *translatio studii,* and it became central to his study of media-related issues and especially of the tetradic laws of media, in which he takes a stance that we have come to know through George Lakoff and Mark Johnson, that is, that metaphor is central to how we interpret and act in the world.

When McLuhan writes that "A man's reach must exceed his grasp or what's a metaphor," he brings forth a smart, almost parodic, variation on the verse of Browning: "Ah, but a man's reach should exceed his grasp, / Or what's a heaven for?" (117). One of his favourite quips, it perfectly illustrates the magnificent power that metaphor held for McLuhan, many layered as the phrase is. In what follows, to attempt to make sense of these layers, I first outline his theory by way of a brief sketch of the metaphors—mind the plural—that he applied to describe the workings of media and technology, calling this the "theoretical" use of metaphor. I then look at his method, finding that it resembles the "structure" of metaphor, calling this the "meta-theoretical" use. I next examine how McLuhan employed metaphor *an sich* as a theoretical tool, calling this the "intra-theoretical" use, which can be categorized into two groups: "technology as metaphor" and "culture as metaphor." Finally, I account for what all these different modes of usage add up to, considering an all-metaphorical outlook.

McLUHAN'S METAPHORS

An examination of the use of metaphor by McLuhan necessarily starts with an overview of some of the metaphors that he created. These figures help to identify the structures and effects of media and technologies, thus being "theoretical": that is, used theoretically to describe and analyze certain situations and events. The following list should be read not as a comprehensive summary of McLuhan's work but as an illustrative encounter with key concepts of his theories. It serves as a guide later on when I dive more deeply into his oeuvre.

Narcissus

According to McLuhan, every technology or medium is an extension of a human sense or body part: the wheel of the foot, script of speech, and so forth. This is not a neutral event: technologies and media "work us over completely" (McLuhan and Fiore 26). But they do so in a subliminal, unconscious way. Media are "make happen" agents, not "make aware" agents (McLuhan, *Understanding Media* 57). In *Understanding Media: The Extensions of Man*, McLuhan employs the Narcissus myth to make sense of this state of unconsciousness: "[M]en at once become fascinated by any extension of themselves in any material other than themselves" (51). But at the same time, all technologies or media, by extending a certain sense or body part and thus "overstimulating" it, cause the amputation and thereby the numbing of that sense or part—"Narcissus," says McLuhan, stems from "narcosis" (51). So we remain completely unaware of the physical, psychological, and social effects that media have on us.

The Medium Is the Message

Those effects nevertheless do not coincide with the media content that we consciously perceive, such as articles in a newspaper or a program on television. The workings of each medium reside in its form or the medium "itself": the newspaper form, the television form. Hence the phrase "the medium is the message" (McLuhan, *Understanding Media* 23–35). This message manifests itself first and foremost in how we perceive, process, and interpret sense data as we extend our senses into our technologies. Every medium-as-extension shakes up the whole sense equilibrium of an individual as well as society, with grave consequences: "A new extension sets up a new equilibrium among all of the senses and faculties leading, as we say, to a 'new outlook'—new attitudes and preferences in many areas" (119). Every technology creates an "environment" (McLuhan and Parker 40). Although "the medium is the message" is not a figure of speech in the proper sense, it should nevertheless be interpreted metaphorically, as societies or cultures in whole are not literally capable of receiving messages or literally in possession of a sense equilibrium that could be altered.

Visual vs. Auditory-Tactile

Phonetic literacy and especially the movable type printing press, introduced by Gutenberg, helped to produce Western capitalist society based on uniformity, segmentation, and visual perspective. But with "electric" technology—McLuhan was writing in the 1960s and 1970s—we return to tribal conditions of simultaneity, instantaneousness, and auditory-tactile ways of interacting. Yet this is not simply a "revolution": the clash between literary and tribal modes can be felt on many different planes and in many different fields, as various sorts of media and technologies exist at the same time. The visual and the auditory-tactile are not equivalent poles. Visuality enhances individual viewpoint and perspective (as in modern novels or Renaissance paintings), but tactility is the synthesis, synesthesia, or interplay among *all* the senses (McLuhan, *Gutenberg Galaxy* 41, 65, 272).

The Global Village

Thus, according to McLuhan, we are now returning to tribal conditions of involvement in others' lives because of the emergence of electric technologies such as the telegraph and television, a situation that inspired him to coin another of his well-known terms: "the global village." "The new electronic interdependence," he says, "recreates the world in the image of a global village" (*Gutenberg Galaxy* 31). Unexpectedly, this does not broaden our worldview—quite the contrary. In the age of electric technology, we have extended our whole nervous system into it: "The effect of extending the central nervous system is not to create a world-wide city of ever-expanding dimensions but rather a global village of ever-contracting size" (McLuhan and Parker 40). The world has become a tribal village.

///

Thus far I have sketched the most central concepts of McLuhan's media theory. Before I move on from this "theoretical" to the "meta-theoretical" plane—that is, his theory of theory—I need to briefly address the question of whether McLuhan used the aforementioned metaphors in a *metaphorical* way, as would be a natural consequence of their use *as* metaphor, or in a *literal* way, as some authors have claimed. For example, in his *McLuhan*, Jonathan Miller reproaches him for taking metaphors literally. Miller claims that, when McLuhan talks about the television image as tactile, this should be interpreted in a literal sense (121–22). However, Gordon retorts in *Marshall McLuhan: Escape into Understanding* that "McLuhan does not refer to the TV image as tactile because of the metaphorical finger scanning the screen, as Miller believes, but because the TV image requires of the eye a degree of involvement as intense as that of touch" (328). Also, William Kuhns remarks about the global village metaphor that, "When McLuhan uses a phrase like 'global village,' he is not speaking literally—even as a metaphor the term founders—but aphoristically" (195). I return to this issue later in this chapter.

THEORY AS METAPHOR

Of McLuhan's method a lot can be and has been said, often to the detriment of McLuhan. But as subversive as his somewhat chaotic approach might have been within traditional academia, he stubbornly kept professing it. He proposed and used an aphoristic style, "packaging" books rather than writing them, as he himself purportedly once said in relation to writing *The Gutenberg Galaxy* (Marchand 165). This was very much a conscious strategy; any good media student, he thought, needs to be subversive in his or her own right.

Central to McLuhan's methodical approach was the "probe." In *The Gutenberg Galaxy*, he does not yet employ this term but refers to his method as a "mosaic approach," implementing a concept from Georg von Békésy. According to von Békésy, there are two different ways of handling a problem. One is the "theoretical approach," in which the problem is described in relation to existing knowledge, elaborated by way of known and accepted principles, and then tested as a hypothesis in an experimental setting (largely the "scientific method," though that concept itself is elusive). Von Békésy continues that "Another, which may be called the mosaic approach, takes each problem for itself with little reference to the field in which it lies, and seeks to discover relations and principles that hold within the circumscribed area" (quoted in McLuhan, *Gutenberg Galaxy* 42).

From *The Medium Is the Massage: An Inventory of Effects* onward, McLuhan formulates this distinction in terms of "fixed point of view" versus "probe." "Probing" is needed to unveil the hidden effects of media—"their message"—while one cannot even begin to comprehend them in taking a fixed standpoint: "The main obstacle to a clear understanding of the effects of the new media is our deeply embedded habit of regarding all phenomena from a fixed point of view" (McLuhan and Fiore 68). All "new" technologies create their own environments, but mostly we are not aware of this happening because we are wrapped up in the "old" environments. Artists pre-eminently are the ones who can raise consciousness of the new environments: "Such environments are invisible and invincible except as they are raised to consciousness by new artistic styles and probes" (McLuhan and Watson 175). Artists, as superb probers, produce "anti-environments," by exploring and focusing their attention elsewhere, by transference. Humour, for example, is a key strategy for doing so: "Humour as a system of communications, and as a probe of our environment— of what's really going on—affords us our most appealing anti-environment tool" (McLuhan and Fiore 92).

Another image that McLuhan deploys to describe the probing attitude is that of the sleuth or detective. A typical detective novel starts with a situation "after the fact"—someone has been murdered, someone has disappeared, something has been stolen. The sleuth then proceeds to question all the persons involved and investigate the crime scene—steadily descending down the causal chain toward the initial event. Likewise, according to McLuhan, the study of media should start from the effects of media and work back to their cause(s) from there. He claims in several texts that the good media student resembles the sleuth, looking for clues in the muddle of media crimes "after the fact" (*Gutenberg Galaxy* 277; McLuhan and Fiore 88; McLuhan, Hutchon, and McLuhan 173).

The dramatic tone that this analogy conveys is not arbitrary. McLuhan seems to think that we really are in danger. He considers technology and media as threatening forces that "beset mankind" and should be exhaustively understood before they are unleashed on the public (*Understanding Media* 67). Because we do not adequately grasp the effects of media, "[w]e may be drowning" (McLuhan and Parker 115). This bedlam cannot be countered by traditional means: that is, the method of uniform rationality. Probing then becomes a highly necessary survival mechanism: "Survival is not possible if one approaches his environment, the social drama, with a fixed, unchangeable point of view—the witless repetitive response to the unperceived" (McLuhan and Fiore 10). "Playing around," on the contrary, could save us from madness.

But how to go about probing practically? Of course, there is no fixed recipe—that is just the "point." As for McLuhan himself, he certainly can be said to have applied his own method well. He never wrote a book or even an article in a clear-cut, linear, logical style, always mixing up pithy phrases, puns, fragments, and quotations almost at random. Of this deliberate non-willingness to construct an all-comprehensive, all-clear story, he himself appears to have said that "People make a great mistake trying to read me as if I were saying something. I poke these sentences around to probe and feel my way around in our kind of world" (quoted in Marchand 195).

Notwithstanding his consistency in practising what he preaches, a paradoxical sleight of hand takes place in the argument. Ultimately, it appears to be the environment created by electric technology that enables us to probe that environment. Employing cybernetic vocabulary, McLuhan observes that, "In the age of the information hunter, feedback yields to feedforward, the point of view becomes the probe" (McLuhan and Parker 80). In other words, "our time" is the best time for probing around: "The method of our time is to use not a single but multiple models for exploration" (McLuhan and Fiore 69). Of course, the word *probe* has a much more tactile resonance than "mosaic approach." This could well be his conscious purpose as he tries to "feel [his] way around in our kind of world." Yet this seems to be begging the question. How can we appropriately attest to the effects of media if these media enable us to attest to them?

Nonetheless, in the context of the "mosaic approach" that McLuhan proposes, this might not be too much of a paradox. What he tries to impart here is that there is no "neutral" place from which to assess phenomena. On the contrary, not leaving our traditional point of view leaves us at the mercy of media. So this "circular reasoning" is not so much a fallacy as a consequence of metaphorical thinking. In a world overwhelming us with media and technology, one *can only* probe or stay forever in a catatonic state. By way of this method of "metaphor instrumentalized"—fooling around, playing around, testing, probing—one can come to grips with a complex, inherently paradoxical reality.

However, whereas McLuhan develops a metaphorically inspired and inclined method on this "meta-theoretical" plane, in the "intra-theoretical" realm he engages the metaphor concept *an sich* to make sense of technology itself and its surroundings.

TECHNOLOGY AS METAPHOR

McLuhan employs an arsenal of metaphors in constructing his theory of media: Narcissus, visual versus auditory-tactile, the global village, and so on. To that list we must add the metaphor of metaphor itself. According to McLuhan, all media and technologies function according to a scheme of translation in the sense of metaphor: transference, *translatio*. Seen from this perspective, "extension" stands for "translation." Already in *The Gutenberg Galaxy* McLuhan points out this connection: "Invention, in a word, is translation of one kind of space into another" (44). Metaphor is a mechanism of translating one thing, concept, sense, image into another. To be sure, language itself is metaphor "in the sense that it not only stores but translates experience from one mode into another" (5). Indeed, language is a technology itself, and one of the first technologies ever, as McLuhan notes in *Understanding Media*: "The spoken word was the first technology by which man was able to let go of his environment in order to grasp it in a new way" (64).

How does this technological translation work exactly? Within it, more or less three "moments" can be distinguished (though McLuhan himself does not literally do so). First, as said, according to him, all technologies and media are extensions of human senses or body parts. So, in the process of extending ourselves into technology, we are translating "more and more of ourselves into other forms of expression that exceed ourselves" (*Understanding Media* 64). Here McLuhan inserts the phrase quoted earlier: "A man's reach must exceed his grasp or what's a metaphor." This is exactly what we do by inventing, developing, and using technology, "alternately grasping and letting go"—as much in a literal sense as in a figurative sense (64). And with electric technology we have extended—"translated"—our nervous system into our technology. The end stage of this evolution is the transfer of our whole consciousness into technology, thereby creating an electronic "collective consciousness" (*Gutenberg Galaxy* 265–79). This notion continues to intrigue us and has been elaborated in recent studies by scholars such as de Kerckhove, Lévy, and Rheingold.

Second, in extending our senses, technologies alter our "sense equilibrium": that is, the balance between the senses, thus exchanging one sense for another. Or, as another one of McLuhan's favourite quips goes, phonetic writing, in stepping down tribalism and orality, gives us "an eye for an ear" (*Gutenberg Galaxy* 26–27; *Understanding Media* 84–90). Thus, metaphor by necessity governs the structuring of our sensory life as well: "the principle of exchange and translation, or metaphor, is in our rational power to translate all of our senses into one another" (*Gutenberg Galaxy* 5). Most exchanges, McLuhan seems to suggest, take place between visuality and tactility, the latter, as said, comprising the interplay of all the senses.

The full extent of what these first two "moments" taken together mean is illustrated well by a quotation from McLuhan and Barrington Nevitt's book "about" management, *Take Today: The Executive as Dropout:* "Every medium imposes its own structure and assumptions upon all data, while each favors either EYE or EAR. . . . All conceptual models or metaphors transfer or transform meaning from one sensory modality or field of being to another, just as the word 'metaphor' itself presents semantic meaning under the guise of transportation" (141). In short, in a mediated world, we are constantly involved in schemes of translation, whether of ourselves into technology or of one sense into another.

But McLuhan goes further. Third, and as a consequence of the previous "moments" of translation, technologies translate modes of perception *beyond* the realm of the individual: "[A]ll media as extensions of ourselves serve to provide new transforming vision and awareness" (*Understanding Media* 66). On a larger, "cultural" plane, we can discern the same sort of processes as those within our sensory lives. Hence McLuhan's principal "historical" distinction: that between the visuality of Western modernity—stressing uniformity, individualism, perspective, and linearity—and the tactility of ancient or contemporary tribalism—enhancing mythicism, involvement, orality, and simultaneity.

CULTURE AS METAPHOR

As mentioned above, according to McLuhan, "the 'message' of any medium or technology is the change of scale or pace or pattern that it introduces into human affairs" (*Understanding Media* 24). The "messages" of media can and do have worldwide impacts. No single technology can be studied independently, or be expected to have clear-cut effects, but neither can environments (39). Just as there are exchanges among the senses as a result of media and technologies, so too the environments created by those technologies interact among each other. McLuhan describes these processes by way of various idioms.

One is "interplay." As we have seen, interplay, or translation, takes place among the senses, but it can be observed among environments as well, and this is a multifarious, complex, all-pervasive process (McLuhan and Parker 31). Media environments are by necessity intertwined: they interact and collide with each other. Various evolutions, processes, and events "conspire" to "make history" (which, of course, is constantly in the making). In that way, the combination of phonetic literacy and Gutenberg's invention of the movable type printing press provided the perfect soil for the growth of Western modernity. But naturally these are only the elementary plot lines of the story. Reality, localized and situated, is far more complex. Myriads of media make for what we can call "media battlefields" that are hardly overseeable. By way of illustration, McLuhan notes that "The United States had built up a large degree of central political controls through the interplay of the railway, the post office, and the newspaper" (*Understanding Media* 226). Many media and their environments must be taken into account.

Another concept that McLuhan provides to come to grips with inter-environmental translation processes is "hybrid energy." The clash between literary and tribal modes can be felt on many different planes and in many different fields, in politics, art, science, popular culture. Wherever technologies, media, modes of perception crash into each other, there is released "hybrid energy," out of which new creations can arise (*Understanding Media* 57–63). And "great periods," those of change because of the collision of cultures, "are always periods of translation" (McLuhan and Parker 110). Of course, McLuhan evidently simplifies things by keying only two main perceptive "schemes": namely, the literary-visual and the tribal-auditory-tactile—often identifying the first with the West and the second with the East. As it stands, this too might be begging the question. Yet again, in a paradoxical way, this relatively crude distinction might work well in creating an interpretive framework for the study of medial complexity—namely, the interaction of environments.

So culture—as the ensemble of the many diverse environments in which we live—is "metaphorical" just as well. In the main, McLuhan argues that "Technologically-created environments are as symbolic as any metaphor could ever be" (McLuhan and Fiore, *War and Peace* 59). McLuhan and co-author Wilfred Watson sum it all up in *From Cliché to Archetype:* "The interplay of environments is translation; the Latin word is *translatio,* and the Greek word is *metaphorein*" (168).

THE UBIQUITY OF METAPHOR

McLuhan's theory is a patchwork of metaphors (theoretical plane). His method and approach are "metaphor instrumentalized" (meta-theoretical plane). He thinks of technologies, and of the interactions among the environments that they create ("culture"), as metaphorical translations (intra-theoretical plane). Clearly, the concept of metaphor was central to his thought. Yet, in some of his later, partially posthumously published, works, he extended all of this even further. Near the end of his life, McLuhan took what Gordon calls a "linguistic turn" (323), actually not so much a turn as, phrased in somewhat McLuhanist terms, a "stepping up" of the "linguistic" "intensity" already present in his work on media.

What McLuhan discovered is that not only media and technologies can be studied as metaphors; all human creations are eligible in principle to this treatment, even more so: all human artifacts are "structurally linguistic." He expressed great enthusiasm for this in a letter: "This discovery, unknown to anybody in any culture, would justify a book without any other factors whatsoever" (quoted in Gordon 224). McLuhan even compared his find to James Watson's discovery of the double helix structure of DNA, favouring his in any case as the "widest": "Literally speaking, this breakthrough about the linguistic structure of all human artifacts is incomparably larger and deeper-going" (quoted 224).

At first sight, such assertions do seem to characterize McLuhan as an outright linguist or structuralist of sorts—despite my suggestion to the contrary at the beginning of this chapter. However, rather than view his "turn" as some kind of linguistic reductionism, we should seize it as an opportunity to re-evaluate language. In that sense, the metaphorical dynamics that media "are" can be seen as the glue keeping our human reality together. The human-made world can be said to have been built out of this "language." In other words, the idea appears to urge us to redefine language as we know it rather than to categorize McLuhan unilaterally under the linguistic rubric. (Elsewhere I have argued that his "linguistic turn" can even be read as an "objective turn." See Van Den Eede 181 ff.)

The alleged "linguistic discovery" relates to several other findings of McLuhan's later years, which have not always been well received or paid attention to within media theorist circles but which certainly bear relevance to my purposes here—namely, an inquiry into his use of the concept of metaphor—for here "metaphor" acquires its full force. From the early to mid-1970s and beyond, McLuhan gradually rephrased his media theory using terms such as "figure" and "ground," "left hemisphere" and "right hemisphere," and, last but not least, "tetrad" and the related notion of "formal cause." With figure and ground, he invoked concepts derived from gestalt psychology: the figure is where our focus of attention lies—the content of the medium—but every figure has a ground, a sort of backdrop to our perception, hidden to our current focus—the unperceived workings of the medium or technology. Thorough study of media, according to McLuhan, should imply looking for their hidden grounds, an investigative procedure that he further explains in *City as Classroom: Understanding Language and Media* (McLuhan, Hutchon, and McLuhan) and *Laws of Media: The New Science* (McLuhan and McLuhan).

The concepts of left hemisphere and right hemisphere Mc-
Luhan borrowed from split-brain theory, which assumes that the
two halves of the brain control different physical and mental functions. He identified the dichotomy between left and right hemispheres, somewhat simplistically, with his own central distinction
between the visual and auditory-tactile, with the left hemisphere
standing for visuality (logical, sequential, intellectual, analytical)
and the right hemisphere representing tactility and the acoustic
(holistic, simultaneous, intuitive, synthetic) (McLuhan and Mc-
Luhan, *Laws* 67–91; McLuhan and Powers 48–56). He also identified figure with the visual and ground with the auditory-tactile.

With the tetrad, McLuhan purportedly found the ultimate formulation of his theory of media evolution. All media—and they
include, as we shall see, all human artifacts—evolve according to
a set of four laws: enhancement, obsolescence, retrieval, and reversal. Every medium, in its effect (its message), enhances something, makes something obsolete, retrieves something that was
obsolesced, and reverses into its "opposite" when pushed to ex-
tremes. When analyzing the workings of a medium, one should
always ask how the medium relates to these four processes (Mc-
Luhan and McLuhan, *Laws;* McLuhan and Powers 167–78).

McLuhan's elaboration of the—originally Aristotelian—notion
of formal cause is also pertinent in this regard. In fact, a more recent publication titled *Media and Formal Cause* (McLuhan and
McLuhan) suggests that this term is the more fundamental one.
Formal cause can be equated more or less with "form," as that
which makes the medium what it is—and the concept in that sense
is to a high degree interchangeable with many of the other notions
that McLuhan deployed, such as tetrad, probe, and ground. As Eric McLuhan remarks, "Our tetrad of laws brings Aristotle up to
date; at the same time, it provides an analytic of formal cause, the
first ever proposed" (123).

All of these ideas, constituting in a way a theory of the func-
tioning of human culture, are heavily intertwined, and they revolve
around the same concept: metaphor. The tetrad itself is a function
of the figure-ground distinction: enhancement and retrieval are
figure qualities, while obsolescence and reversal are ground aspects (though one can discuss whether this categorization does

not actually go against the grain of McLuhan's ideas, as Graham Harman has suggested in "The McLuhans and Metaphysics"). Looking back on his findings in one of his last papers, "Man and Media," McLuhan notes that "This pattern of four aspects of change—enhancing, obsolescing, retrieving, and flipping—happens to be the pattern of a metaphor" (*Understanding Me* 288–89). Figure-ground and tetrad are four-part structures, just as metaphor is. It might be worth noting that as early as 1948 McLuhan was giving this four-part structure its due. In a letter to Ezra Pound, he wrote that "America is 100% eighteenth century. The eighteenth century had chucked out the principle of metaphor and analogy—the basic fact that as A is to B so is C to D. AB:CD. It can see AB relations. But relations in four terms are still verboten" (Molinaro, McLuhan, and Toye 207). Conversely, metaphor can be explained using the figure-ground distinction: the figurative element in a metaphor acts like a ground for the figure of the literal element (McLuhan, Hutchon, and McLuhan 21).

Throughout his later research, McLuhan eventually came to realize that all media are essentially "linguistic": "I was gradually forced to conclude that all human extensions are utterings or outerings of our own beings and are literally linguistic in character" (*Understanding Media* 289). But "language" itself, as we have seen, is metaphor. In *Laws of Media,* this insight even gets strengthened: "All words, in every language, are metaphors" (McLuhan and McLuhan 120). Moreover, media include all human-made artifacts, and artifacts include all "utterings" and "outerings." McLuhan hints at this point when he observes in *Culture Is Our Business* that "Make-up is metaphor. It translates one face through another via transparency" (280). That no one had reached a similar conclusion thus far McLuhan imputed to a "left brain" mentality, regarding metaphor strictly as verbal and not as structural or operational, as would be more appropriate from a "right brain" point of view (see also the above point with regard to our supposed understanding of language). This harks back to his method, which I have sketched above. Through the heavy stress on visuality and conceptuality, brought forth by modernity, "the sense was lost of metaphor as perceptual technique for seeing one whole situation *through* another whole situation" (McLuhan and McLuhan, *Laws*

225). In fact, McLuhan claims that the tetrad, as metaphor, is this perceptual technique: "[T]he tetrad, like the metaphor, performs the same function that the camera did in the *Apollo 8* mission: it reveals figure (moon) and ground (earth) simultaneously" (McLuhan and Powers 4). It thus constitutes a way of probing "formal cause"; again Eric McLuhan: "[A]ll of the elements of the tetrad, the four processes, are both formal and causal" (McLuhan and McLuhan, *Media* 124). The tetrad as perceptual technique can be applied to everything "nonnatural," and all can be "linguistically" analyzed: "Our new dictionary includes all human artefacts as human speech, be they hardware or software, physical or mental or aesthetic entities, arts or sciences. Such former distinctions have no scientific relevance. As utterances, our artefacts are submissible to rhetorical (poetic) investigation; as words, they are susceptible to grammatical investigation" (McLuhan and McLuhan, *Laws* 224). But not only can artifacts be analyzed *as* words; they also *are* words. And vice versa: "Just as all artifacts are words, all words and languages are artifacts; each of which manifests a four-part structure in the form of double-ends joined" (McLuhan and Powers 7). Thus, metaphor is a technique by which one can analyze artifacts that are words, that are artifacts, that are metaphors—through the use of metaphors. It appears that in the work of McLuhan metaphor is ubiquitous.

Here I must return briefly, before reaching my conclusion, to the aforementioned question: does McLuhan employ his metaphors in a literal way? As we have seen, Gordon does not think so. Nevertheless, he does concede that "there is clear evidence for key McLuhanean notions where literal interpretation is demanded" (352). The only evidence that he presents, though, in a footnote, is an interview in which McLuhan refers to "discarnate man": "[W]hen you are on the air, you are literally disembodied" (435). However, can we call this a literal application of the metaphor "discarnate man"? One should first ask what it means to "be on the air," for is this not a metaphor itself? Still, in investigating the question concerning the literality of McLuhan's use of metaphor, we might just be looking in the wrong direction. The literal-metaphorical distinction itself has become obsolete, for reasons that we can clarify by examining McLuhan's argument.

First, as seen above, McLuhan interprets metaphor not just in a verbal (left brain) way but also and even more so in a structural, operational (right brain) way. Asking if a metaphor is applied literally, according to McLuhan, is a left brain way of looking at things.

Second, either consciously or not, McLuhan makes even the distinction between verbal and structural obsolete. In a self-referential move, he analyzes the concept of metaphor itself in a tetradic manner (McLuhan and McLuhan, *Laws* 234–35). This move attests perfectly to the circularity of the concept in his theoretical framework. Yes, one can say "so media are not *as* words, they actually *are* words," as Eric McLuhan does in the preface to *Laws of Media* (ix), and this is a literal application of the metaphor concept to media. But this concept itself is an artifact, thus applicable to metaphorical analysis, and so on, *ad infinitum.* So McLuhan sketches a metaphorical view of metaphor itself, probing his probing, never reaching a place from which to judge literality or resemblance to "neutral data" whatsoever. Such an epistemological attitude is at last neatly demonstrated by these sayings of McLuhan: "Truth is not matching. It is neither a label nor a mental reflection. It is something we make in the encounter with the world that is making us. We make sense not in cognition, but in replay. That is my definition of intellection, if not, indeed, scholarship. Representation, not replica" (McLuhan and Powers xi).

Norman Mailer said of McLuhan that "He had a mind that could only think in metaphors" (quoted in Gordon 301), capturing his linguistically inspired worldview, revolving around metaphor as a central notion. McLuhan employs various metaphors to make sense of the effects and functions of media. There is metaphor in his method, too, but "metaphor instrumentalized": metaphor as a tool, a probe. He describes the workings of media and their environments by way of the metaphor concept itself: media, technologies, senses, spaces, and cultural environments interact according to a scheme of translation. All of these various uses—theoretical, meta-theoretical, and intra-theoretical—culminate in the ubiquity of metaphor, specifically noticeable in McLuhan's later works. In them, "media" are extended to include all human artifacts, which appear to have linguistic structures. They *are* metaphors, should be studied *as* metaphors, *by using* metaphors: that is, the theoretical framework circumscribed by the notions of figure-ground and tetrad.

WORKS CITED

Browning, Robert. *Selected Poems.* London: Penguin, 1999. Print.

Gordon, W. Terrence. *Marshall McLuhan: Escape into Understanding.* New York: Basic Books, 1997. Print.

Harman, Graham. "The McLuhans and Metaphysics." *New Waves in Philosophy of Technology.* Ed. Jan Kyrre Berg Olsen, Evan Selinger, and Søren Riis. Basingstoke, UK: Palgrave Macmillan, 2009. 100–22. Print.

Kuhns, William. *The Post-Industrial Prophets: Interpretations of Technology.* New York: Harper and Row, 1971. Print.

Lakoff, George, and Mark Johnson. *Metaphors We Live By.* Chicago: U of Chicago P, 1980. Print.

Lévy, Pierre. *Collective Intelligence: Mankind's Emerging World in Cyberspace.* Trans. Robert Bononno. Cambridge, MA: Perseus Books, 1999. Print.

Marchand, Philip. *Marshall McLuhan: The Medium and the Messenger.* Cambridge, MA: MIT P, 1998. Print.

McLuhan, Marshall. *The Gutenberg Galaxy: The Making of Typographic Man.* Toronto: U of Toronto P, 1962. Print.

———. *Understanding Me: Lectures and Interviews.* Ed. Stephanie McLuhan and David Staines. Cambridge, MA: MIT P, 2005. Print.

———. *Understanding Media: The Extensions of Man.* New York: New American Library, 1966. Print.

McLuhan, Marshall, and Quentin Fiore. *The Medium Is the Massage: An Inventory of Effects.* Corte Madera, CA: Gingko, 2001. Print.

———. *War and Peace in the Global Village.* Corte Madera, CA: Gingko, 2001. Print.

McLuhan, Marshall, Kathryn Hutchon, and Eric McLuhan. *City as Classroom: Understanding Language and Media*. Agincourt, ON: Book Society of Canada, 1977. Print.

McLuhan, Marshall, and Eric McLuhan. *Laws of Media: The New Science*. Toronto: U of Toronto P, 1988. Print.

———. *Media and Formal Cause*. Houston: NeoPoiesis, 2011. Print.

McLuhan, Marshall, and Barrington Nevitt. *Take Today: The Executive as Dropout*. New York: Harcourt Brace Jovanovich, 1972. Print.

McLuhan, Marshall, and Harley Parker. *Counterblast*. London: Rapp and Whiting, 1970. Print.

McLuhan, Marshall, and Bruce R. Powers. *The Global Village: Transformations in World Life and Media in the 21st Century*. Oxford: Oxford UP, 1989. Print.

McLuhan, Marshall, and Wilfred Watson. *From Cliché to Archetype*. New York: Viking, 1970. Print.

Miller, Jonathan. *McLuhan*. London: Fontana/Collins, 1971. Print.

Molinaro, Matie, Corinne McLuhan, and William Toye, eds. *Letters of Marshall McLuhan*. Toronto: Oxford UP, 1987. Print.

Rheingold, Howard. *Smart Mobs: The Next Social Revolution*. New ed. New York: Basic Books, 2002. Print.

Van Den Eede, Yoni. *Amor Technologiae: Marshall McLuhan as Philosopher of Technology—Toward a Philosophy of Human-Media Relationships*. Brussels: VUBPRESS, 2012. Print.

IMAGE / FIGURE / GROUND

CHAPTER 4

SPACE ON THE EDGE:

MARSHALL McLUHAN'S MARGINALIA AND ANNOTATIONS OF SIGFRIED GIEDION AND ERNST GOMBRICH

James F. Scott

After the publication of Richard Cavell's comprehensive analysis of *McLuhan in Space: A Cultural Geography* in 2002, it might seem presumptuous to open the topic of space to further discussion, except that access to Marshall McLuhan's personal library brings to light a considerable body of new information that deserves to be placed within the continuum of his media theory.[1] My exploration of these sources leaves in place

---

1   The material on which I am drawing is now archived in the Thomas Fisher Rare Book Library in the Marshall McLuhan Library Collection, University of Toronto (fisher.library.utoronto.ca/sites/default/files/mcluhanFA-june2014.pdf). When I was using the collection, it was under the custodianship of Eric McLuhan, Marshall's eldest son, and housed on the family farmstead near Wellington, Ontario. The books were unsorted and uncatalogued but totalled well over 100 volumes, many of them

Cavell's conclusion that "understanding McLuhan in terms of acoustic space clarifies a number of aspects in his intellectual career and provides a unifying approach to an otherwise unwieldy output" (225). But I would argue that, by looking at McLuhan's ongoing conversation with his favourite intellectual contemporaries, a conversation made available to us in summary comments, coded notations, and detailed underlinings or bracketings of selected passages from his favourite books, we gain fuller insight not only into acoustic space but also into the visible spaces of typographic culture from which McLuhan sought to escape but never fully separated himself. Of particular importance to this topic are Sigfried Giedion and Ernst Gombrich, towering presences in the fields of art and architecture. In his extended dialogue with these men, two of the most sensitive readers of "space" that the twentieth century produced, McLuhan bent their constructs of geometric and perspectivist space toward the support of his own favourite speculation about literacy: namely, that writing evolves in sync with Euclidian geometry and depends for its intelligibility on linearity and sequence within the Euclidian rectangle. Giedion and Gombrich also helped to convince him that writing gave way to electric discourse at about the same moment that the elliptical and multidimensional geometries of Bernard Reimann, among others, began answering the needs of modern physics. Approaching McLuhan through the spaces of architecture, sculpture, and painting, while relating these disciplines to the evolving culture of literacy, adds to our understanding of what Mario Neve calls "the concept of *spatial information*," by which he means not merely "the communication through space or with spatial media, but the *production of the space as information*" (153).

---

crucial texts of literary and cultural modernism heavily annotated with commentary in McLuhan's own hand. In addition to the seminal works of Giedion and Gombrich, covered in this chapter, the library includes the works of other space-oriented thinkers such as Gaston Bachelard, Harold Innis, and Lewis Mumford. Also included are works by Walter Ong, Eric Havelock, and psychologist Julian Jaynes, as well as works by Joyce, Eliot, Pound, Wyndham Lewis, and many others. I am much in the debt of the McLuhan family for access to this collection, without which this chapter could not have been written. The collection will hereafter be cited as Marginalia and Annotations, short-titled as M&A.

In my judgment, the best starting point for a deeper under-standing of how McLuhan appropriates the spatial concepts of these (and other) thinkers[2] is the model from contemporary neuroscience provided by researchers such as Lawrence Shapiro, David Chalmers, and Andy Clark. Shapiro speaks of "the mind incarnate" (the title of his 2004 monograph) and insists that "the body is profoundly involved in mental operations" (187). This em-bodied cognition is elaborated more fully in Clark's *Supersizing the Mind: Embodiment, Action, and Cognitive Extension.* Here Clark argues on behalf of "blurrings of the mind-world boundary," the work of what he calls "the negotiable body" and the "negoti-ability of our own embodiment" (30, 43). In other words, we not only adapt to our environment but also assimilate into our being the environment to which we are adapting. "Our bodies," Clark says, "are essentially open to episodes of deep and transformative restructuring in which new equipment (both physical and 'men-tal') can become quite literally incorporated into the thinking and acting systems that we identify as our minds and bodies" (31). In an earlier work, *Being There: Putting Brain, Body, and World Together Again,* Clark sets out to describe "situated reasoning," a cognitive agency that presupposes "reasoning by embodied beings acting in a real physical environment" (4). Here he identifies our minds as "organs exquisitely geared to the production of actions laid out in local space and real time" (8). Hence, he speaks of "scaf-folded minds" that use "special external structures (symbolic and social-institutional) . . . to complement our individual cognitive profiles and to diffuse human reason across wider and wider so-cial and physical networks" (179). More specifically, he tells us that "advanced cognition depends crucially on our abilities to *dissipate* reasoning," which means "to reduce the loads on individual brains by locating those brains in complex webs of linguistic, social,

---

2   One can easily make a case for including several other students of space in this conversation that I have restricted to Giedion and Gombrich. Inn-is, Mumford, and Ong would be ideal choices since McLuhan made mar-ginal notes on some of the volumes that they authored. But Innis is well covered elsewhere, while Mumford was a passing interest that diminished over time, as noted by Glenn Willmott (92–100). Ong, on the other hand, is so central as to require separate treatment.

political and institutional constraints" (180). For Clark, "the ultimate artifact," the most decisive scaffold, is language, the tool/medium that not only gives us "added powers of communication" but also "enables us to reshape a variety of difficult but important tasks into formats better suited to the basic computational capacities of the human brain" (193).

This model, I think, applies to McLuhan in two closely related ways. First, it describes accurately how he assimilates the constructs of Giedion and Gombrich, subtly distinguishing between the one and the other while excerpting their thoughts from the original contexts and inserting them into the web of his own thinking. Second, the model throws light on McLuhan's conception of media and their impacts on the "ratio" of the human sensorium. Like McLuhan, Clark understands media as "extensions of man," information systems and plastic structures that augment the domain of the human senses while invisibly guiding those senses toward "*highly scaffolded choices*" (*Being There* 181) of which the human agent might be only subliminally aware.

The "scaffolds" of language that supported McLuhan's constructs of space were erected with the help of Giedion and Gombrich, though their vocabularies and analytical tools were modified and repurposed as McLuhan imported them from art and architectural history. It would be wrong to call this appropriation a distortion. Rather, it is an ideal instance of Clark's point that "we self-engineer worlds in which to build better worlds to think in" (*Supersizing* 59). Actually, McLuhan felt comfortable with the controlling ideas of Giedion and Gombrich, particularly with the assumption that space is a human invention, a frame or container brought into being by a trick of the eye. Giedion and Gombrich helped McLuhan to understand how and when the eyes began to play those tricks on the human species, literally setting the stage for the emergence of the figure at the centre of *The Gutenberg Galaxy: The Making of Typographic Man*. This figure fit perfectly into the ground of the Euclidian rectangle, as explored with unprecedented nuance by Giedion in *The Beginnings of Architecture* and *Space, Time, and Architecture: The Birth of a New Tradition*. Gombrich's *Art and Illusion: A Study in the Psychology of Pictorial Representation* helped McLuhan to define a new kind of interiority, the mediated interiority of print culture, what we might call the objectivized subjectivity of literate man, the perfect icon of the Gutenberg era.

Our insistent immersion in McLuhan's effort to chart the formation of "visual space" reduces our ability to take hold of this space dialectically, as the diametric opposite of "acoustic space," in which McLuhan was equally interested. Like other thinkers within his circle, notably Edmund Carpenter and, later, Edward Wachtel, McLuhan understood the work of Giedion and Gombrich as historicizing the erasure of acoustic space, the space that preceded the all-powerful Euclidian rectangle. In one of his most penetrating essays, Wachtel asks, "Did Picasso and DaVinci . . . see the same thing when they faced the east at dawn?" (123). And his answer is clearly "no." McLuhan's would be the same. Both men believed that Picasso's war on classical space was inspired by his familiarity with the "acoustic space" of prehistoric art, which viewed objects from multiple perspectives at once, in the way that they might have been apprehended by the ear rather than the eye. And both men learned this powerful lesson in part from Giedion.

In *McLuhan, or Modernism in Reverse*, Glenn Willmott names Giedion as the thinker who carried McLuhan beyond Lewis Mumford's "essentially negative critique of modern culture" toward "a historical object in which is impressed or encoded all aspects of human reality in the existential history of a period" (100–01). For Giedion, architectural structures—the built spaces of humankind—were texts that might be used to read the world, hence "a means to discover the existential wholeness of a world history conventionally divided up and understood only piecemeal according to politics, economics, ideas, artistic styles or moods, or events in the march of time" (Willmott 102). When McLuhan met Giedion in the 1940s, he knew that he had found a kindred spirit, whose example he recommended to Edmund Carpenter when they founded the journal *Explorations: Studies in Culture and Communications* (1953–59). During this decade, Giedion's English-language translator, Jaqueline Tyrwhitt, became McLuhan's colleague at the University of Toronto and a participant in his cross-disciplinary symposia on communication theory.

Giedion published three volumes on the social space of architecture, all of which McLuhan carefully read and annotated. Giedion's magisterial analysis of architectural space—from the temples, tombs, and monuments of Egypt and Babylon to the work of the Bauhaus—ties in closely with McLuhan's most fundamental thoughts about the spaces that give us our social and psychic bearings.

Although Giedion's impact on McLuhan resonates in many directions, what these men share most crucially is a concern for the disruptive impact of modernism and a need to reknit the organic fibres of Western culture. McLuhan also found in Giedion the implicit belief that horizontal and vertical space, first articulated in the architecture of Egypt and Babylon, created the preconditions for Western literacy and the visual bias of Greco-Roman civilization. What Denise Schmandt-Besserat characterizes in McLuhan's thinking as "the interface between writing and art," in other words "our inclination to organize information in a linear way" (109), owes much to McLuhan's reading of Giedion. The social space that Giedion describes in *The Beginnings of Architecture* is in effect a Euclidian space, which McLuhan thought pointed inevitably toward the linearity of writing and its enclosure within a schematic of up/down, left/right.

McLuhan first quotes from Giedion in *The Mechanical Bride: The Folklore of Industrial Man,* citing a passage from *Mechanization Takes Command: A Contribution to Anonymous History,* in which the architectural historian discusses the application of assembly line techniques to the slaughter of hogs in the abattoirs of Chicago. McLuhan's context in his own book is a riff on metallic caskets: McLuhan chides the makers of the "Metal Grave Vault" for blurring the line between life and death by turning the embalmed corpse into an industrially produced mummy whose virtual immortality is assured by "25 to 35lbs. of *zinc*" and "Clark's *exclusive* process" (15). He continues to explore this trespass of boundaries in mechanized modernism by considering how "scientific techniques of mass killing" might be "applied with equal indifference in the abattoirs, in the Nazi death camps, and on the battlefields" (15). In his personal notes on *Mechanization Takes Command,* McLuhan describes this process as "the mechanization of death"

(M&A). But beyond his distaste for metallic products (whether caskets, machine gun barrels, or cylinders that dispense zyclon gas), McLuhan finds in Giedion a much more crucial concern for the "dissociation of sensibility" (M&A) that industrial culture has bequeathed to the modern world. In the passage that McLuhan marks for attention, Giedion speaks of "our epoch" as "unaccustomed to assimilating processes of thought into the emotional domain" (30). McLuhan's gloss of this passage is simply "Gerontion," presumably anchoring Giedion's theme to T.S. Eliot's anti-hero, bedevilled by "thoughts of a dry brain in a dry season."

Before he read *Mechanization Takes Command*, McLuhan had met Giedion and read *Space, Time, and Architecture*, in its fourth printing by 1943, the year on the volume in McLuhan's personal library. This book obviously meant much to McLuhan, not simply because it is richly annotated but also because it contains a personal memento, a postcard that Giedion evidently sent to McLuhan sometime in the 1940s requesting that he send him "whatever you publish."

Space, Time, and Architecture recounts the demise of Greco-Roman classicism under the pressure of industrial and electrical culture, which had fragmented, during the nineteenth century, the social spaces of Europe and the United States. Giedion lays out his conception of architectural organicism and how it might be applied to a world of assembly lines and electrical dynamos. In this volume, we find an even richer dialogue between McLuhan and Giedion concerning the challenge of industrial culture and the dissociated sensibility of modernism.

Amid McLuhan's profuse marginalia in *Space, Time, and Architecture*, one comment points particularly toward his unique angle of entry into the debate over modernism. Anticipating the methodology of *The Mechanical Bride*, McLuhan notes "real nature of the period found in popular culture" (M&A). The remark glosses Giedion's observation that the artistic side of industrialism first "manifested itself in the creation of odd mechanical contrivances and of marvelous automatons, lifelike mechanical dolls capable of performing the most amazing feats, from walking to playing musical instruments and drawing pictures" (100). That is, even in a fragmented age, a society might satisfy some of its emotional needs through its sense of play, not only the play related to children's toys but also the play that adult America finds in comic strips and the wit of radio puppets. Hence the inclination in *The Mechanical Bride* to draw a serious cultural critique from the casual comedy of Chic Young's "Blondie" or Edgar Bergen's "Charlie McCarthy." Noting that in the latter show the puppeteer Bergen speaks for the General Electric corporation and the puppet Charlie for the alienated individual, McLuhan glosses the conflict as "real authority versus the ghost of freedom" (*Mechanical Bride* 16). The program vents authentic anger without challenging the power of corporate capitalism.

It is also relevant to note that pop culture works outside Euclidian space, as does modernism generally, especially from cubism forward. Comic strips deal with stick figures and use colour expressionistically, without reference to perspective or the conventions of realism. Even the advertisement for General Electric rejects Renaissance space. The signage promoting "G-E LAMPS" is inserted into a canted rectangle that violates the perspectivist illusion of Bergen and Charlie talking. Moreover, Charlie has grown to human proportions, in fact has shoulders that are wider than Bergen's, having lost all resemblance to his real-world status as a hand puppet (McLuhan, *Mechanical Bride* 17). Since we are in Giedion's world of ingenious mechanical dolls, we need not worry about modernism's affront to the organic visual fabric.

The opposite face of concern over dissociated sensibility is the hope for a new "organicism" that Giedion and McLuhan share. "Thought and feeling must communicate," urges McLuhan in a marginal note that compresses Giedion's introductory remarks on "architecture as an organism" (M&A, *Space*). For Giedion in *Space, Time, and Architecture*, the builder's art is both an index and an agent of social cohesion "because it is so bound up with the life of the period as a whole." More fully than other arts, architecture is "the product of all sorts of factors—social, economic, scientific, technical, ethnological." According to Giedion, "we are looking for the reflection in architecture of the progress our own period has made toward consciousness of itself—of its special limitations and potentialities, needs, and aims" (19). In other words, as both McLuhan and Giedion would have it, we seek in our built environment resources to diffuse the impact of an "industrial revolution [that] destroys inner security and order" (M&A). Mc-Luhan's marginalia follow the thread of Giedion's analysis, clearly supporting his fundamental point that architecture has lost its organic character, its iconic capacity to represent the cohesion of thought and feeling. Of particular importance is Giedion's attention to housing, where social space most obviously touches human feeling. "Around 1900," says Giedion, "most of the buildings from which modern development stems lacked all connection with human residence" (25). The single exception was the residential architecture designed by Frank Lloyd Wright, a man of towering importance to both Giedion and McLuhan.

Searching for organic filaments in the work of modern builders, Giedion asserts that "throughout history there persist two distinct trends—the one toward the rational and the geometrical, the other toward the irrational and the organic: two different ways of dealing with or mastering the environment" (*Space* 336). In his judgment, Wright represents the intuitive and organic, apprehending form without clearly referencing geometry and sensing human need without necessarily calling on immediate historical precedent. That is why, according to Giedion, Wright is ideally positioned to bring modernism into the home, grasping—with an analogy to the factory—"the house as one room," where "inner space is differentiated to meet special needs" (322). Using "the central chimney as the core of the house, as the point about which the whole is organized" (323), Wright can use lessons learned from the steel-frame skeletons of Chicago's skyscrapers without surrendering to industrial utilitarianism. Following Giedion's analysis, McLuhan acknowledges the "industrial impact on the home through factory architecture" (M&A). But Giedion also introduces a disclaimer, remarking that as Wright "conceives of his interior spaces" (322) he prefers stone to metal and generally avoids the light-giving window space characteristic of warehouses and department stores. Giedion reads this inclination not as an anachronism but as a more primal impulse: "For Wright, the house is a shelter, a covert into which the human animal can retire as into a cave, protected from rain, and wind and—light. There he may crouch, as it were, in complete security and relaxation, like an animal in its lair." Rather than call this a mistaken homage "to the shadowed dimness that prevailed in the late nineteenth century," Giedion suggests that it might be "an urge toward primitive eternal instincts which sooner or later must be satisfied" (339).

McLuhan accepts the latter interpretation, making a note on this page of "FL Wright's houses as wombs" or "caves" (M&A). Moreover, he recalls this point nearly two decades later in *Understanding Media: The Extensions of Man* (1964) when he speaks not only of "housing as shelter" but also of "the house with its hearth as fire altar ... ritually associated with the act of creation" (123, 124). From his standpoint, there was little doubt that Wright had caught hold of a deep-seated human need. Furthermore, because this architect had an inborn respect for the organic, especially in his understanding of the home, he could—as Giedion maintains— help European builders to withstand the new spatial conception.

The most specialized tangent from McLuhan's commentary on *Space, Time, and Architecture* also comes with reference to Wright and celebrates the value of private interior space, as evidenced by the home as "womb." Anticipating thoughts that he would develop later, particularly after his careful reading of Julian Jaynes, McLuhan associates Giedion's sense of the organic with the right hemisphere of the human brain. Referencing Giedion's homage to Wright, on the back flyleaf of the volume McLuhan writes "2 hems, geometric vs. organic = permanent conflict," and then—as if to further underscore this distinction—he adds in the margin on page 336 "two hemispheres" (M&A). The right hemisphere, of course, is intuitive, hence outside engineering, perhaps even outside history. That is why Wright can design a dwelling inspired by the functional shape of a factory yet conspicuously not a factory. That is why, too, according to Giedion, "Wright reached solutions to the dwelling problem which furnished the basis of further developments in Europe at the hands of the post-war generation" (26). In McLuhan's language, this meant that Wright's design principles could withstand the impact of "cubism" and its "great leap to architecture in 1910" (M&A).

In the homage to Wright, we can see McLuhan's propensity to psychologize social space; McLuhan goes well beyond Giedion to make the secluded, dimly lit interior an analogue of the primal "cave," where "darkness = the acoustic" (M&A, *Beginnings*), an environment in which the sacred power of collective human subjectivity is first released and revealed. This relationship of structure to consciousness provides a smooth transition to the third Giedion volume that McLuhan annotated, *The Beginnings of Architecture*. Here, in this 1964 revision of his 1957 Mellon lectures, Giedion discusses the evolution of interior space, beginning with its effacement in Babylon and Egypt, where monumental structures with negligible interiors replaced the rich interiors of caves and firepits from prehistoric times. This subject was of keen interest to McLuhan, as evidenced by his abundant underscorings. Following the argument closely, he assimilates Giedion's view of social space in historical perspective—from the pyramids and ziggurats of Egypt and Babylon to the more complex interiors of Greco-Roman and Renaissance builders. What McLuhan finds here—as is clear in his sparse but pointed comments—is a confirmation through architecture of the visual/acoustic binary so forcefully declared in *The Gutenberg Galaxy,* in which we are told that "media . . . may alter the ratio among our senses and change mental processes" (24).

McLuhan was so eager to absorb *The Beginnings of Architecture* that he pulled it from the author's hands two years before its formal publication to paraphrase one of its key arguments in *The Gutenberg Galaxy:* Giedion's claim for "the close interrelation between the world and art of the cave man, and the intensely organic interdependence of men in the electric age" (65).[3] As if still meditating on the right-brained intuition that models the home on the primal cave, McLuhan turns Giedion's comments on prehistoric architecture into a probe on behalf of acoustic/tactile space, which is also sacred space. The earliest structures,

---

3   McLuhan goes to some length here to acknowledge his debt to Giedion, saluting the "great art historian" whose "massive work" (*Beginnings*) will thoroughly explain "the new art approaches to space since Cezanne" (*Gutenberg Galaxy* 65). This explanation, as McLuhan remarks a few pages later, when he references James Joyce and *Finnegans Wake,* requires that we see this consummate master of modernist space "making his own Altamira cave drawings" that carry us back "into the night of sacral or auditory man" (75).

says Giedion, reflect the life worlds of primal communities, "the circle around the fire, the circle around the hearth, . . . even soul houses or ancestor houses for the spirits of men or animals" (*Beginnings* 179). Giedion also notes that the system of perception of the earliest human societies included no sense of perspective: the cave artists of southern Europe drew beautifully accurate animal figures without respecting up or down or attempting to create a three-dimensional illusion. "The eyes of primeval man," Giedion says, "held all directions in equal esteem. Representations that are to our eyes vertical—animals that seem to be falling or standing on their heads—were not so intended" (502). This is a world that McLuhan describes as acoustic, as "vertical-horizontal—not yet" (M&A), a phrase that echoes Giedion's remark that in this primal environment "vertical and horizontal had not yet achieved predominance" (502). That was to change, for the worse, McLuhan would argue, with the raising of the ziggurats of Ur and the pyramids of the Nile Valley.

The Beginnings of Architecture gives tangible support to Mc-Luhan's belief that the priority of the visual is tightly interwoven with the concentration of power, what Giedion characterizes as "the means of production . . . concentrated in the hands of a single man" (216). McLuhan's marginal notes read "central power = move to visual from acoustic" (M&A). Giedion also supplies McLuhan with information on spatial geometry that seems to promote the eye over the ear. The crucial term is the "squared grid" (M&A), which Giedion introduces in his discussion of "the supremacy of the vertical" (435), a subject to which he devotes a whole chapter (435–92). Although he makes no effort to associate these new monumental spaces with literacy, or the Phoenician alphabet, he insists that they imply a "far reaching change . . . in the development of vision . . . nothing less than an optical revolution" (437). Furthermore, at least as McLuhan would have it, this transformation of "seeing," anchored in a new sense of authority and hierarchy, points directly to the emergence of Euclidian space.

Scanning his source for telling words and phrases, McLuhan boldly underscores the lines where Giedion asserts that "the beginning of architecture coincides with the rise of the supremacy of the vertical, the right angle, the axis, and symmetry" (*Beginnings*

522), in other words those relationships that Euclid would make famous. As he examines the designs of ziggurats and pyramids, Giedion insists on "the vertical as directive," pointing out that "we automatically organize the structure of a building, a sculpture, a relief, or a painting with reference to its relation to the vertical" (436). But we find that "vertical and horizontal belong together [and] cannot be thought of independently," because the "origin of verticality is deeply anchored in mythopoeic thinking"; it is "an upward glance transmuted into stone" (445). Giedion illustrates this point through his detailed analysis of a stone relief from a tomb commemorating Sety I at Abydos and dating from the Nineteenth Dynasty of Egypt (thirteenth century BCE). Here the god of the air, Shu, a vertical figure at the centre of the image, holds up the sky, personified as his daughter Nut, while he himself stands on the horizontal earth, all of these lines combining into a trapezoidal shape that could easily morph into a rectangle. This paradigmatic example proves that the vertical is "a universal organizing principle," not "limited to the field of art" but "basic to the development of the science of geometry, from which arose the perception of the axis, symmetry, and the sequence" (445). And the "squared grid" that fascinated McLuhan and from which Giedion extracts "far reaching relationships between human forms, proportions, and the Egyptian system of measurement" (470) is simply an extension of the power of the vertical. It is a formula for proportioning the human figure and fitting such figures into a complex skein of vertical and horizontal lines (482–88).

The companion phrase that McLuhan also underscores is the one that Giedion uses to connect classical Greece to the Near East, via their shared preference for massive structures and powerful vertical lines: "[T]he first architectural space conception was concerned with the emanating power of volumes, their relations with one another and their interaction. This binds the Egyptian and the Greek elements together" (*Beginnings* 522). As an interpretive comment, McLuhan adds "Cornford" (M&A), referencing Francis Cornford, whose essay on the invention of Euclidian space had greatly influenced him. In that essay, Cornford puzzles over the fact that "such space does not exist of its own right, in nature, [and] the construction does not come immediately from observation"

(218). McLuhan, it seems, had found in *The Beginnings of Architecture* the answer to this riddle: Euclidian space had been created by the vertical/horizontal bias among builders in Egypt and Babylon, a bias that had committed Western culture for the next three millennia to up/down, right/left, and segmented linearity. Thus, Giedion, through his analysis of the all-powerful rectangle, had given McLuhan a sense of social space into which literacy was almost predestined to fit. Looming, almost literally, like a gigantic proscenium, the Euclidian rectangle set the stage for individualism, rationality, and the alphabetizing of Europe. In turn, this priority of the visual led, over the course of centuries, to Gutenberg, Ramus, and the perspectivist aesthetic of the Renaissance.

While immersed in the thinking of Giedion, McLuhan also began to read Ernst Gombrich, the Austrian expatriate from Nazi Europe, whose *Art and Illusion,* published in 1960, became one of the defining statements of mid-century art history. For McLuhan, Gombrich fit snugly within the Giedion paradigm, as is clear from one of the marginal notes that simply reads "GIEDION" (M&A). The link was their shared interest in Euclidian space and McLuhan's conviction that both writers bolstered his belief in the close tie between geometry and literacy. But Gombrich also conveyed a respect for "illusionism" (i.e., painting in the perspectivist framework) that survived his critique of its artifice. And, like Gombrich, McLuhan valued the art and literature of the Gutenberg era more highly than was sometimes apparent.

In *Unthinking Modernity: Innis, McLuhan, and the Frankfurt School,* Judith Stamps notes that Gombrich confirmed McLuhan's belief in "the formative powers of senses." This meant that "perception is an historical phenomenon" characterized by "choices that are historically conditioned" (104–05). In concrete terms, "Gombrich arrived at his unique media theory by tracing the historical transition from schematic to representational forms of art." In doing so, Stamps concludes, "he offered a historical account that paralleled the transition from oral to literate societies" (105). Gombrich looms large in McLuhan's thinking, particularly in *The Gutenberg Galaxy,* because he provides more evidence, and another kind of evidence, of changes in the human sensorium that gave the Renaissance mind a radically different way to take hold of the world.

At its most obvious level, *Art and Illusion* relativizes perspectivist art, the three-dimensional illusion executed within the Euclidian rectangle. In a spoofing passage that McLuhan cites in *Through the Vanishing Point: Space in Poetry and Painting* (McLuhan and Parker), Gombrich uses the comic drawings of *New Yorker* cartoonist Saul Steinberg to show the flexibility and complete arbitrariness of perspectivist drawing. In one of the drawings, which appears on the page from which McLuhan and Parker quote, a piece of graph paper is turned into a Plexiglas skyscraper with Steinberg's insertion of a street with autos and pedestrians in front of it and another structure, drawn in perspective, immediately to its right. In a drawing on the preceding page, an extended horizontal line becomes, in quick succession, a horizon line that creates a landscape, then a railway track, then a rope that holds wet wash, and then a desk with a chair pushed up against its edge (Gombrich 238–40). Each effect is achieved by changing the array of related objects. McLuhan quotes Gombrich on the significance of this playfulness: "Steinberg's trick drawings serve as a welcome reminder that it is never space which is represented but familiar things in situations" (McLuhan and Parker 6). In their own voices, McLuhan and Parker then add that, "as painters well know, space is created or evoked by all manner of associations among colours, textures, sounds, and their intervals" (6), indicating innumerable ways "through the vanishing point" or avenues of escape from Euclidian confinement.

When Gombrich strikes a more serious philosophical chord, it is to argue against art as "imitation." The artist does not look at the world; he looks at his paints, his brushes, and his drawing pencil. In a passage that McLuhan underscores, Gombrich describes painting as a "history of inventions," an exercise in the mastery of "representation" (11). He wonders if we can recover "the innocent eye" of which Ruskin spoke with epistemological gusto; McLuhan shares these doubts as he writes marginally that "innocent eye of Ruskin = abstract mysteries of perception" (M&A). Without fully grasping the mystery of perception, the artist will presumably fall back on "the reliance on construction, not imitation," another phrase that McLuhan underscores (62). A few pages later Gombrich challenges the view that gesture or body language is painted from the observed world: "Even Dutch genre paintings that appear to mirror life in all its bustle and complexity will turn out to be created from a limited number of types and gestures, much as the apparent realism of the picaresque novel or of Restoration comedy still applies and modifies stock figures that can be traced back for centuries" (87). McLuhan confirms this point with a marginal note: "[T]here is no neutral naturalism" because "the language of art [is] a projection—a reading" (M&A). He also seems to accept Gombrich's summary, which immediately follows, underlining one of the key phrases: "All art originates in the human mind, in our reactions to the visible world *rather than in the visible world itself,* and it is precisely because all art is conceptual that all representations are recognizable by their style" (87; emphasis added by McLuhan). McLuhan gains the last word with the marginal remark "output, not input" (M&A).

When Gombrich examines the history of mimesis in the Western arts, he draws a line from Greece through Rome to fifteenth-century Italy, just as Giedion does in *The Beginnings of Architecture.* Both were fascinated with what Gombrich calls "the Greek Revolution," which softened and individuated the monumental forms of the Near East, making place for interiority and subjectivity. "*There is,*" says Gombrich, in a passage that McLuhan highlights, "*the history of Greek painting, as we can follow it in painted pottery, which tells of the discovery of foreshortening and the conquest of space early in the fifth century and of light in the fourth*"; then he adds that "the discovery of appearances was not so much due to careful observation of nature as to the invention of *pictorial effects*" (330). McLuhan clearly accepts this historical narrative and even lends it his ultimate seal of approval, with the catchphrase "the medium is the message" (M&A). Missing from the Gombrich account, however, is the issue of a cause or motive. Leaning heavily on the work of Walter Ong, whom he was also reading closely at this time, McLuhan thought that the creative impulse that subjectified Greek painting and sculpture must have come from the triumph of literacy in classical Athens.[4] Hence his determination to affiliate art history with the emergence of a literary culture, the world of theatre for example, that could produce "characters" and even critical commentary, à la Aristotle and his students, on a figure with enough interior life to have a "tragic flaw." As Ong and Eric Havelock had pointed out, these are figures with "motives" and even "personalities," very different from their counterparts in the tradition of oral sagas, such as *The Iliad*.

Many of McLuhan's annotations in *Art and Illusion* seem to be intended to pull art history toward the world of words, not the sounded words of oratory and bardic recitation, which operate in the entirely different realm of acoustic space, but the fixed spaces of script, where they are available for review, reconsideration, and possible revision. This helps to explain McLuhan's annotational coinages, which speak of "art as [a] *translation* of relationships from nature" and "Renaissance styles as adoption of [a] new visual *language*" (M&A; emphasis added by me). Once, in a direct intervention that seems to lack an immediate connection to the text, McLuhan reminds himself that "medieval law and art used [the word] *simile*" to reference "visual information [that] is entered on a pre-existing blank or formulary" (M&A). In other words, visual material—like its verbal counterpart—is made to be slipped into pre-assigned space, probably harmonious subdivisions of the Euclidian rectangle. McLuhan slightly warps Gombrich in the direction of a painterly analogy to language. But in some ways Gombrich himself encourages this reading by his scrupulous attention to tools, methods, and the artist's "vocabulary" of resources.

As Gombrich brings painting into the Renaissance, McLuhan is even more eager to associate perspectivist illusion with movable type. His marginal notes are dense with comments such as "alphabet" and "phonetic alphabet < pictorial mode" and "Euclid—space via the alphabet" (M&A). One of the most revealing comments

---

4   At this stage of his career, Ong had published only *Ramus, Method, and the Decay of Dialogue*. But this seminal work sets up a schematic to describe the foundation of the West's culture of literacy as a revolt of the technology of writing against an older, less individualistic oral tradition. And for Ong as for McLuhan, literacy culminated in the print technology of Gutenberg. Havelock argues in the same direction in *A Preface to Plato*.

comes apropos of "naturalism in art from the Greeks to the impressionists" (326), where McLuhan intrudes to say that "what he calls illusionism [i.e., "naturalism"] is Euclidian space" (M&A). At this point, his intellectual leaps might seem too strenuous to follow, but the core perception drawn from Gombrich is that "the injunction to 'copy appearances' is really meaningless unless the artist is first given something which is to be made like something else" (313). As far as McLuhan is concerned, this "something else" is a Euclidian rectangle, that window on the world championed by Leonardo da Vinci when he spoke of "seeing a place behind a pane of glass, quite transparent, on the surface of which the objects behind the glass are to be drawn" (299). Glossing this comment, McLuhan writes "HD—via print" (M&A). HD denotes "high definition," here associated with print, presumably because naturalism requires explicit forms, careful details, and intelligible relationships that respect the horizontal/vertical axis, all of which are found in print culture as well as the manuscript culture that preceded it. These assumptions find their way into *The Gutenberg Galaxy* when McLuhan notes that young Battista Alberti presented his "geometrical scheme for depicting objects in a unified space . . . in 1435, a mere decade before typography" (112). Whether or not Gombrich would follow McLuhan all the way into a Euclidian rectangle, he is convinced that "illusionist art grew out of a long tradition and that it collapsed as soon as the value of that tradition was questioned" (313). Indeed, "far from being the basis, it is a kind of alternative to ordinary perception" (328).

That said, Gombrich treats the perspectivist illusion respectfully, as a vehicle to convey human subjectivity and interiority. "*The history of art,*" he says, in a passage that McLuhan underscores, "*may be described as forging the master keys for opening the mysterious locks of our senses to which only nature herself originally held the key*" (359). What legitimates this comment for McLuhan is that it touches "our senses" instead of referencing the "real" world. Although McLuhan showed no particular interest in the paintings of Constable, of which Gombrich was particularly fond, he seems to concede that painting might conjure up an "inner landscape," apprehensible as "synesthesia." In considering Gombrich's admiration of Constable's *Wivenhoe Park*, McLuhan cites in his marginalia the comment that paintings (even perspectivist paintings) give us "access to traditional symbols like Yin and Yang in China, for instance, or light and darkness" (371). In this frame of reference, Constable's synesthetic landscape becomes for McLuhan an instance of "syn=relationships=ratios" (M&A), which I would translate as Constable's iconography triggers responses from other senses that neutralize the visual bias and invite participation from the entire human sensorium. Expressing his own preferences, however, McLuhan then adds "so too with Joyce" (M&A). This comment comes at the moment when Gombrich refers the "figure" of Constable's images to the "ground" of genre, noting that "the subject of Constable's choice . . . could be reflected in the various genres of poetry, the epic, or the idyll" (377). The insight that McLuhan draws from this point entails "traditional rhetoric's relevance to painting" (M&A). In effect, this is to say that perspectivist painting justifies itself when it connects analogically not with "reality" but with the "formal space" (M&A) carved out in the *topoi* of the oral tradition.

Our best insight into the complexity of McLuhan's response to the visual bias of print culture might be gained by looking closely at the opening of *The Gutenberg Galaxy* (11–18), in which McLuhan implicates Gombrich in his brilliant if highly eccentric reading of *King Lear*. Remarking how "the illusion of the third dimension is discussed at length in E. H. Gombrich's *Art and Illusion*" (11), McLuhan shows how perspectivist painting is wildly spoofed in the notorious scene at Dover, in which Edgar convinces his blind father that he has fallen from an immense height yet miraculously survived. He does so by orally constructing a perspectivist landscape painting, conventional in every detail, particularly in its effort to lay several distinct planes into the recesses of space to ensure the impression of depth. The language of the passage even teases us with other sensory information, very crucial to McLuhan's thinking about the ratio of the senses. As Edgar and Gloucester approach the illusory "steep cliff," Edgar asks, "Do you hear the sea?" When Gloucester says, "No, truly," Edgar immediately rejoins, "Why then your other senses grow imperfect by your eyes' anguish." The missing dimension of sound is referenced again when Edgar reminds his father of the stunning height of the cliff: "[T]he murmuring surge, that on the unnumbered idle pebbles chafes, cannot be heard so high" (Shakespeare IV.vi.3–6, 20–23).

This example nicely encapsulates McLuhan's sense of the inescapable bond between Euclidian geometry, perspectivist drawing, and the culture of print, apprehended in both their positive and their negative aspects. We might also read into it, as a subtext, McLuhan's respect for the Shakespearean moment, when print culture had installed itself sufficiently to produce intricate analytical metaphor (e.g., seeing and blindness) but when the social system still felt the force of oral tradition, its chants and mnemonic devices adumbrated in the subtle rhythms of blank verse. In glossing this passage, McLuhan points out that the perspectivist illusion that Edgar has conjured up is possible only if we "fix the gaze" (*Gutenberg Galaxy* 16): that is, deny the eye the opportunity to scan beyond the arc of the magic rectangle, where it will drift outside the frame of the painting or mural. Data from the other senses would also explode the illusion, notably the sense of touch that Gombrich stresses is crucial to the reliable use of the eye. (One thing that makes the scene ridiculous is our realization that one could not fall from a high cliff without experiencing the tactile sensation of falling.) And, finally, there is the fascinating treatment of language. In this scene, voice is redemptive: both the supportive words and, above all, the kindly tone of Edgar persuade his afflicted father that together they can survive their exile and perhaps restore Lear's kingdom. When Edgar says, "Give me your hand," Gloucester replies, with newfound confidence provided by his son, "henceforth I'll bear affliction till it cry out, 'Enough, enough' and die" (Shakespeare IV.vi.77).

As in the oral tradition from the Hebrew prophets to the great political orators of Greece and Rome, the voice is the organ of human interiority, the font of trust and belief, our only non-invasive access to the depths of the human spirit. It is the domain of all qualities not susceptible to measurement, ultimate concerns such as faith, love, and courage. Gloucester is saved because under his son's loving supervision he is abruptly extracted from the threatening world of the eye and thrust into the primal darkness of "acoustic space," a space far removed from Gutenberg and Euclid but the same space in which Giedion and Gombrich found the sacred in the dark but resonant caves of Altamira and Lascaut.

In his important essay published in 2004, "Making Sense of Mc-Luhan Space," Gordon Gow cautions against too literal a reading of McLuhan's "spatial metaphors," especially phrases such as "acoustic space." He asks us to be wary of the McLuhan who moved "beyond human sensory experience as the informational structure of equivalence and began to draw upon more abstract equivalences when referring to visual and acoustic space." It is in these cases that "acoustic space is attributed with qualities that bear little relation to the experience of sound, such as those associated with electricity and quantum physics" (200). This seems to be remarkably good advice as we attempt to carry analysis beyond where I am leaving it at this time. It makes McLuhan a little less a prophet and rather more a man of his own times who, like Giedion and Gombrich, glanced at a vast sea whose tides and currents often perplexed him.

Undoubtedly, sight and sound are his most crucial concepts, which McLuhan handled with admirable nuance. But only up to a point are they intelligible as spatial metaphors. I am not sure, for example, whether the emerging electronic culture of the twenty-first century is best described as "acoustic." The data from an MRI scan are fully visible, as are the global positioning systems that guide missiles and drones to their targets. Even the timeline of a video editor, which might position and synchronize more than a dozen tracks of audio, is elaborately laid out in space, so that the operator can see the audio as space spread across a screen, allowing every fade-in, cut, lap-dissolve, or voice dip to be calibrated down to one-thirtieth of a second. It seems to be more productive to understand sound as Jerry Harp presents it in *Constant Motion: Ongian Hermeneutics and the Shifting Ground of Early Modern Understanding*. Harp ties sound to the uttering/outering of human subjectivity because "both vision and touch become problematic in rendering interiors as interiors" (18). Only the human voice, he concludes, allows the deepest self of the human person to be revealed in the public world. But as McLuhan (like Ong) would have it, over the course of roughly three millennia, the technology of writing, supported by geometry and numeration, evolved to fix the voice in space, hence objectify its subjectivity, as in the "bright ink" of a Shakespearean sonnet. Giedion and Gombrich assure us that similar processes took place in architecture and painting, yielding the intimate spiritual space of Borromini's Sant'Ivo chapel in Rome as well as the emotionally expressive spaces of Constable's *Wivenhoe Park*. These spaces, therefore, are spaces of paradox, where we must constantly search for equilibrium, taking advantage of print, perspective, and Euclidian proportions as communicative instruments without losing a sense of the wider arc that allows us to perceive what is outside the visual rectangle, beyond the realm of measurement.

What made Giedion and Gombrich so valuable to McLuhan was that their framing constructs bridged the gap between the spatial theories of Cornford and Innis, which captivated his imagination, and the rhetorical research of Ong and Havelock, which more fully reflected the education that McLuhan himself had received. Less abstract than Cornford and more broadly historical than Innis, Giedion gave McLuhan a space anchored in the social world, which invited him to connect the alphabet with the spread of commerce, the building of empires, and the advancement of bureaucratic record keeping. Similarly, Gombrich made painting a language, fundamentally a set of conventions, yet like alphabetic language empowered with the capacity to find correlatives to subjective experience, opening up and objectifying the interior of the human psyche. All three were classic specimens of "typographic man." Their thinking hinted at an electronic, perhaps digital, future but was solidly grounded in a literate past. Although some still imagine that McLuhan fully embraced the electronic maelstrom, sacralizing the "Woodstock Nation" of the late 1960s, Douglas Coupland is much closer to the mark when he says that "Marshall *did* foresee a long painful process in which technology shifts would trigger massive identity collapses around the world," which "would generate new and terrifying sources of disassociation between the reality of what was physically available to individuals and the unreality of a world depicted by electronic media" (164–65). Similarly, W. Terrence Gordon's *McLuhan: A Guide for the Perplexed* warns that "electricity has not unified the world into a global village. Where McLuhan speaks of the global village, his key word is *interdependence,* a far different matter from *unity*" (24). Ironically, McLuhan's last great metaphor was the tetrad, which uncomfortably resembles a Euclidian rectangle, or a Ramistic diagram, even if McLuhan did his best to conceal their similarity. Although acculturated to the rectangle of rational discourse, he recognized the need to cope with the electronic maelstrom. But, like the mentors who instructed him in the poetics of space, he worried about the violence of its whirling vortex.

WORKS CITED

Cavell, Richard. *McLuhan in Space: A Cultural Geography.* Toronto: U of Toronto P, 2002. Print.

Clark, Andy. *Being There: Putting Brain, Body, and World Together Again.* Boston: MIT P, 1997. Print.

———. *Supersizing the Mind: Embodiment, Action, and Cognitive Extension.* Cambridge, MA: Harvard UP, 2011. Print.

Cornford, Francis. "The Invention of Space." *Essays in Honour of Gilbert Murray.* Ed. James Thomson and Arnold Toynbee. London: George Allen and Unwin, 1936. 215–35. Print.

Coupland, Douglas. *Marshall McLuhan: You Know Nothing of My Work!* New York: Atlas, 2010. Print.

Giedion, Sigfried. *The Beginnings of Architecture.* Princeton, NJ: Princeton UP, 1964. Print.

———. *Mechanization Takes Command: A Contribution to Anonymous History.* New York: Oxford UP, 1948. Print.

———. *Space, Time, and Architecture: The Birth of a New Tradition.* Cambridge, MA: Harvard UP, 1943. Print.

Gombrich, E.H. *Art and Illusion: A Study in the Psychology of Pictorial Representation.* New York: Random House, 1960. Print.

Gordon, W. Terrence. *McLuhan: A Guide for the Perplexed.* New York: Continuum Press, 2010. Print.

Gow, Gordon. "Making Sense of McLuhan Space." Morra and Moss 185–206.

Harp, Jerry. *Constant Motion: Ongian Hermeneutics and the Shifting Ground of Early Modern Understanding.* Cresskill, NJ: Hampton, 2010. Print.

Havelock, Eric. *A Preface to Plato.* Cambridge, MA: Harvard UP, 1963. Print.

McLuhan, Marshall. *The Gutenberg Galaxy: The Making of Typographic Man.* Toronto: U of Toronto P, 1962. Print.

——. *The Mechanical Bride: The Folklore of Industrial Man.* Corte Madera, CA: Ginko, 2002. Print.

——. *Understanding Media: The Extensions of Man.* Boston: MIT P, 1994.

McLuhan, Marshall, and Harley Parker. *Through the Vanishing Point: Space in Poetry and Painting.* New York: Harper and Row, 1968. Print.

Morra, Linda, and John Moss, eds. *At the Speed of Light There Is Only Illumination: A Reappraisal of Marshall McLuhan.* Ottawa: U of Ottawa P, 2004. Print.

Neve, Mario. "Does the Space Make Differences? Some Geographical Remarks about Spatial Information between Harold Innis and Marshall McLuhan." Morra and Moss 153–64.

Ong, Walter. *Ramus, Method, and the Decay of Dialogue.* Cambridge, MA: Harvard UP, 1958. Print.

Schmandt-Besserat, Denise. "The Interface between Writing and Art." Strate and Wachtel 109–22.

Shakespeare, William. *The London Shakespeare.* Vol. 4. Ed. John Munro. New York: Simon and Schuster, 1958. 4 vols. Print.

Shapiro, Lawrence. *The Mind Incarnate: Philosophical Issues in Biology and Psychology.* Boston: MIT P, 2004. Print.

Stamps, Judith. *Unthinking Modernity: Innis, McLuhan, and the Frankfurt School.* Montreal: McGill Queen's UP, 1995. Print.

Strate, Lance, and Edward Wachtel, eds. *The Legacy of McLuhan.* Cresskill, NJ: Hampton, 2005. Print.

Wachtel, Edward. "Did Picasso and DaVinci, Newton and Einstein, the Bushman and the Englishman See the Same Thing When They Faced the East at Dawn? Or, Some Lessons I Learned about Perception, Time, Space, and the Order of the World." Strate and Wachtel 123–35.

Willmott, Glenn. *McLuhan, or Modernism in Reverse.* Toronto: U of Toronto P, 1996. Print.

CHAPTER 5

SELLING VIA THE "FIVE SENSE SENSORIUM":
BERTRAM BROOKER, MARSHALL McLUHAN, AND THE SENSORY MEDIA CULTURE OF TORONTO 1921-55

Adam Lauder

The sources of Marshall McLuhan's aesthetic approach to the study of media have usually been traced to the techniques of New Criticism, which he encountered as a student at Cambridge University during the 1930s (see Katz and Katz 104–05; Marchand 34–35; Marchessault 27; Rhodes 374; Theall 4). The influence of American theorists such as Edward T. Hall has also been explored (see Rogers). Yet investigation of the specifically Canadian origins of McLuhan's ideas has been restricted, for the most part, to his engagement with the communication studies of fellow University of Toronto professor Harold Adams Innis (Blondheim and Watson; Carey; Kroker; Stamps), with detours through the work of peers Eric Havelock and Northrop Frye (see Siegel). Only Richard Cavell has sketched a more comprehensive picture of the cultural and speculative landscape of early-twentieth-century Canada out of which McLuhan's media explorations evolved.

In addition to the radical psychiatrist Richard Maurice Bucke (1837–1902) and the Canadian-born artist and author Wyndham Lewis (1882–1957), Cavell identifies the Toronto-based advertising executive and multimedia artist Bertram Brooker (1888–1955) as indigenous sources for McLuhan's theories (15, 178). But as in the scholarship of Gregory Betts and Glenn Willmott, the relationship between Brooker and McLuhan remains little more than a footnote to Cavell's text. This chapter fills this gap through a close reading of selected marketing texts in which Brooker developed his groundbreaking analysis of advertising as a multimodal media system. The texts analyzed here were published in the influential Toronto business journal *Marketing,* which Brooker owned and edited from 1924 to 1927, or appeared in the textbooks *Layout Technique in Advertising* (1929) and *Copy Technique in Advertising* ... (1930): collections of essays originally published in *Marketing* and other trade papers, including the leading American journal *Printers' Ink.* Analysis of these texts uncovers striking parallels with the early writings of McLuhan.

Brooker's writings represent a significant precedent for the analyses of McLuhan and provide a more nuanced picture of what I term the "sensory media culture" of Toronto that developed in the decades prior to and during the interdisciplinary Communication and Culture Seminar organized by McLuhan with colleagues at the University of Toronto from 1953 to 1955 (see Darroch; Marchand 119, 125). The picture of a proto-McLuhanesque Toronto media culture that emerges from this study of Brooker's innovative practice and theory amplifies Paul Tiessen's description of "a pre-McLuhan body of media discourse." But where Tiessen's analysis of the interwar situation focuses on links between the Canadians Gerald Noxon (1910–90) and Graham Spry (1900–83) and their British contemporaries John Grierson (1898–1972) and Wyndham Lewis (1882–1957)—both of whom spent sojourns in Canada during the 1940s—with an emphasis on British media initiatives and policy, this chapter posits an indigenous tradition exemplified by the advertising writings and commercial designs of Brooker. The Toronto artist-advertiser's multidisciplinary output evinces a sensory and time-based paradigm derived from his reading of the philosopher Henri Bergson (1859–1941) as well as representations of transpersonal affect and the "ratio" of the senses as a form of visionary cognition found in the poetry of William Blake (1757–1827) (see Grace 8; Lauder; Luff; Zemans 30).

The Canadian media culture sketched here nonetheless intersects with the transatlantic discourse network traced by Tiessen at several junctures. Although Brooker directly cites Bergson several times in his published writings beginning in 1924 ("Are Statistics"; *Copy Technique* 217; "Make Advertising Believable"; "Making Orders Flow Downhill"), it is clear that his aesthetics of flux largely developed out of a reading of former Bergsonists from Britain such as Katherine Mansfield (1888–1923), Walter de la Mare (1873–1956), and John Middleton Murry (1889–1957) (Lauder 92). Wyndham Lewis also served as a touchstone for Brooker, beginning in at least 1927, albeit as a source of information on the very Bergsonian time-based paradigm that Lewis critiqued—much as he later did, according to Tiessen, for McLuhan and Spry (Brooker, "Blake"). It must be stressed that Lewis was a highly ambivalent reference for Brooker, who—like later McLuhan—read the British author's "spatial" paradigm against the grain (Marchessault 214–16).

Cavell and Willmott have persuasively argued that Brooker's application of the tools of literary criticism in his influential textbooks on advertising provided a model for McLuhan's interdisciplinary approach in *The Mechanical Bride: Folklore of Industrial Man* (1951) (Cavell 15; Willmott xii). I want to propose that Brooker's conception of advertising as a multisensory media system addressed to an active and synesthetic consumer set the stage for McLuhan's mature interest in shifting sensory "ratios" under the impact of electronic media and an associated return to participatory—oral and tactile—forms of communication (see McLuhan, "Age of Advertising"; "Notes on the Media"; "Radio and Television"). Earlier studies interpreted Brooker's synesthetic concerns as either evidence of the artist's alleged mysticism (see Betts, "*Destroyer*"; Davis; Reid) or as an expression of his musical interests (see Williams). However, Joyce Zemans has definitively demonstrated that the textual evidence does not support a mystical reading of Brooker's production (21). And, while Brooker's marketing texts repeatedly discuss the auditory and musical orientation of his synesthetic experiments, to date commentary on synesthesia in his practice has neglected the critical function of the multimodal strategies deployed by the artist's commercial designs and writings on advertising as a sound-based alternative to hegemonic print media. This chapter investigates the sources of the sensory and time-based paradigm put forward by Brooker during the 1920s in the writings of Bergson and Blake—shared points of departure for McLuhan. This study thus answers Janine Marchessault's call for a more contextualist reading of McLuhan that would situate his media studies within their immediate Toronto milieu: "McLuhan's work needs to be understood as arising out of collective engagement, conversations, letters and dialogue. Just as *The Mechanical Bride* grew out of courses he taught at St Louis University, so too did *The Gutenberg Galaxy* grow out of an interdisciplinary confluence of students, scholars, scientists, artists and journalists in Toronto" (77). Despite this rallying cry, this chapter represents one of the first attempts to excavate the Canadian media culture that thrived beyond the boundaries of the University of Toronto campus in the period that nourished McLuhan's discoveries.

BIOGRAPHY

Brooker was born in Croydon, England, in 1888 (Reid 9). He immigrated to Canada in 1905 (Lee 287), settling in Portage la Prairie, Manitoba. After relocating to Neepawa in 1912, Brooker purchased a movie theatre—the Neepawa Opera House—that he operated with his brother prior to moving to Winnipeg in 1915 (Betts, "Introduction" xv–xvi). It is from this Neepawa period that some of his earliest surviving experiments in visual art and commercial design probably date (Zemans 18). They include studies with overtly biological themes that reveal an awareness of modernist art and possibly of Bergson's influential notion of "creative evolution," such as the drawing *Ultrahomo, the Prophet* (ca. 1912). Other works consist of all-over compositions based on corporate logotypes such as *The Romance of Trademarks* and *Reznor* (both ca. 1912–15), pointing to the influence of his contemporaneous career as a commercial illustrator (see Wagner 46; Zemans 23, 34n14). The Neepawa period was extremely fertile for Brooker. In addition to working as an illustrator and journalist, his contact with cinema inspired him to write more than half a dozen scenarios for silent films that were produced by the Brooklyn-based Vitagraph Company of America (see Lauder 96). In counterpoint to these activities, Brooker was also writing and producing theatrical works (see Grace; Wagner). As in later life, his practice during his years in Neepawa was characterized by a radical fusion of popular culture and modernism—a "confluence of advertising and artistic technique" that would later define McLuhan's experiments, as Cavell underlines (15).

By 1912, Brooker had formulated a non-Christian belief system, which he termed "Ultimatism," that drew on his earlier speculations on physics, which he had submitted to the Royal Society in England as a youth (see Wagner 45). The artist's vision of the universe as composed of a finite body of "sparks" or "electrons" set in motion by an affective force, which he dubbed the "First Desire," might account for the pointillist flicker of his early drawings (quoted in Wagner 45). Brooker's subsequent commentaries on Blake and Bergson, following his move to Toronto to take a position with *Marketing* magazine in 1921, built on these earlier investigations of physics and spirituality. The artist-advertiser's highly idiosyncratic *bricolage* of these diverse sources provided an unlikely framework for his parallel activities in advertising and visual art during the period of his synesthetic experiments in the 1920s, discussed below.

During the years of McLuhan's studies at the University of Manitoba from 1928 to 1934, Brooker would have been a prominent figure in Winnipeg, which he continued to visit on business and family vacations (Cavell 233n40). Subsequently, he was a leading player in Toronto during the period of McLuhan's media explorations of the 1950s. Brooker—awarded the first Governor General's Award for Fiction (then the Lord Tweedsmuir Award) in 1937—would have been an inescapable presence in cultural, intellectual, and business circles during the critical early phase of the *Explorations* project (the interdisciplinary journal that Mc-Luhan and Carpenter founded in 1953 with funds from a Ford Foundation grant) (Darroch; Darroch and Marchessault). The publication of Brooker's 1950 novel *The Robber*—adapted for radio by the Canadian Broadcasting Corporation—secured an ongoing place for the artist-advertiser at the centre of the Toronto literary scene well into the mature phase of McLuhan's media studies (Betts, *"Destroyer"* xxviii, 46). An acquaintance of Northrop Frye and Barker Fairley (University of Toronto faculty members with ties to, respectively, McLuhan and his mentor Wyndham Lewis), from the mid-1920s until his death, Brooker belonged to an elite circle of artists, intellectuals, and businessmen for whom the Arts and Letters Club in downtown Toronto served as a regular meeting place and forum for intellectual and creative exchange (Betts, *"Destroyer"* 214; Frye 200, 327; Mastin 28).

As late as 1940, Brooker continued to contribute articles to *Printers' Ink*, a publication that McLuhan referenced in a 1947 article on advertising (see Brooker, "Six Primary Ingredients"; Marchand 107; McLuhan, "American Advertising" 13). Judith Stamps observes that McLuhan employed his extensive personal archive of advertisements as a teaching aid for a course on mass culture and propaganda that he taught in the early 1940s (110). This collection of advertisements subsequently laid the foundation for *The Mechanical Bride*. The multiple pseudonyms under which Brooker published both his advertising texts and literary writings probably ensured that McLuhan encountered his work without recognizing it as that of a single author. In any case, Brooker's retirement as vice-president of MacLaren Advertising in 1955—the same year that McLuhan's brief commercial venture with William Hagon, Idea Consultants, rented office space in downtown Toronto—situates the artist-advertiser squarely within the same milieu into which McLuhan was busily insinuating himself (Betts, *"Destroyer"* 29; Marchand 100). It therefore seems improbable that McLuhan would have been unaware of Brooker, even if he did not associate his name with the advertisements that he studied as artifacts of "anonymous history" (*Gutenberg Galaxy* 65). Even so, no definitive evidence of a meeting between Brooker and McLuhan has been unearthed to date. Therefore, the innovations of the former were likely absorbed indirectly by McLuhan.

DIALOGICAL MEDIA

Long before McLuhan's conceptualization of the advertisement as "a piece of abstract art" ("Age of Advertising" 555), Brooker had argued that "art has a place—and a very important one—in advertising" ("Pictorial Salesmanship" 347). Setting the stage for McLuhan's dialogical media theory, the function of art in advertising, according to Brooker, is to paint a participatory scene "where the prospect feels at home, where he enters into the action, where he is a *character* in the play" ("Pictorial Salesmanship" 349). Reflecting on the interactive and multisensory approach to advertising that he promoted in the pages of *Marketing* for nearly a decade, Brooker wrote in 1929 that "I debated . . . using ink and paper to stimulate the palate or to cause the mind to 'auditionize' unheard sounds in the same way that it 'visualizes' unseen sights" ("Hoist the Sales" 212). Clearing a path for the subsequent writings of McLuhan, Brooker emphasized the advantages of countering the optical bias of traditional print media by communicating acoustic "tone" and involving readers in the process of textual production ("Help the Prospect" 131). The auditory concerns of this article endorse Cavell's interpretation of the artist's contemporaneous visual art, notably the monumental canvas *Sounds Assembling* (1928)—one of the earliest examples of abstract art exhibited in Canada—as effecting a "spatialization of the sonic" (15).

Stamps argues that the communication writings of Innis and McLuhan were motivated by a shared commitment to preserving cultural traditions perceived as threatened by the spatial and visual bias of modern Western society—particularly as embodied by the proprietary media of a neocolonial United States. These concerns led the Toronto theorists to develop what Stamps terms a "sound-based paradigm," which set out to revive oral traditions and forms (11). Innis and McLuhan alike opposed the participatory, open-ended characteristics of the spoken word to the spatial abstraction privileged by mathematics and quantitative social science. Brooker's exploration of techniques of "musical visualiza-tion" in his pioneering abstract paintings, ably described by Glenn Williams (113), points to an allied search for a critical language with which to oppose the spatial paradigm endorsed by modern science and the Western metaphysical tradition. Brooker's search for "pictorial equivalents for such musical qualities as rhythm and volume" in his visual art was complemented by synesthet-ic experiments in his contemporaneous advertising texts and commercial designs intended to oppose and explode the crude quantitative methodologies and mechanistic theories—particu-larly behaviourist—that dominated the advertising industry of the 1920s (Williams 120; see also Johnston 173).

Notes for a talk on William Blake delivered by Brooker at the University of Toronto's Hart House in 1927 reveal that the art-ist's representations of "formlessness" in his contemporary paint-ings were derived, in part, from a careful reading of the Romantic poet (Brooker, "Blake" 19). This genealogy resonates in McLuhan's later gloss on Blake's critique of Newtonian mechanism in *Under-standing Media: The Extensions of Man:*

> [P]oets like Blake were far ahead of Newton in their re-sponse to the challenge of the clock. Blake spoke of the need to be delivered 'from single vision and Newton's sleep,' knowing very well that Newton's response to the challenge of the new mechanism was itself merely a mechanical rep-etition of the challenge. . . . Blake's counterstrategy for his age was to meet mechanism with organic myth. (25)

McLuhan's invocation of Blake's belief that "truth is a ratio between the mind and things, a ratio made by the shaping imagination," has been overshadowed by commentary on the role of Thomas Aquinas's sensory philosophy in his media theory (*Understanding Media* 268). Brooker's search for what we would now recognize as a "complete media system" in his synesthetic advertising writings can be explained as an application of Blake's concept of "spiritual sensation" as the ratio of the senses to concrete problems in ad-vertising (Kittler 245; Murry 15).

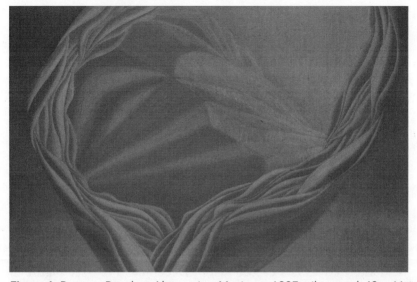

Figure 1: Bertram Brooker, *Abstraction-Music,* ca. 1927, oil on card, 43 × 61 cm. Collection of Museum London, F.B. Housser Memorial Collection, 1945.

Brooker's texts on advertising and marketing similarly marshal the non-dual philosophy of Bergson to critique spatial systems and, in particular, the visual bias of traditional print media. Brooker's representations of musical content in abstract canvases such as *Abstraction-Music* (ca. 1927; see Figure 1), *Chorale (Bach)* (ca. 1927), and *Toccata* (ca. 1927) recall Bergson's deployment of "melody" as a metaphor for the non-rational temporality of embodied *duration*—which the French philosopher opposed to the "spatial" (sequential and linear) model of temporality associated with mechanistic science and Cartesian metaphysics:

> There is simply the continuous inner melody of our inner life—a melody which is going on and will go on, indivisible, from the beginning to the end of our conscious existence. Our personality is precisely that. This indivisible continuity of change is precisely what constitutes true duration. . . . *[R]eal duration* is what we have always called *time,* but time perceived as indivisible. That time implies succession I do not deny. But that succession is first presented to our consciousness, like the distinction of a

> "before" and "after" set side by side, is what I cannot admit.
> When we listen to a melody we have the purest impression
> of succession we could possibly have—an impression as far
> removed as possible from that of simultaneity—and yet it
> is the very continuity of the melody and the impossibility
> of breaking it up which make that impression upon us.
> (Bergson, *Key Writings* 26)

Consonant with the "new kind of orality" subsequently articulated by McLuhan (Stamps 137), Brooker drew on Bergson's philosophy of duration to formulate a vision of advertising as itself
suspended in a perpetual state of "flux" (*Copy Technique* 216).

Perhaps Brooker's most incisive statement on the visual bias of
conventional print media and the desirability of exploring non-optical alternatives is a cartoon from December 1925 (see Figure 2).
Published to accompany an article by Charles W. Stokes on the un-
tapped potential of synesthetic strategies in advertising, Brooker's
cartoon portrays the bust of a man with comically enlarged eyes.
The caption reads "Our tame cartoonist predicts what the race
will look like a few generations hence if eye-mindedness is carried
much further" (quoted in Stokes 353). Brooker's playful representation of the physiological effects of media in this image coincides
with McLuhan's subsequent recognition in *Understanding Media*
that "The effects of technology do not occur at the level of opinions
or concepts, but alter sense ratios or patterns of perception" (18). It
is striking that McLuhan employed the same language as Brooker
to describe the dominant sensory orientation of Western culture—
as being "eye-minded"—in one of his earliest expositions of this
theme ("Notes on the Media" 11).

Strengthening the parallels between Brooker's and McLuhan's
respective descriptions of technology's entanglement with the
senses is the former's attentiveness to the somatic effects of the
new medium of radio in the 1920s—a theme that would preoccupy
McLuhan as early as *Counterblast* (1954; see McLuhan and Parker). Brooker's analysis of an advertisement for Philco radio batteries in 1930 (see Figure 3) focuses on the synesthetic associations
of photographs of musicians, strategically distorted to resemble
reflections in fun house mirrors:

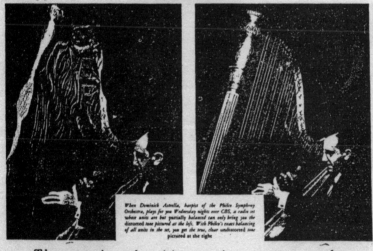

Figure 2: Philco, "More . . . better . . . daytime programs with Philco Screen Grid-Plus," 1930. Courtesy *Marketing* magazine.

By **CHARLES W. STOKES**

Our tame cartoonist predicts what the race will look like a few generations hence if eye-mindedness is carried much further.

Figure 3: Bertram Brooker, "Our tame cartoonist predicts what the race will look like a few generations hence if eye-mindedness is carried much further," 1925. Courtesy *Marketing* magazine.

[T]he distortion idea, as pictured in these twisted photographs, ingeniously duplicates the feeling a radio listener has when he hears a voice that is familiar to him—a singer he has heard on the concert stage, for example—distorted by bad reception. [I]nstruments stretched into thin and monstrously warped shapes, with curious u n n a t u r a l [sic] bulges where they shouldn't be, do somehow correspond to the effect produced on one's hearing when the radio starts to "act up." These thematic illustrations are perhaps as close as it is possible to go, pictorially, in representing an auditory experience. In other words, as a friend of mine remarked recently—not intending a pun—they constitute *"a sound idea."* (Brooker, "Aggressive Advertising" 102)

Clearing a path for McLuhan's dictum "the medium is the message," Brooker's analysis draws attention to the medium-specific characteristics of radio rather than the "content"—or product—of the Philco advertisement (i.e., batteries).[1] Moreover, Brooker's

---

1   A comparable conception of the selling power of media *as* media emerges
     from an anonymous 1924 *Marketing* interview with Alex MacKenzie,
     sales manager of Canadian National Carbon, likely authored by Brooker:
     "Our advertising has not been to sell batteries," MacKenzie states, "but to
     sell radio. Its aim has been to spread the gospel of radio, to multiply the
     number of fans both in town and country" (131).

interest in the potential for "auditory experience" to be translated from one medium (i.e., radio) into another (i.e., print) suggests
parallels with McLuhan's subsequent theorization of the "media
as translators" in *Understanding Media* (56–61). "[T]echnologies,"
proposes McLuhan, "are ways of translating one kind of knowledge into another" (56). The same text famously posits that "the
'content' of any medium is always another medium" (8). Anteced-
ing this insight by almost four decades, Brooker's analysis of the
advertisement for Philco radio batteries explores how the content
of successful print advertising is speech—or, as Brooker would
have preferred, "tone of voice" (*Copy Technique* 270). His comments on the residual aural properties of print media simultaneously anticipate the meditations of McLuhan's graduate student
Walter J. Ong (1912–2003) on "secondary orality," which abandons
the linear and sequential characteristics of speech shaped by the
conventions of writing (Ong 3). As such, Brooker's *Marketing* analyses provide compelling evidence that the artist-advertiser's insights served as one point of departure for the sound-based paradigm that Stamps identifies as a unifying theme of later Innis and
McLuhan.

The radio craze that captivated Canadian consumers beginning in 1922 appears to have provided the immediate stimulus
for Brooker's sustained exploration of the synesthetic qualities of
"'sonorous' words" in subsequent years ("Rhythmical Headings?"
39; see also Weir 2). Rather than placing radio in competition
with print, Brooker conceived of multiple media as generating
an integrated media system—what he elsewhere termed an "environment"—requiring multimodal techniques to reach a synesthetic consumer ("Idolaters of Brevity" 264). His holistic alternative to the either/or dichotomy advanced by some early analysts
and partisans of radio cleared a path for McLuhan's later vision
of the electronic media as effecting a reintegration and rebalan-
cing of the senses: "Telephone, gramophone, and RADIO are the
mechanization of post-literate acoustic space. . . . By surpassing
writing, we have regained our WHOLENESS" (McLuhan and
Parker, *Counterblast* n. pag.). Moreover, Brooker's descriptions
of radio and print as forming an integrated media environment
suggest comparisons with Stamps's discussion of Innis's belief

that "a successful community called for a multiplicity of media" (138). In McLuhan's reworking of this formulation, particularly in *Understanding Media,* a diverse media ecology is the precondition for the reintegration of the senses vis-à-vis the constitution of a prosthetic "common sense" (60). According to McLuhan, such an intelligent ratio of the senses can only be achieved in a technological milieu through an artificial "extension" of the sense organs (4).

MEDIA EXTENSIONS

Parallels between Brooker's Blakean conception of advertising as a synesthetic media system and McLuhan's subsequent neo-Aquinian formulation of the electronic media as a prosthetic *sensus communis* are supplemented by their common representation of technologies as physical "extensions" of the body (McLuhan, *Understanding Media* 60). McLuhan first advanced his influential notion that media are "extensions of the mechanisms of human perception" in the "Media Log" section of *Counterblast,* later reprinted in the February 1955 volume of *Explorations.* Brooker had earlier hinted at a similar conception of media as augmentations or prostheses of the human sensorium in an inspired cartoon of a cowboy "riding" a car modified to resemble a bucking bronco—with eyes in place of headlights and tires arching like legs (see Figure 4). Brooker had subsequently commented on this image in a 1926 article for *Printers' Ink* (writing in the third person, though it is all but certain that the artist-advertiser was involved in the design's conception and/or execution):

> The only thing that was remarkable about this booklet was its cover. I remember it very distinctly. . . . It was an illustration of a cowboy riding a bucking automobile. Yes, it was really bucking! Not just tilted up at the back with its rear wheels in the air—but with a really spirited sweep to the arched hood, and plenty of zip in the up-slanting lines terminating in a frenzied spare tire, which served as a swishing tail. . . . After he'd gone I sat looking at it, and though I may

have had inklings before, it was there and then that the idea, of the greatest use to me in advertising work since, suddenly crystallized in my mind. *Talk about dead things—inanimate products—as though they were living!* ("Life" 3)

Figure 4: *Winnipeg Free Press, A Survey of Western Canada's Motor Market,* 1920. Courtesy *Winnipeg Free Press.*

This striking image of a bucking automobile would have been highly visible in Winnipeg during the period of McLuhan's late adolescence. It was a constant feature of Brooker's regular humour and traffic column for the *Winnipeg Free Press*, "Gasograms by 'Honk,'" and appeared on the cover of a January 1920 publication issued by the *Winnipeg Free Press, A Survey of Western Canada's Motor Market*. Brooker's animistic rendering of the automobile suggests parallels with one of McLuhan's favourite figures for his extensions thesis: "the wheel as an extension of the foot" (*Understanding Media* 42). We can only speculate whether McLuhan's deployment of the phrase "wild broncos of technological culture" to describe the new media in the same "Media Log" in which he introduced his extension metaphor reflected an awareness of Brooker's once ubiquitous image of technological prosthesis (182). In keeping with Brooker's sound-based paradigm discussed above, his harnessing of the cartoon to communicate the non-optical possibilities of print media additionally suggests comparisons with McLuhan's later understanding of the cartoon as a specifically *auditory* medium: "cartoon and sculpture," he argued, "are not visual forms" (quoted in Gordon 121).

Like Brooker's subsequent representation of the somatic effects of media in his cartoon for Stokes's 1925 article on synesthetic advertising, his depiction of the automobile as an extension of human physiology suggests that bodies and technologies are inextricably entangled in processes of "creative evolution" consistent with the central thesis of Bergson's popular text of that title (which we know Brooker to have owned and underlined) (see Luff). In *Creative Evolution*, Bergson famously posits that the eye of the organism and the photographic apparatus respond to a common "problem," whose solution requires ongoing evolutionary adaptation—a formulation that suggests analogies with Brooker's hypertrophied representation of the eye as a commentary on the interaction of human bodies and technological media in his cartoon for Stokes's *Marketing* text (70–71). In *Copy Technique in Advertising*, Brooker further develops these evolutionary speculations, likening language itself—the first technical artifact according to McLuhan—to a "*vitalizing germ* of sufficient fecundity to enliven and thicken reams of copy" (177; emphasis added). Similarly, the artist-advertiser's idealized representations of bodies and abstracted body parts in canvases dating from the same years as his synesthetic advertising writings, including *Endless Dawn* (1927), *Green Movement* (ca. 1927), and *The Dawn of Man* (ca. 1927), coincide with the perpetually embryonic status, and enduring potential for creative self-fashioning, of the human subject in Bergson's theory of creative evolution. The fluid contours of Brooker's bodies in these paintings correspond with the persistent elasticity of the consumer in his Bergsonian-inspired advertising writings.

Marchessault has initiated the project of tracing the influence of Bergson's writings on McLuhan's thought during the post-*Mechanical Bride* period, starting with the Communication and Culture Seminar. She argues that "McLuhan's relation to Bergson could help us to better understand what is meant by 'cosmic consciousness'" (214). She suggests that Bergson's theories informed the dynamic spatial paradigm that McLuhan elaborated as he gradually complicated his early identification with the static perspective of Wyndham Lewis's "vortex" (215–16). In particular, Marchessault (213) draws attention to McLuhan's invocation of the philosopher of duration in his discussion of cosmic consciousness in *Understanding Media:*

> Bergson argues in *Creative Evolution* that even consciousness is an extension of man that dims the bliss of union with the collective unconscious. . . . The computer . . . promises by technology a Pentecostal condition of universal understanding and unity. The next logical step would seem to be, not to translate, but to by-pass languages in favor of a general cosmic consciousness which might be very like the collective unconscious dreamt of by Bergson. (79–80)

Clearing a path for McLuhan's subsequent meditations on the condition of perpetual adaptation characteristic of subjects in an electronic environment, Brooker's representations of embryonic bodies reflect a Blakean understanding of sensory intelligence as a nascent "cosmic consciousness" allied to a Bergsonian conception of creative evolution as the generative entanglement of organisms and technological artifacts (Brooker, "Blake" 23; "Mysticism Debunked" 202).

CONCLUSION

McLuhan—whose interdisciplinary approach to the study of communication drew sharp criticism from some circles—might have been at pains to distance himself from Brooker, whose visionary media analyses and experimental, multimedia art practice were likely perceived as tainted by his association with commerce (see Marchand 84–85). It is possible that Brooker's friendship with Frye—McLuhan's long-standing rival in the English department at the University of Toronto—also contributed to his absence from McLuhan's bibliographies (Marchand 105). Whether or not Brooker was an unacknowledged or, more likely, indirect source for some of McLuhan's insights, his speculative writings for *Marketing* add greater detail and nuance to our picture of the sensory media culture of Toronto that served as the immediate backdrop to the theorist's early explorations.

WORKS CITED

Bergson, Henri. *Creative Evolution.* Trans. Arthur Mitchell. 1911. Mineola, NY: Dover, 1998. Print.

——. *Key Writings: Henri Bergson.* Ed. Keith Ansell Pearson and John Mullarkey. New York: Continuum, 2002. Print.

Betts, Gregory. *"The Destroyer": Modernism and Mystical Revolution in Bertram Brooker.* Diss. York U, 2005. Ann Arbor: UMI, 2006. Print.

——. "Introduction." *The Wrong World: Selected Stories and Essays of Bertram Brooker.* Ed. Betts. Ottawa: U of Ottawa P, 2009. xi–xlix. Print.

Brooker, Bertram [Philip E. Spane]. "Aggressive Advertising, Merchandising under Way for Philco Radio." *Marketing* 30 Aug. 1930: 101–03. Print.

———. [Richard Surrey]. "Are Statistics More Convincing than Words or Pictures?" *Printers' Ink* 7 Jan. 1926: 115–25. Print.

———. "Blake." 1927. MS. University of Manitoba Archives and Special Collections, Winnipeg. Print.

———. [Richard Surrey]. *Copy Technique in Advertising, Including a System of Copy Synthesis, a Classification of Copy Sources, and a Section on Copy Construction.* New York: McGraw-Hill, 1930. Print.

———. [Honk]. "Gasograms by 'Honk.'" *Winnipeg Free Press* 4 Dec. 1920: 44. Print.

———. [Richard Surrey]. "Help the Prospect to Visualize What the Product Does." *Marketing* 1 Sept. 1928: 131–32. Print.

———. [Mark E. Ting]. "Hoist the Sales." *Marketing* 30 Mar. 1929: 212. Print.

———. "Idolaters of Brevity." *Sewanee Review* 39.3 (1931): 263–68. Print.

———. [Richard Surrey]. *Layout Technique in Advertising.* New York: McGraw-Hill, 1929. Print.

———. [Richard Surrey]. "Life vs. Lingo." *Printers' Ink* 9 Sept. 1926: 3–6, 165–71. Print.

———. [Philip E. Spane]. "Make Advertising Believable." *Marketing* 4 Feb. 1928: 75–76, 96. Print.

———. [Richard Surrey]. "Making Orders Flow Downhill." *Printers' Ink* 21 Feb. 1924: 3–8. Print.

———. "Mysticism Debunked." *Canadian Forum* 10.114 (1930): 202–03. Print.

———. [Richard Surrey]. "Pictorial Salesmanship: Its 12 Main Functions." *Marketing* 12 Dec. 1925: 347–50. Print.

———. [Richard Surrey]. "Rhythmical Headings? No!" *Marketing* 19 Jan. 1929: 39–40. Print.

———. "Six Primary Ingredients in Layout." *Printers' Ink* 40.3 (1940): 14–15, 53–54. Print.

Blondheim, Menahem, and Rita Watson. "Introduction." Watson and Blondheim 7–26.

Carey, James. "Harold Adams Innis and Marshall McLuhan." *Antioch Review* 27.1 (1967): 5–39. Print.

Cavell, Richard. *McLuhan in Space: A Cultural Geography.* Toronto: U of Toronto P, 2002. Print.

Darroch, Michael. "Bridging Urban and Media Studies: Jaqueline Tyrwhitt and the *Explorations* Group, 1951–1957." *Canadian Journal of Communication* 33.2 (2008): 147–69. Print.

Darroch, Michael, and Janine Marchessault. "Anonymous History as Methodology: The Collaborations of Sigfried Giedion, Jaqueline Tyrwhitt, and the *Explorations* Group, 1953–1955." *Place Studies in Art, Media, Science, and Technology: Historical Investigations on the Sites and Migration of Knowledge.* Ed. Andreas Broeckmann and Gunalan Nadarajan. Weimar: Verlag und Datenbank für Geisteswissenschaften, 2009. 9–27. Print.

Davis, Ann. *The Logic of Ecstasy: Canadian Mystical Painting 1920–1940.* Toronto: U of Toronto P, 1992. Print.

Frye, Northrop. *The Diaries of Northrop Frye, 1942–1955.* Ed. Robert D. Denham. Toronto: U of Toronto P, 2001. Print.

Gordon, W. Terrence. *Marshall McLuhan: Escape into Understanding.* New York: Basic Books, 1997. Print.

Grace, Sherrill. "'The Living Soul of Man': Bertram Brooker and Expressionist Theatre." *Theatre Research in Canada* 6.1 (1985): 1–22. Print.

Johnston, Russell. *Selling Themselves: The Emergence of Canadian Advertising.* Toronto: U of Toronto P, 2001. Print.

Katz, Ruth, and Elihu Katz. "McLuhan: Where Did He Come from, Where Did He Disappear?" Watson and Blondheim 98–113.

Kittler, Friedrich A. "Universities: Wet, Hard, Soft, and Harder." *Critical Inquiry* 31.1 (2004): 244–55.

Kroker, Arthur. *Technology and the Canadian Mind: Innis, McLuhan, Grant.* New York: St. Martin's, 1984. Print.

Lauder, Adam. "It's Alive! Bertram Brooker and Vitalism." *The Logic of Nature, the Romance of Space.* Ed. Cassandra Getty. Windsor, ON: Art Gallery of Windsor, 2010. 81–105. Print.

Lee, Thomas R. "Bertram Brooker 1888–1955." *Canadian Art* 13.3 (1956): 287–91. Print.

Luff, Carole F. "Progress Passing through the Spirit: The Modernist Vision of Bertram Brooker and Lionel LeMoine FitzGerald as Redemptive Art." Unpublished MA thesis, Carleton U, 1991. Print.

MacKenzie, Alex. "Taking Radio Tide at the Flood." *Marketing* 8 Mar. 1924: 131–32. Print.

Marchand, Philip. *Marshall McLuhan: The Medium and the Messenger.* Toronto: Vintage, 1990. Print.

Marchessault, Janine. *Marshall McLuhan: Cosmic Media.* London: Sage, 2005. Print.

Mastin, Catherine. "The Talented Intruder." *The Talented Intruder: Wyndham Lewis in Canada, 1939–1945.* Ed. Robert Stacey. Windsor, ON: Art Gallery of Windsor, 1992. 24–104. Print.

McLuhan, Marshall. "The Age of Advertising." *Commonweal* 11 Sept. 1953: 555–57. Print.

———. "American Advertising." *Essential McLuhan.* Ed. Eric McLuhan and Frank Zingrone. 1947. Toronto: Anansi, 1995. 13–20. Print.

———. *The Gutenberg Galaxy: The Making of Typographic Man.* Toronto: U of Toronto P, 1962. Print.

———. *The Mechanical Bride: Folklore of Industrial Man.* New York: Vanguard, 1951. Print.

———. "Media Log." *Explorations* 4 (1955): 56–62. Print.

———. "Notes on the Media as Art Forms." *Explorations* 2 (1954): 6–13. Print.

———. "Radio and Television vs. the ABCED-Minded." *Explorations* 5 (1955): 12–18. Print.

———. *Understanding Media: The Extensions of Man.* New York: McGraw-Hill, 1964. Print.

McLuhan, Marshall, and Harley Parker. *Counterblast.* Toronto: n.p., 1954. Print.

Murry, J. Middleton. *William Blake.* 1933. London: Jonathan Cape, 1936. Print.

Ong, Walter J. *Orality and Literacy: The Technologizing of the Word.* 1982. Abingdon, UK: Routledge, 1988. Print.

Reid, Dennis. *Bertram Brooker.* Ottawa: National Gallery of Canada, 1973. Print.

Rhodes, Neil. "On Speech, Print, and New Media." *Oral Tradition* 24.2 (2009): 373–92. Print.

Rogers, Everett R. "The Extensions of Men: The Correspondence of Marshall McLuhan and Edward T. Hall." *Mass Communication and Society* 3.1 (2000): 117–35. Print.

Siegel, Arthur. "Northrop Frye and the Toronto School of Communication Theory." Watson and Blondheim114–44.

Stamps, Judith. *Unthinking Modernity: Innis, McLuhan, and the Frankfurt School.* Montreal: McGill-Queen's UP, 2001. Print.

Stokes, Charles W. "Selling via All Five Senses." *Marketing* 12 Dec. 1925: 353, 364. Print.

Theall, Donald. *The Virtual Marshall McLuhan.* Montreal: McGill-Queen's UP, 2001. Print.

Tiessen, Paul. "From Literary Modernism to the Tantramar Marshes: Anticipating McLuhan in British and Canadian Media Theory and Practice." *Canadian Journal of Communication* 18.4 (1993). Web.

Wagner, Anton. "'God Crucified Upside Down': The Search for Dramatic Form and Meaning." *Provincial Essays* 7 (1989): 38–51. Print.

Watson, Rita, and Menahem Blondheim, eds. *The Toronto School of Communication Theory: Interpretations, Extensions, Applications.* Toronto: U of Toronto P; Jerusalem: Hebrew U Magnes P, 2007. Print.

Weir, E. Austin. *The Struggle for National Broadcasting in Canada.* Toronto: McClelland,1965. Print.

Williams, Glenn. "Translating Music into Visual Form: The Influence of Music in the Work of Bertram Brooker." *RACAR* 37.1–2 (2000): 111–22. Print.

Willmott, Glenn. "Introduction." *Think of the Earth.* By Bertram Brooker. Toronto: Brown Bear, 2000. ix–xx. Print.

Zemans, Joyce. 1989. "First Fruits: The World and Spirit Paintings." *Provincial Essays* 7 (1989): 17–37. Print.

CHAPTER 6

BUFFALO TRACKS AND CANOE CODES:
MARSHALL McLUHAN AND ABORIGINAL MEDIA'S DISSIDENT GENEALOGY IN CANADA

Kathleen Buddle

"AN INDIAN IS THE SERVOMECHANISM OF HIS CANOE"?

It is the continuous embrace of our own technology in daily use that puts us in the Narcissus role of subliminal awareness and numbness in relation to these images of ourselves. By continuously embracing technologies, we relate ourselves to them as servomechanisms. . . . An Indian is the servomechanism of his canoe, as the cowboy of his horse or the executive of his clock. —MARSHALL McLUHAN (BBC INTERVIEW, 1964, 59, 55)

The "servomechanistic" relationship of Indians to canoes, cowboys to horses, and businesspeople to their clocks, Marshall McLuhan explains, is best characterized as a feedback loop. People shape tools, and later those tools shape those people. His concern with the *determining effects* of technologies led him to conclude that television, for example, has altered the form of news and entertainment, transformed social relations and social institutions, transfigured our perceptions of reality and our relationships with each other and the world, and modified the scale and pace of our societies. *Understanding Media: The Extensions of Man,* a work that Mc-Luhan co-wrote with lifetime collaborator and anthropologist Edmund Carpenter, employed a method that Carpenter called "'mystical' or 'subjective' or 'insight without method'" (Prins and Bishop 117). In *Understanding Media,* the authors declared that the centralization of power attending the invention of print media had the effect of homogenizing regional groups and promoting nationalism. The spread of vernacular languages by print replaced tribal communities with new associations of individuals. The speed and breadth of electronic media, they charged, would un-make nationalism, rendering national groups unworkable (159–61). Media, for McLuhan and Carpenter, were at once the cause and effect of social change (see Askew and Wilk 15).

Critics of his work have suggested that McLuhan was able to hoodwink followers by elevating vagueness to a virtue (Williams, *Television;* Winston). He played with words and ideas, his detractors have charged, unencumbered by the messy business of real people, empirical facts, and scientific proofs (Miller; Stearn). By ignoring valid concerns regarding reliability, those who praise his contributions as prophetic would better understand them as rhetorical insights. Even McLuhan resisted asserting the truth value of his claims and preferred to consider them as probes for probabilities. In a *Playboy* interview in 1964, he explained his approach:

> But I've never presented such explorations as revealed truth. As an investigator, I have no fixed point of view, no commitment to any theory—my own or anyone else's. As a matter of fact, I'm completely ready to junk any statement I've ever made about any subject if events don't bear me out, or if I discover it isn't contributing to an understanding of the problem. The better part of my work on media is actually somewhat like a safe-cracker's. I don't know what's inside; maybe it's nothing. I just sit down and start to work. I grope, I listen, I test, I accept and discard;

I try out different sequences—until the tumblers fall and the doors spring open. (*"Playboy* Interview" 134)

McLuhan's assessment of an "electronic revolution" emerged around the same time that feminists, environmentalists, and civil rights activists were trading on telegenic images of "the Indian" for political capital. They became popular long after the many and often conflicting images of "Indianness" had been put to strategic use via print and radio through moral, commercial, and political discourses—by missionaries, settlers, anthropologists, and Native peoples themselves. These phenomena were of no consequence in McLuhan's estimation. In a work that McLuhan co-authored with Carpenter—*Oh, What a Blow That Phantom Gave Me!*—Native people, Inuit people, indeed all preliterate "tribal people" are purported to inhabit "acoustic space." This space, they explain, "isn't pictorial, boxed-in, framed: it's resonating, in flux, creating its own dimensions moment by moment. It's a world in which the eye hears, the ear sees, & all the five & country senses join in a concert of interweaving rhythms" (Carpenter 31). One might expect Carpenter's contributions to have served as correctives to McLuhan's generalizations given the former's fieldwork experience in Canada's north, but this was not the case.

Although some scholars read McLuhan's media evolution as "recursive" rather than linear, McLuhan himself posited contemporary tribal peoples as windows into the West's past, which betrayed the evolutionary schema undergirding his work:

Tribal cultures even today simply cannot comprehend the concept of the individual or of the separate and independent citizen. Oral cultures act and react simultaneously, whereas the capacity to act without reacting, without involvement, is the special gift of "detached" literate man. Another basic characteristic distinguishing tribal man from his literate successors is that he lived in a world of acoustic space, which gave him a radically different concept of time-space relationships. . . . (*"Playboy* Interview" 135)

The power of television to transform capitalistic colonists in-to "empathic" "tribal" participant-activists living "mythically" has not been borne out historically, if current relationships between Canadians and Native peoples are an accurate gauge. Nor has the introduction of syllabic literacy radically inflected the sensory environment of "Indian country" or undermined tribal solidarity therein. Instead, like the World Fairs and Wild West shows of the nineteenth century, the "global village" might represent a recent incarnation of a long-standing human tendency to offset controversy at home by romanticizing (or demonizing) the remote. The Wild West shows glamorized the farthest away "Indians"—from the plains, in the south, or farther west—depending on the site of the spectacle. This permitted settlers to engage in imagined admiration of strangers while continuing to exploit the local indigenous population. Similarly, "global villagers," pierced modern-primitives, and past-life-emburdened neopagans might fashion themselves as net-Nuer and ritually attend powwows, usually shirtless and with hacky sacks, yet most are no more "connected" with the objects of their fantasies now than were the masses of yore with the inhabitants of World Fair indigenous exhibits then. The scholarly attention lent to this so-called unified global village often distracts us from the fatigue of the apparently unending unruliness in our own backyards. Western scholars, moreover, highly mobile and multiconnected, might be tempted to overestimate the role of electronic and transnational media because they are readily available to them in their narrow and privileged circles while remaining unavailable for many "others."

Even if one sets content aside, however, the *meanings* that technological forms take in concrete settings remain mostly invisible in McLuhan's accounts. His analyses privileged the determining effects of media hardware, not software. From his starting point, one cannot assess the ways in which print, radio, and television hardware, for example, might operate as sites of ideological and political struggle, or emerge with or from non-conventional publics and spheres, or circulate through unpredictable processes and trajectories of dissident networks. McLuhan's projection for tribal peoples was pessimistic and misinformed, ignoring more than a century of work by Aboriginal media activists to promote literacy across Canada (see Smith). Native newspaper-men and other scribes sought to arm Native polities with weapons that they could use to fight battles over land and rights that were waged in printed texts. McLuhan saw literacy as detribalizing:

> It has been the sad fate of the Negro and the Indian to be tribal men in a fragmented culture—men born ahead of rather than behind their time. . . .
>
> I mean that at precisely the time when the white young-er generation is retribalizing and generalizing, the Negro and the Indian are under tremendous social and economic pressure to go in the opposite direction: to detribalize and specialize, to tear out their tribal roots when the rest of society is rediscovering theirs. Long held in a totally sub-ordinate socioeconomic position, they are now impelled to acquire literacy as a prerequisite to employment in the old mechanical service environment of hardware, rather than adapt themselves to the new tribal environment of soft-ware, or electric information, as the middle-class white young are doing. Needless to say, this generates great psychic pain, which in turn is translated into bitterness and violence. . . . They are angry because they understand . . . that the source of their psychic and social degradation lies in the *mechanical technology* that is now being repudi-ated by the very white overculture that developed it—a re-pudiation that the majority of Negroes and Indians cannot, literally, afford because of their inferior economic position. (*"Playboy* Interview" 137; emphasis added)

McLuhan did not consider the ways in which media technol-ogies can operate both as cultural products and as social pro-cesses through which living individuals and groups negotiate the constraints of the *unique* material conditions, discursive frame-works, power relations, and ideological environments in which they live. He thus miscalculated the relative import of hardware and software in diverse scenarios of cultural change. As a result, he misread the critical forces impinging on cultural transforma-tion in Aboriginal circles. His entrancement by form elided any engagement with methods, including any accounting of the substantive complexities between a Native person and "the Indian" or between the symbolic and the semiotic—a theme developed later in Baudrillard's work. For these and other reasons discussed below, McLuhan is better understood as a stylist as opposed to an architect in the narrative of communications history.

This chapter is informed by two decades of ethnographic research with urban Aboriginal peoples in Ontario, Manitoba, and Alberta and more specifically with the Aboriginal media communities found therein. It illuminates the ways in which Native community radio, the Aboriginal People's Television Network, and inner-city Aboriginal gang graffiti not only represent different *uses* of technology but also constitute identifiably different *technological inventions,* which support, are constrained by, and must be negotiated across demonstrably different sensorial orders, cultural information systems, discourses, and relations of power.

EVOLUTION OF SENSORY PROGRAMMING

McLuhan sought to explain all of human history, as well as the differences in social organization between "tribal" and no-longer-"tribal" societies, in terms of transformations in the ratio between the senses brought on by changes in the technology of communications (*Understanding Media* 3–4, 152, 42–43). According to him, different communications media distort our experience of the world because of the unique way in which each medium calls the senses into action (18). New extensions reorganize "the whole psychic and social complex" (4). In the same way that Narcissus was both fascinated with and anesthetized by the extension of his own image, people, McLuhan insisted, are becoming "servomechanisms" of their own technologies (46).

Whole cultures, he suggests in *The Gutenberg Galaxy: The Making of Typographic Man,* can be classified as belonging to one of four kinds or stages: oral-aural, chirographic, typographic, and electronic. In his tribal/oral-aural environment, individuals are mutually involved in direct, face-to-face communications, and the senses are equally engaged, producing a "seamless web of experience" (*Understanding Media* 335). The invention of the phonetic alphabet, he argues, however, abstracted and diminished the resonance of these relationships and shared experiences, replacing them with the assent of the visual—to the exclusion of the other senses—along with the capacity to individually manipulate external signs and culminating in an individualized consciousness (*Essential McLuhan* 240–44). The invention of mechanical typography, McLuhan says, created the conditions for the emergence of the modern, industrial world (*Understanding Media* 3). Finally, the electric telegraph permitted a replacement of mechanical mediation with a direct sensory experience, which operates at electronic speed, extending the central nervous system and consciousness, "imploding" the world's temporal and spatial dimensions into a "global village" (3). The resulting field of simultaneity engages all peoples "in a total field of interacting events in which all men participate" (254), becoming "one tribe again" (172). Building on the work of his graduate student Walter Ong, McLuhan characterized electronic societies as approximating a return to the conditions of orality and tribalism.

Despite his appropriation of certain anthropological terms—notably the "sacred" character that television imprints on a participant (*Understanding Media* 336), allowing one to live "mythically" ("What TV Does Best" 133) as a "hunter-gatherer of information" ("Television" 100–01) and to "ritually" unite humankind as a "tribe" ("What TV Does Best" 248)—McLuhan tends to interpret media history as an evolutionary process that is problematic from an anthropological perspective. His notion that all "tribal" cultures display the same "overwhelming tyranny of the ear over the eye" (*Gutenberg Galaxy* 28), moreover, makes all oral cultures sound identical and literate ones look the same. Moreover, because McLuhan views technology as an apolitical actor neutral to class and other interests, all "non-literate" cultures, in his scheme, invariably develop a similar perceptual style as a result of employing particular communications media.

His ideas gain clarity in reference to the work of his predecessor Harold Adams Innis. Extending Innis's theories of technological and societal change, which trace the impacts of the introduction of the telegraph, the train, and the automobile, McLuhan developed the idea of an altered sensory environment. Like McLuhan, Innis was quick to locate the cue for cultural change in the hardware. In his work, the imposition of "Western" technologies, including television, onto hunter-gatherer societies *alone* is sufficient to cause the destruction of "traditional" ways of life. Although McLuhan retained this idea in his own work, his views of cultural shift were not based on any concrete political economy. Much like the arguments that assert a causal relationship between contemporary social media and democracy, the logic conflates the idea of the global diffusion of communications *technology* with a global diffusion of communications *ideology* (Appadurai; Williams, *Marxism*).

ANTHROPOLOGICAL INTERVENTIONS

These media effects are simply not borne out in the sorts of studies that media anthropologists conduct, which ask questions about human need, interest, value, and goals and look for the political, economic, cultural, and military dimensions of power and ownership and class interests of mass media. Where Aboriginal people in Canada are concerned, the selective application by settlers of invented traditions in the realm of memory, politics, and history has allowed them to derive their authority and act as agents of change in Indigenous settings rather than any technological hardware per se. As Neu and Therrien and Bell, Butlin, and Heffernan assert, for instance, technologies of governance, as opposed to mass communications, including the courts, bureaucracy, police, and military, have historically served as the most formidable forms (hardware) allowing the Canadian government to deploy its software. The deployment of disciplinary knowledges such as bureaucratic and Christian discourses (i.e., the software) has induced the most fundamental changes in Aboriginal life to date.

In general, anthropologists tend to view media engagement as a skilled accomplishment—that is, media technologies and products are presumed to be actively "appropriated"—worked over within specific socio-historical contexts by individuals who are diversely situated interpreters. The tendency is to view cultural

information systems as shaped also by class, race, and other ethnic markers that have different salience in different geographic contexts and that denote more than mere abstract epistemological ideals. These variables imply conditions for who is likely
to communicate with whom, when, under what conditions, and
via which channels. Each system of communication involves a negotiated set of relations and alliances, characteristically gathering only certain people together while excluding others, thus protecting communication pathways and the information that they
carry. Viewed through an anthropological lens, media technologies are not seen to arrive with a set of prefabricated meanings in
indigenous contexts; rather, their place in social life must be defined. And it is generally found that the production and consumption of newspapers, radio, television, and other media forms are
only partly about consuming modernity; they are also about establishing what modernity *means* in each context—or constructing modernity.

Early media anthropologist Eric Michaels, for instance, argued
that, among Australian Aborigines, local systems of information
ownership, exchange, and control had far more resilience in the
face of new communications technologies than McLuhan might
have anticipated. Michaels's studies show that the sorts of social
relations governing tribal Australian communities were not rendered obsolete but enhanced by the introduction of radio, telephone, and other electronic communications media (509). More
recently, media anthropologists have advanced similar arguments: Daniel Miller and Don Slater regarding Internet use and
the enhancement of *selective* network structures among Trini-
dadians; Debra Spitulnik regarding the relative unimportance of
audibility to radio practice in Zambia; Bart Barendregt regarding the "domesticization" of cell phone practices in Indonesia;
and Terrence Turner regarding the Kayapo schemas guiding the
making of videos in Brazil. Among the Kayapo of Brazil, cultural categories appear in their essential social character as forms
of activity rather than static textual structures or tropes. Turner illuminates the ways that the production of the medium itself
"mediates" the indigenous categories and cultural forms that also
constitute its subject matter.

In Canada, the introduction of new communications technologies in the First Nations and Inuit communication ecologies did not cause radical shifts in epistemology or in the pace or scale of Aboriginal social relations. Instead, already operative communicative regimes informed the ways in which novel media extensions would be bent to local bidding (see Buddle, "Alterity" and "Transistor Resistors"). Historically, Native peoples socially produced media forms by folding traditional communication technologies into their everyday forms of media practice (cf. Deleuze). This blending of assets and practices generally has the effect of adding new materials with which to distinguish the uniqueness of Aboriginal peoples, supporting the theory of a more "villagized globe" rather than its obverse. The tradition of selective adaptation that Native peoples historically deployed when confronted with new technologies provides clues to interpreting current Native media practices and products.

DISSIDENT GENEALOGIES OF PROGRESS

Long before the arrival of Europeans in the "New World," Aboriginal mediators were at work "imaging" or orchestrating and communicating images of, and information on, themselves and negotiating them across local sensorial orders, cultural information systems, discourses, and relations of power. They did so by employing the digital-like, binary code switching of smoke signals and wampum as well as drumbeats, runners, town criers, and the moccasin telegraph. They innovated pictographic codes bitten into sheets of bark from birch trees and rolled into scrolls. The interpretation of petroglyph, gestural sign language, sculpture, and sand painting required rigorous training in visual literacy, multisensory trail or tracking praxis, and oral history pedagogy, among other competencies, for which the issues of imprimatur and censorship were subject to proprietary classifications by kinship lineages and secret societies, personal rank or status categories, and other situational factors (Buddle, "Media").

In postcontact times, Native peoples incorporated alphabetic and syllabic literacies into pre-existing communicative forms to do battle in the war that newcomers waged with words and images. Despite the devastating constraints that Indian Department policies and Indian legislation placed on Native peoples' access to official channels of communication with each other and the world beyond, Native polities persisted in circulating consciously cultural narratives, among themselves and others, to promote collective rather than individual aims and divergent modernities. Shifting among a number of registers, they performed their own versions and directions of progress through agricultural exhibits and fairs; by selectively engaging mainstream presses and museums in projects of their own making; by creating Native presses and authoring books that employed alphabetic and/or syllabic alphabets (Smith); and by performing unique collective identities, for instance, through Inuit and Dene political organizations (Kulchyski), urban friendship centre events, and Aboriginal communications societies.

By the 1950s, alphabetic and syllabic literacy were deeply ensconced in Native communities across Canada, and English-language films and public radio had arrived in the Canadian north. The way that radio was introduced more than its technology made it possible for Native people to be involved in radio production from the beginning. And, like print, radio was incorporated into an already changing web of relations, in which material tools were subordinated to the social goal of balance among land, body, community, and spirit world. These processes of change are indivisible from the evolution of storytelling, dancing, feasting, and so on.

Radio and television were initially installed in northern areas by the Canadian government with "modernization" as the goal: namely, to bring the north and the "undeveloped" regions of Canada into the mainstream of Canadian life. Electronic media hardware, however, arrived without missionaries, forced schooling, or directions for its use or incorporation into the daily rhythms of Native life. With radio and later television came the possibility for Native communities to override the Western-style consumer capitalism of so-called globalizing media and to fight for and achieve the power to frame and implement their own communicatory agendas and priorities and control the parameters of their evolution (see Roth).

Native peoples innovated forms of trail, community, and seafaring radio as part of a broader social project of communicating cultural knowledge for political and social ends, which included overcoming prejudice through intercultural understanding and reproducing Aboriginal cultural consciousness and political cohesion. The media initiatives served to repair the communication corridors that colonial projects had short-circuited (Buddle, "Transistor Resistors").

As Faye Ginsburg instructs, the tendency among Aboriginal communicators has been to accentuate the *activities* of production and reception—the social relations ("Aboriginal Media" 575). The general emphasis in Indigenous *consumption* practices, moreover, remains on what is *done* with objects. Early Native newspapermen in the nineteenth century, and more current community radio and television producers, regarded writing and audio-video documentation not as passive recording or reflection of already existing facts but as helping to establish the facts that they recorded. Each has, in other words, a performative or culturally mediating function.

NATIVE CULTURAL MEDIATORS AS MEDIUM

Aboriginal orators, political leaders, and elders have often been the first to assume authoritative positions at Native radio outlets, showing how Indian radio is produced and consumed in ways that both give expression to cultural categories and express differences in social location. Native mediators reworked audiovisual technologies to enable locally controlled, innovative, and community-supported radio production. This can have a revitalizing effect on certain cultural values. However, it can also provide a means of cultural invention in enabling the selective appropriating of the new and idiosyncratic blending of the old. A transformation of sorts was to occur through this recombination, and a new compound was to come about.

PERFORMING NATIVE NEO-TRADITIONALITY

Native peoples have combined the neo-traditional participatory principles and practices innovated for northern radio development with emerging televisual practices. In northern Manitoba, for example, Cree peoples first incorporated television as a tool of divination, naming it Koosbachican after the "shaking tent" ceremony. Television watching in the early 1960s, moreover, was usually a group affair, with whole communities sharing a set and simultaneously "watching" for messages from worlds beyond the empirical realm while engaging in discussion, playing traditional games, and listening to radio programs—in much the same way as old school storytelling sessions or shaking tent ceremonies would transpire (Granzberg; Granzberg, Steinbring, and Hamer).

As with Native radio, Aboriginal television did not suddenly emerge because of shifts in the technical environment and new transmission possibilities. Rather, the technologies were made to fit within a changing social and political environment characterized by increased mobility and information exchange between reserves and urban areas and the diminishing control of Indian agents to filter all information flowing into and out of reserves. These factors coincided with the slow erosion of the gerontocratic style of information management within Native communities, with widespread closures of residential schools, and with the lifting of the code of silence surrounding the abuses experienced therein.

Aboriginal cultural drift is tied to these factors and to the greater freedom that exists today to embrace discourses such as neo-traditional Native spiritualties and international human rights discourse and for Native peoples to recover their histories, land rights, and knowledge bases as their own cultural property. Media technologies have merely cleared the paths for pursuits already under way in Native societies. This is an important distinction because the same technology can and often does lead to different outcomes in different Aboriginal societies.

By the 1970s, Canadian agents of development were forced to reconcile social plurality with the failed Enlightenment goal of fulfilling history through modernization. It had become abundantly clear to Canadian government officials by this time that technology and economy alone were not the driving forces behind "development." This was proven when technology alone neither purged the problems that colonial policies brought into being nor eliminated cultural differences. If anything, Aboriginal peoples' engagements with a variety of media had highlighted the experiential and class differences within and between Canadian First Nations. As Mike Featherstone might posit, cultural imperialism, media homogenization, or assimilation would acquire little traction. Instead, "diversity, variety and richness of popular and local discourses, codes and practices which resist . . . order" were to persist (167).

SILENCE IS THE MESSAGE

Contemporary graffiti offers a case in point. In Winnipeg, tagging graffiti remains the preserve of poor, usually Native, disenfranchised youth and often of youth gang subcultures. Gang members are the poster children of the "discarnate" youth, whom McLuhan describes as "aimless, undisciplined, and illiterate" (*Essential McLuhan* 379), whose existence is marked by violence as a last-ditch effort to achieve meaning and identity. He writes that, "As electric media proliferate, whole societies at a time become discarnate, detached from mere bodily or physical 'reality' and relieved of any allegiance to or a sense of responsibility for it. . . . The alteration of human identity by new service environments of information has left whole populations without personal or community values" (379). It cannot be denied that "the violent criminal" has become iconic of urban Aboriginal male youth collective identity in Canada. However, this ubiquitous image has little to do with any all-powerful autonomous social force that television might represent in youth's lives or with the ways in which "the Native male youth," like "the Indian" who preceded him, has been socially organized as a construct by mainstream mediators. What McLuhan's formulation of media-produced social relations obscures are gang members' relationships with the disciplinary and regulative protocols and apparatuses of the state. The focus on media effects effectively deflects attention from the deviant positionality through which the state produces these errant subjects.

In the lives of the gang members with whom I work, who, not incidentally, are also marginalized within the *Aboriginal* mainstream, graffiti tends more often than not to announce invisibility, to mark erasure, and to signal silence (see Buddle, "Urban Aboriginal Gangs"). These messages, which cannot be read outside street subcultures, offer no solution to the placelessness and civic exclusion of urban Aboriginal youth. Graffiti, as with certain other forms of "underground" Aboriginal media, continues to be confined to a particular locus of enunciation, as Ricouer might contend; it does not generally make understood as discourse what can only be heard as *noise* (see Dikeç).

DIGITAL VISION QUESTS

On the other hand, contemporary Native and Inuit film units, whose programming and workplace organization give structure to the Aboriginal People's Television Network (also based in Winnipeg), have been very effective in referencing mainstream filmic forms without surrendering to them and in speaking across cultures to fairly receptive non-Native audiences. This is so even though Inuit television, for example, does not correspond with the "society of the spectacle" in which a large gap between producers and receivers is extant. With Inuit television, performers are the main audience. Inuit video makers operate with the same set of cultural categories, notions of representation, aesthetic values, and notions of what is socially and politically important as those whose actions they are recording (Ginsburg, "Screen Memories"). There is a specifically Inuit visual language to film and video that shows no presuppositions for mainstream Canadian standards of what films should look like.

The Native films and videos disseminated via the national Aboriginal People's Television Network (which began broadcasting in 1999) and through a growing Indigenous film festival network are often made to perform archival acts—recording and storing memories, texts, and objects. Native screenwriters and novelists alike are often cultural and political visionaries. They play a prestigious role in the community and mediate cultural and political relations with Western society (Turner). They write stories that serve to counter intrusive pedagogies from residential school systems and mainstream media images of vanishing Natives—selectively recombining traditional narratives and historiographies with adapted Western image-making technologies. Their contributions are thus not to the retrieval of an idealized vision of pre-contact culture but to "processes of identity construction" in the cultural present.

Indigenous film units must accommodate the annual ceremonial cycle that schedules an appropriate time of year for storytelling. Moreover, the film units invariably train shadow youth staff both to engage them in the process of cultural production and to provide opportunities for vision questing—a coming of age, or rite of passage, in the way that a first kill or vision quest operates in hunting societies. Directors also travel with their films into Native communities to organize media-training opportunities, to mobilize community members politically, and to create discursive space for the amelioration of social justice for Native peoples.

In Indian Country, writers are invariably embedded in their narratives, highlighting the relationship between teller and story: this exposes the book's or script's mode of production, for the story is always attached to its author. Yet Native electronic media do not correspond neatly with some multisensory acoustic space that is simultaneous, immediate, resonant, natural, and analogical. The circumstances of their production and reception are quite a bit messier, more situational, local, partial, and relational. Indian country is not governed by McLuhan's visual/acoustic dualism. Aboriginal technological evolution therefore ought not to be doubly romanticized since it marks neither the mourning of a lost golden age nor the forecasting of a connected future that is somehow inscribed in the unified logic of global developments. As Waisbord rejoins, the notion of a global mediated public sphere is often declared or prophesied but lacks sufficient empirical evidence: "The notion that global media technologies have fundamentally reshaped collective action is intriguing, but it is too general to capture the vast universe of experiences concerning media and participation.... Interest in transborder media assumes, rather than demonstrates, the disappearance or the porosity of political and cultural borders" (133).

The simple presence of electronic technologies does not ensure the development of truly transnational media platforms or even dialogue across boundaries. Instead, linguistic, cultural, and digital divides along with enduring regional practices have tended to reinforce those boundaries. The notion of the global village is too blunt an analytical tool to assess the interaction between media hardware and local cultural dynamics. The panoramic view supported by McLuhan that references the very sorts of grand master narratives that the postmodernists sought to disassemble steers media and cultural analyses away from a fine-grained approach that carefully attends to the cultural screens and filters that imprint local media practices and policies.

CONCLUSION: MEDIATION AS MEDICINE

In the 1960s, studies of television "effects" in northern Native communities by Canadian scholar Gary Granzberg predicted that Cree sociality would be destroyed with the introduction of the medium. Presuming that the form of the technology itself was the operative agent of change, like McLuhan, Granzberg saw the steam engine, automobile, television, and atomic bomb as the makers of modern humans and *the* modern condition. What his and other accounts failed to consider, however, was that Cree people in northern Manitoba, and Aboriginal peoples in general, would selectively incorporate aspects of the television complex into their already existing communication systems, reinventing television in the process. Whereas McLuhan posited that the serious artist alone was inured against passivity, individualization, and consumerism, it appears that Indigenous groups were, and remain, equally aware of possible changes in sense perception and apt at devising strategies to mitigate the formal effects of new media.

This is an important consideration because McLuhan's concept of the global village—a world psychically connected through a common communications network—continues to be advanced in conjunction with assertions about global homogenization. The issue is more critical when it is nested in master narratives of modernization, progress, and development. Hence, social evolution, glossed as "cultural modernity," comes to be measured using a continuum along which traditional/modern and poor/rich societies can be identified and rated using indicators such as rate of literacy, level of urbanization, availability of education, and degree of media exposure. And communications media are envisioned as instruments to be employed to promote economic and other Western-authorized notions of development and democracy, in other words to push modernization.

McLuhan's scenario misconstrues humans as merely sensing or perceiving, as opposed to interpreting, subjects (Poster 15). Indigenous reconfigurings of media forms, on the other hand, suggest that social processes are not given in the technology but constitute a "discursive formation" that has to be negotiated in and across other discursive fields. And, outside its mobilizations in specific discourses, practices, institutions, and relations of power, a technology on its own has no inherent value. As John Tagg insists, "Import and status have to be produced and effectively institutionalized and such institutionalizations do not describe a unified field or the working out of some essential causality. Even as they interlink in more or less extended chains, they are negotiated locally and discontinuously and are productive of value and meaning" (158–59).

Aboriginal cultural persistence and continuing divides in global modernity clearly undercut any notion of a logically unified humanity or global village. Instead, the human race continues to constitute itself as an assemblage of multiple, mutually exclusive peoples (Ang 27). For those pressed to exist in virtual obscurity behind a settler-imposed "buckskin curtain," the glitter of the global village might not be as powerful or attractive as imagined by those who have historically shone *through*—following McLuhan's own metaphor—the limelight.

WORKS CITED

Ang, Ien. "Ethnicities and Our Precarious Future." *Ethnicities* 11.1 (2011): 27–31. Web.

Appadurai, Arjun. *Modernity at Large: Cultural Dimensions of Globalization.* Minneapolis: U of Minnesota P, 1996. Print.

Askew, Kelly, and Richard R. Wilk, eds. *The Anthropology of the Media: A Reader.* Malden, MA: Blackwell. 2002. Print.

Barendregt, Bart. "Sex, Cannibals, and the Language of Cool: Indonesian Tales of the Phone and Modernity." *Information Society* 24.3 (2008): 160–70. Print.

Baudrillard, Jean. *For a Critique of the Political Economy of the Sign.* St. Louis: Telos, 1981. Print.

——. *"Revenge of the Crystal": Selected Writings on the Modern Object and Its Destiny, 1968–1983."* Ed. P. Foss and J. Pefanis. London: Pluto, 1990. Print.

Bell, Morag, Robin Butlin, and Michael Heffernan. *Geography and Imperialism: 1820–1940.* Manchester: Manchester UP, 1995. Print.

Buddle, Kathleen. "Alterity, Activism, and the Articulation of Gendered Cinemascapes in Urban Indian Country." *Film, History, and Cultural Citizenship.* Ed. T. Chen and D. Churchill. New York: Routledge, 2007. 159–78. Print.

——. "Media, Markets, and Powwows: Matrices of Aboriginal Cultural Mediation in Canada." *Cultural Dynamics* 16. 1 (2004): 29–69. Print.

——. "Transistor Resistors: Native Women's Radio and the Social Organization of Political Space in Manitoba." *Global and Indigenous Media: Cultures, Practices, and Politics.* Ed. P. Wilson and M. Stewart. Durham: Duke UP, 2008. 128–44. Print.

——. "Urban Aboriginal Gangs and Street Sociality in the Canadian West: Places, Performances, and Predicaments of Transition." *Aboriginal Peoples in Canadian Cities: Transformations and Continuities.* Ed. H.A. Howard and C. Proulx. Waterloo: Wilfrid Laurier UP, 2011. 171–202. Print.

Carpenter, Edmund. *Oh, What a Blow That Phantom Gave Me!* New York: Holt, Rinehart, and Winston, 1972. Print.

Deleuze, Gilles. *Foucault.* Minneapolis: U of Minnesota P, 1988. Print.

Dikeç, Mustafa. "Space, Politics, and the Political." *Environment and Planning D: Society and Space* 23.2 (2005): 171–88. Print.

Featherstone, Mike, ed. *Global Culture: Nationalism, Globalization, and Modernity.* London: Sage, 1994. Print.

Ginsburg, Faye. "Aboriginal Media and the Australian Imaginary." *Public Culture* 5.3 (1993): 557–78. Print.

———. "Screen Memories: Resignifying the Traditional in Indigenous Media." *Media Worlds: Anthropology on New Terrain.* Ed. F. Ginsburg, L. Abu-Lughod, and B. Larkin. Berkeley: U of California P, 2002. 39–57. Print.

Granzberg, Gary. "Television as Storyteller: The Algonkian Indians of Central Canada." *Communication* 32.1 (1982): 120–29. Print.

Granzberg, Gary, Jack Steinbring, and John Hamer. "New Magic for Old: TV in Cree Culture." *Journal of Communication* 27.4 (1977): 154–57. Print.

Kulchyski, Peter. *Like the Sound of a Drum: Aboriginal Cultural Politics in Denendeh and Nunavut.* Winnipeg: University of Manitoba Press, 2005.

McLuhan, Marshall. BBC Interview with Frank Kermode. 1964. www. viceomcluhan.com/inte.htm. Web.

———. *Essential McLuhan.* Ed. Eric McLuhan and Frank Zingrone. New York: HarperCollins, 1995. Print.

———. *The Gutenberg Galaxy: The Making of Typographic Man.* Toronto: U of Toronto P, 1962. Print.

———. "The *Playboy* Interview: Marshall McLuhan." With Eric Nolden. *Canadian Journal of Communication* (Dec. 1989): 134–37. Print.

———. "Television in a New Light." *The Meaning of Commercial Television.* Ed. S.T. Donner. Notre Dame, IN: U of Notre Dame P, 1967. 95–108. Print.

———. *Understanding Media: The Extensions of Man.* 1964. New York: Mentor, 1994. Print.

———. "What TV Does Best: An Interview with Marshall McLuhan." With Tom Synder. *Marshall McLuhan, Understanding Me: Lectures and Interviews.* Ed. Stephanie McLuhan and David Staines. Toronto: McClelland, 2003. 244–55. Print.

Michaels, Eric. *The Aboriginal Invention of Television in Central Australia 1982–1986: Report of the Fellowship to Assess the Impact of Television in Remote Aboriginal Communities.* Canberra: Australian Institute of Aboriginal Studies, 1986. Print.

Miller, Daniel, and Don Slater. *The Internet: An Ethnographic Approach.* Oxford: Berg, 2000. Print.

Miller, Jonathan. *McLuhan.* London: Fontana, 1971. Print.

Neu, Dean, and Richard Therrien. *Accounting for Genocide: Canada's Bureaucratic Assault on Aboriginal People.* Halifax: Fernwood, 2003. Print.

Ong, Walter. *Ramus, Method, and the Decay of Dialogue: From the Art of Discourse to the Art of Reason.* Cambridge, MA: Harvard UP, 1958. Print.

Poster, Mark. *The Mode of Information: Poststructuralism and Social Context.* Chicago: U of Chicago P, 1990. Print.

Prins, Harold E.L., and John Bishop. "Edmund Carpenter: Explorations in Media and Anthropology." *Visual Anthropology Review* 17.2 (2001–02): 110–40. Print.

Roth, Lorna. *Something New in the Air: The Story of First Peoples Television Broadcasting in Canada.* Montreal: McGill-Queen's UP, 2005. Print.

Smith, Donald B. *Sacred Feathers: The Reverend Peter Jones (Kahkewaquonaby) and the Mississauga Indians.* Toronto: U of Toronto P, 1987. Print.

Spitulnik, Debra. *Media Connections and Disconnections: Radio Culture and the Public Sphere in Zambia.* Durham: Duke UP, 2002. Print.

Stearn, Gerald E. *McLuhan: Hot and Cool.* London: Penguin, 1968. Print.

Tagg, John. "Globalization, Totalization, and the Discursive Field." *Culture, Globalization, and the World-System.* Ed. Anthony B. King. Minneapolis: U of Minnesota P, 1997. 155–60. Print.

Turner, Terrence. "Defiant Images: The Kayapo Appropriation of Video." *Anthropology Today* 8.6 (1992): 5–16. Print.

——. "Representation, Politics, and Cultural Imagination in Indigenous Video: General Points and Kayapo Examples." *Media Worlds: Anthropology on New Terrain.* Ed. Faye Ginsburg, Lila Abu-Lughod, and Brian Larkin. Berkeley: U of California P, 2002. 75–89. Print.

———. "The Social Dynamics of Video Media in an Indigenous Society: The Cultural Meaning and the Personal Politics of Video-Making in Kayapo Communities." *Visual Anthropology Review* 7.2 (1991): 68–76. Print.

———. "Visual Media, Cultural Politics, and Anthropological Practice." *Independent* 14.1 (1991): 34–40. Print.

Waisbord, Silvio. "Media Policies and the Blindspots of Media Globalization: Insights from Latin America." *Media, Culture, and Society* 35.1 (2013): 132–38. Print.

Williams, Raymond. *Marxism and Literature.* Marxist Introductions Series. London: Oxford UP, 1977. Print.

———. *Television: Technology and Cultural Form.* London: Routledge, 1990. Print.

Winston, Brian. *Misunderstanding Media.* Cambridge, MA: Harvard UP, 1986. Print.

SPACE / PLACE / TOOLS

CHAPTER 7

McLUHAN AND THE CITY

Jaqueline McLeod Rogers

n *Counterblast,* in headline style, Marshall McLuhan forecasts the death of the city: "The city no longer exists. . . . The city is obsolete. . . . [A]sk the computer" (McLuhan and Parker 12). In *Understanding Media: The Extensions of Man,* in a chapter on weaponry and war, McLuhan makes another direct reference to the city as "obsolete": "With instant technology, the globe itself can never again be more than a village, and the very nature of the city as a form of major dimensions must inevitably dissolve like a fading shot in a movie" (454). Coupling these rather extreme pronouncements with his frequent and now famous references to the coming of the "global village" has led some urban theorists to depict him as the spokesperson for a wave of dystopian scholars who have decreed various deaths of the city (from the mid-twentieth century onward). For example, according to British urban theorists Ash Amin and Stephen Graham, McLuhan was an early dystopian voice leading an eventual chorus of those who anticipated "a progressive dissolution or erosion of cities, as advanced transport and telecommunications infrastructures released economic, social, and cultural activities from the need for spatial propinquity and metropolitan cooperation" (412).

Yet characterizing McLuhan as a theorist against urban living and settlement does not make sense if we take into account
the life that he chose, living sociably in cities all his life: in several
American cities and in Canada in Edmonton, Winnipeg, and Toronto. His biographer W. Terrence Gordon notes that McLuhan
was well pleased with his family home in Toronto's Whychwood
Park, a neighbourhood with an artesian-fed pond and "centuries
old oaks lining its streets" (232). He was known for working col-
laboratively, seldom in a solitary manner. He was not known for
seeking wilderness escapes and indeed noted that the space that
we broadly conceptualize as "nature" is a state of mind, only another human construction: "Twenty-five centuries ago the Greeks
invented Nature by abstracting it from total existence" (McLuhan
and Nevitt 2). When McLuhan spoke of the death of the city, there
was neither expectation of nor longing for a return to simpler and
more natural ways of living but a call for us to notice that city
life keeps changing as technologies change it and us. The following passage from archival notes is helpful in capturing both his
sense of how life has changed as we leave mechanical-industrial
for electric-digital times and his seldom-expressed sense of optimism about the advantages that such changes might offer to those
committed to learning from and growing with the times: "[T]he
whole globe has been compressed to the dimensions of a village.
This global extension of the human brain is as involuntary as seeing when one's eyes are open. It represents a new kind of continuous learning and *an enormous upgrading of man*" (quoted in Wigley 115; emphasis added).

Rather than anticipating the death of the city, McLuhan devoted considerable time and thought to theorizing possibilities
for urban growth, with his intellectual energy aimed as always
at understanding change in a world "where nothing is stable but
change itself" (McLuhan and Nevitt 1). His reference to obsolescence of the city was tied to his broader vision of cycles of change
and transformation (cycles that he observed to have sped up in
contemporary electric life), so that, if the city as we know it dies,
it will eventually return in a revised form, likely one that bears
resemblance to a previously outmoded form. Certainly, a sense
of historical throwback can be glimpsed in his depiction of our

lives becoming more nomadic than settled. Archaic return and transformation are also discernible in his vision of the changing structure of work and communications, with individualized literate acts of reading and writing being replaced by a new orality supported by invisible networks of mass media communication linking us to others around the planet. We are, McLuhan says in *Understanding Media,* "poised between two ages—one of detribalization and one of retribalization" (456). He makes statements about recurrence in many places. For example, in the 1973 article "The Argument: Causality in the Electric World," co-written with Barrington Nevitt, he states that, if "innovation scraps its immediate predecessor," it "retrieves still older figures" (2).

In this chapter, I look at several forms of evidence that discourage reading McLuhan as a spokesperson for the mid-twentieth-century backlash against cities and urban living and that reveal instead how his theories about technological change directly and implicitly anticipated several themes informing current planning—in particular, how replacing a concept of non-mechanical mobility with one of invisible networked mobilities connects to contemporary visions of urban structures and living. When McLuhan spoke of city dissolution, he had a particular kind of city structure in mind, one organized by traffic grids, specifically the city as it had grown up to accommodate transportation traffic. He believed that the modernist city of visible grids connecting concrete places had had its day, and he referred disparagingly to contemporaries who continued to want cities to be such places as "earnest men, rather nineteenth-century types, still preoccupied with bricks and mortar" (quoted in Wigley 113). Instead of taking shape around material roadways and tracks—around transportation and communication networks that are visible and material—the city of the future that McLuhan pictured was more responsive to invisible interconnectivity, such as flight paths and digital networks. Although he did not dictate the forms of buildings, he referred to structures being less permanent in response to increasing human mobility. The global village can be understood as a world city of electronic linkages, connecting people across and around the globe.

McLuhan's urban theory is not as well known or fully developed as his reflections on history and technological change, but some of it is accessible through the article "Network Fever" by scholar and architect Mark Wigley, who draws from archival documents to explore McLuhan's commitment to the Ekistics movement of the 1960s—"the science (or art and science) of planning and designing the [shared planetary] home" (Pyla 27). According to Wigley, McLuhan engaged the attention of architects and planners because his claims about technology and the changing human body implied the need to reframe architectural terms and concepts; his contemporaries working in architecture and urban design responded to the architectural implications of his claim that technology had extended the body so that we had outgrown the confines of old housing and cities, requiring "a new architecture," "creating a 'tremendous opportunity' for planners" (86). Wigley provides evidence that McLuhan shared at least some of Buckminster Fuller's enthusiasm for envisioning cities as becoming more modular and mobile than fixed in place.

There is also evidence that his association with this group of thinkers made McLuhan more aware of the need for sustainability and green space cultivation. He recognized the opportunity and desirability of designers balancing the built environment with natural or green spaces in the world city of the future. By attending several of the Delos Symposia in the 1960s convened to explore the ideals of Ekistics, McLuhan engaged with the interest of founders in matching urban expansion with plans "to control land use, regulate buildings' shape and scale, and manage access to nature" (Pyla 16). This futuristic nature, more than ever, is planned and managed, nature not as wilderness but as "forces of the countryside" to be designed in precision against counterforces (18). Lending further support to the hypothesis that McLuhan recognized the need for planned and built green spaces was his interest in the theory of Lewis Mumford, which often advocated for urban planners to integrate more gardens and green space in the built environment. Mumford wrote, for example, that "we must think of a new form of the city, which will have the biological advantages of the suburb, the social advantages of the city, and new esthetic delights that will do justice to both modes"

(88). McLuhan had direct collaborative involvement with figures such as Jaqueline Tyrwhitt, a planner and professor who became a latter-day exotic gardener, and activist Jane Jacobs, both of whom were committed to planning practices that balanced built infrastructures with nature.

To examine McLuhan's observations about how technology is likely to change the city of the future is not to unearth blueprints of how cities have actually evolved so far or of the shapes that they will assume in the future. His prescience in these matters should not be overstated. Yet the themes and elements that McLuhan distinguished as key are arguably those that continue to dominate discussions of city life and urban planning in the twenty-first century: the expanding importance of invisible networks and human mobilities and the importance of balancing development with nature. Perhaps it is not too fanciful to add that many of his predictions of urban futures were aimed at defining life in the twenty-second century—and that bearing this future-oriented time frame in mind, we need to postpone making final assessments of the fit between his city imaginary and urban reality.

FROM TRAIN TO CAR TO PLANE CITY: OUTWARD MOBILITIES

In *Understanding Media,* McLuhan offers his take on the argument that cities—particularly new North American cities—were formed by and around transportation technologies. He describes the life and death of the "train city," designed to accommodate tracks within the physical landscape because these tracks allowed for the movement of people and goods that influenced all aspects of human development and culture. McLuhan links the dissolution of the train city to the advent of air travel, which changed our connections to people and places by accelerating our ability to move through time and space:

> The railway did not introduce movement or transportation or wheel or road into human society, but it accelerated and enlarged the scale of previous human functions, creating totally new kinds of cities and new kinds of work

and leisure. . . . The airplane, on the other hand, by accelerating the rate of transportation, tends to dissolve the railway form of city, politics and association. (20)

The changes that McLuhan observed in mid-twentieth-century
urban patterns because of air travel continue to affect development. Most cities are still in the process of changing shape to allow for the growth of airport industry and air travel. As our cities
spread outward, airports need to be relocated, demanding per-
imeters rather than hubs to do business. This process of airport
renewal and redesign has spawned deliberative replication of airport terminal buildings, in a move toward symmetry that has led
theorist Marc Augé to warn that these buildings have lost local
character and been stylized as non-placed replicas of each other.
This development away from creating monumental airports bearing the signature of the city corresponds with McLuhan's forecast
that buildings should be less grand and permanent and become
more shell-like to mark points of access to global transportation;
McLuhan conceptualized shell buildings as enabling patterns of
movement, reaching out from these shells and circling the globe
in invisible grids or networks.

If we rebuild our cities to accommodate growing airports
and give some consideration to flight path networks and housing, the influence on city design is relatively small compared with
how transportation grids such as railway tracks and automobile
roads defined city shape and life in the past. While many modern
North American cities were initially built to accommodate rail
transportation, the next stage of their growth and development
was aimed at accommodating cars and roads. In *The Mechanical Bride: Folklore of Industrial Man*, McLuhan examines the role
of the automobile in shaping culture and landscape; more than a
commodity, the fetishized car became a marker of status, freedom, and identity, the thing that we loved so dearly as to make it
our "mechanical bride." In *Culture Is Our Business*, he spells out
in sweeping terms the importance of the road as "our major architectural form" (132). The following passage from the chapter on
the car in *Understanding Media*—"The Motor Car: The Mechanical Bride"—conveys in a few sentences his sense of how fully the

car has fashioned not only our physical environment but also our psychic and social lives:

> The motorcar ended the countryside and substituted a new landscape in which the car was a sort of steeple-chaser. At the same time the motor destroyed the city as a casual environment in which families could be reared. Streets, and even sidewalks, became too intense a scene for the casual interplay of growing up. As the city filled with mobile strangers, even next door neighbors became strangers. This is the story of the motorcar and it has not much longer to run. (300)

This passage is profoundly resonant—in four sentences, "the story of the motorcar" reveals not only how the automobile connected urban to rural regions and shaped cities around roads but also how it affected our views of distance, personal mobility, rooted-ness, home, and wilderness, as well as our tolerance for hordes of strangers. McLuhan depicts car-happy, inner cities, amass-ing crowds of strangers, most of whom had undertaken the daily obligation of travelling to and from work, going home at night to ever-spreading suburbs.

After summing up the thoroughgoing influence of the car on both urban and psychic landscapes, McLuhan goes on in this passage to forecast that we are about to replace our mechanical bride—the car—with a new, as yet unknown, partner: "The car in a word has quite refashioned all of the spaces that unite and sep-arate men, and it will continue to do so for a decade or more, by which time the electronic successor to the car will be manifest" (301). Interesting here is that he does not specify exactly what the successor to the car will be. McLuhan might have had the com-puter in mind and with it our shift from material grids to more virtual forms of flow and mobility. He develops this theme in some detail in "Inside the Five Sense Sensorium," referring to how new communication technologies have changed our sense of the division between being inside and being outside, so that "With Electric media any place is a centre" (48).

At the same time, McLuhan might also have been predicting the increasing influence of air transportation on our sense of place and connectedness. Far from being a technological innovation whose influence peaked in the twentieth century, as some cultural geographers have argued, air travel continues to be the dominant means of geographic and social mobility, according to Tim Cresswell in his recent book *On the Move: Mobility in the Modern Western World.* McLuhan recognized air transportation as ascendant and replacing road transportation, despite integrative efforts to reconfigure roads as cities offering services to those routinely travelling them: "The road ceases to be a link between different social spaces, town and country, city and suburb. . . . But as [the] road tries to become the city, the further speed up of vehicle traffic occurs not on the road but in the air, and the logic of the jet plane would seem to render even the wheel obsolete" ("Inside" 50). In a passage from *Understanding Media,* McLuhan also pinpoints the airplane as the transportation innovation that bumped the car from its position of dominance and reduced our concern with road building and expansion: "With the plane, the cities began to have the same slender relation to needs that museums do. They became corridors of showcases echoing the departing forms of industrial assembly lines" (132). The city that is obsolete, then, is "the car city" built for internal mobility of citizens dependent on the sustenance of local industry.

Another way in which McLuhan challenges city planning centred on roads and highways is to link the arrangement of transportation grids to the linearity and lineality of "typographic man"—roadway grids belong in a "Gutenberg galaxy," not in a networked electric environment that thrives on non-hierarchic, changeable, and often invisible interconnections. In *The Global Village: Transformations in World Life and Media in the 21st Century,* he talks about the link between alphabet literacy and linearity, affecting how we both think and live, our work, and our culture: "The alphabet created a lineal and visual environment of services and experiences (everything from architecture and highways to representational art) which contributed to the ascendency or dominance of the left . . . or lineal hemisphere" (McLuhan and Powers 58). Here is how McLuhan dismisses linearity in culture, a pattern that he links to the design of the transportation matrix: "We have all noticed how lineality has faded from the current scene. The chorus line, the stag line, the assembly line, all have gone the way of the clothes line" ("Inside" 43). He admired the Whychwood Park neighbourhood in which he lived from 1968 till his death for its non-lineal development and relative disregard for roads—for its unusual and even old-fashioned arrangement, out of sync with the design elements generally shaping industrial and modernist Toronto. Gordon reports that the park was not the product of urban design but an artists' community that had grown up around the rambling house of the area's founder. The park was out of step with modernist tendencies to build around roads and grids. Yet, rather than calling for replication of its anti-lineal design, in "Inside the Five Sense Sensorium" McLuhan charges architects and designers with making adaptations: "How to breathe new life into the lineal forms of the past five centuries while admitting the relevance of the new organic forms of spatial organization . . . is not this the task of the architect at present?" (51).

McLuhan might have been drawn into hyperbole in declaring that our love affair with cars and car cities was on the wane. Yet we must remember that he was not talking merely about the number of vehicles on the road but also about the psychic and symbolic power of the automobile as a shaping force of urban culture in the early twentieth century. Supporting his story of how the automobile lost its cultural grip is the story of Detroit, Motor City itself, whose death has been declared by many as its factories have closed, its businesses shut down, and its infrastructures decayed to the point that the downtown core has become an urban wasteland—perhaps no more than "a museum way of life," with its former main streets turned into mostly deserted "corridors of showcases echoing the departing forms of industrial assembly lines" (to borrow the language that McLuhan used to depict city recession). In a recent book studying the demise of the city, *Detroit: An American Autopsy*, Charlie LeDuff links urban decay to the automobile industry: "The car made Detroit and the car unmade Detroit. Detroit was built in some ways to be disposable. The auto industry allowed for sprawl. It allowed a man to escape the smoldering city, with its grubby factory and steaming smokestacks" (80–81). In an article called "Detroit Arcadia: Exploring the Landscape of Post America," Rebecca Solnit similarly links the death of car culture to the death of Motor City:

> The city, once the fourth largest in the country, is now so depopulated that some stretches resemble the outlying farmland and others are altogether wild. Downtown still looks like a downtown, and all of those high-rise buildings still make an impressive skyline, but when you look closely at some of them, you can see trees growing out of the ledges and crevices. . . . Even Ford's old Highland Park headquarters, where the Model T was born, is now just a shuttered series of dusty warehouses with tape on the windows and cyclone fences around the cracked pavement. Once upon a time, the plant was one of the wonders of the world—on a single day in 1925 it cranked out 9,000 cars, according to a sign I saw under a tree next to the empty buildings. (n. pag.)

Although these urban reporters might be oversimplifying the cause of Detroit's decline by linking it to the stalled automobile industry, it remains the sad case that Detroit, the prototypical car city, has gone from boom to bust in half a century. In entirely literal terms, its fate fulfills McLuhan's prediction of the death of the city built for cars. Although many North Americans have been aware that Detroit—along with other automobile-producing and industry-based cities—has been in economic turmoil, news headlines during the summer of 2013 indicated that economic downturn has resulted in the city's filing for bankruptcy (Dolan).

Solnit also points out that Detroit has recently struggled for rebirth in new ways; she notes the urban creativity of public activism and art projects that have led to its greening, with "artists in particular see[ing] the potential, the possibility of bringing the country back into the city": "After all, the city is rich in open space and—with an official unemployment rate in the mid-teens—people with time on their hands. The land is fertile, too, and the visionaries are there" (n. pag.). This story of Detroit's struggle for regeneration—of its death followed by its struggle to transform and rebuild—is a modern-day representation of McLuhan's view that, while the new replaces the old, the old returns in a reworked way, in this case a new agrarianism. A related story of city renewal makes a similar point about how new developments manifest older ways. Like other mid-continent North American postindustrial cities, Memphis suffered economic depression and downturn in the late twentieth century, but it has recently begun to revive "due to heavy flows of transnational migration" (Garvin 252). Urban renewal and transition rest on modern-day populations abandoning models of settlement and fixity in favour of increased nomadism, in a world undergoing what Gordon calls "the dramatic reversal" of compression in which "the globe is no more than a village" (6).

Many of us are familiar with McLuhan's fascination with Poe's short story "The Maelstrom," which McLuhan often presented as a metaphor for contemporary individuals facing a storm of technological change. While the protagonist's ability to survive the storm conveys McLuhan's abiding commitment to human agency—so that, if we cannot take technology out of our world, we can learn with conscious effort to work with it—what the story contributes to my argument is a depiction of the overwhelming and relentless force of change. This powerful force, however, does not have to destroy everything in its path, but it can work a sea change, so that what re-emerges is the same but different—a "re-presentation." In McLuhan's view, change is not a balanced or measured process— not, say, occurring with the evenness of a pendulum swing, from thesis to antithesis to synthesis and forward. Instead, McLuhan asks us to think about historical linkages in terms of networks that crisscross at a rate of constant speedup, but even this crazy-paced crossing allows for a constancy and recurrence. For him to say that the city is dead is not to say that it is gone but to predict its revival in some future form.

THE DELOS SYMPOSIA:
PLANNING THE NETWORKED WORLD CITY

Apart from envisioning how cities might grow and change in response to human forces of transportation technology, McLuhan's thinking about the direction of urban settlement was also influenced by the interdisciplinary perspectives of architects, designers, and scholars who attended the Delos Symposia beginning in 1962. These symposia were organized by Greek architect Constantin Doxiadis, founder of the Ekistics movement committed to predicting and controlling human settlement patterns on a global scale. This movement was in favour of a single planned city of the future, one mobile and responsive to layers of invisible life-sustaining networks. Wigley describes the prediction of Doxiadis of "the emergence of a single city covering the whole earth like a lava lamp network, a fluid biomorphic growth extending itself everywhere" (88). Called "Ecumenopolis," a neologism that scholar Panayiota Pyla tells us is a conflation of "the home (*oikos*) with the globe (*oicumene*)" (27), it is like a "single continuous living space, a vast urban network that looks like a nervous system" (Wigley 102). Doxiadis was struck by the similarity of his conception of architectural form and McLuhan's descriptions of how the human body had experienced prosthetic extensions brought about by technology; as Wigley summarizes, McLuhan often spoke in terms of networks of communication as "new body parts" that "constitute a new organism, a new spatial system, a new architecture" (86). Doxiadis adopted a similar belief in networks as being like human biological systems, which led to his statement that design decisions should be based "on the internal operations of the body. The architect elaborates the human body rather than houses it" (quoted in Wigley 94). McLuhan was also aware of being drawn into conversations about housing and changing settlement patterns; Wigley quotes his reference to being interested in "matters of immediate concern in housing and town planning" (86).

To discuss models of future human settlement, Doxiadis assembled international and interdisciplinary experts on a yearly basis (from 1961 to 1975), convening the Delos Symposia on a yacht sailing the Aegean Sea to discuss city theory and practice away from mundane work. After reading *The Gutenberg Galaxy: The Making of Typographic Man*, Doxiadis was determined to add McLuhan to a guest list that included Buckminster Fuller, Barbara Ward, and Margaret Mead, and he sent him a flattering invitation outlining his contribution to the event: "I have just finished reading your wonderful book 'Gutenberg Galaxy,' in which I found so many of the things that we also believe in and so many of the ideas which I think are relevant and essential to human settlements and their problems" (quoted in Wigley 115). The participants debated ways to reshape cities to better accommodate growing populations, avoid sprawl, and share resources by cultivating an ecology of networks. McLuhan's primary contribution to this group was to share and elaborate his vision of the ways in which technologies extend human lives across space and around the globe.

A key concept of the Delos Symposia was that the futurist single city would be organized around an understanding of its being connected by layers of mostly invisible networks—of its being "a continuous network of centers and lines of communication" in which "all parts of the settlement and all lines of communication will be interwoven into a meaningful organism" (Wigley 88). Whereas modernist cities were replete with visible roads and boundaries—"modern architects like Le Corbusier only used the word 'network' to describe the old street pattern and the new ones they proposed" (94)—Ecumenopolis would be bound by layers of mostly invisible networks. Moreover, in this world city, houses would no longer be permanent structures but more like "'shells' for movement patterns that reach out far beyond them" (88). Thus, the world city was conceptualized as being organized in an orderly yet mobile framework around what had been up till then mostly invisible networks. The flow of electricity, for example, exemplifies the sort of invisible network that Doxiadis believed needed to be made visible in plans and designs and coordinated with all other flows: "We must coordinate *all* of our Networks *now*. All networks, from roads to telephones" (quoted 94). Seen from above at night, city lights hint at arrangements and networks that connect settlements across the globe, a theme that Doxiadis picked up and explored in attempting to make invisible networks visible by finding ways to depict them in charts and graphs.

To adopt a view of buildings as mobile and disposable, and of architecture and networks as increasingly invisible, is to abandon the widely held modernist model of "settlements held together by transportation networks" and to adopt instead "the idea of inhabitable information networks" (Wigley 97). When, in the early twentieth century, modernist architects such as Giedion and Le Corbusier met in the International Congresses of Modern Architecture, they identified as the main functions of cities dwelling, working, and recreation. To these functions they added, at a later meeting, traffic, with the qualification that this function was "to bring the other three into communication with one another" (95). Traffic introduced a concept of networking, yet the modernist planners envisioned it as visible, as somewhat subservient to the other functions, and primarily as a "word to describe the old street patterns and the new ones" (94). In contrast, the Ekistics movement of the 1960s and 1970s recognized networks as one of five elements of settlement, added to "'Nature,' 'Man,' 'Society,' and 'Shells'" (93). Moreover, this became the trump term, so that "Everything was seen to be networked" (93).

In addition to emphasizing the importance of organizing the networks linking the global city, Doxiadis emphasized the importance of balancing urban and non-urban green worlds, "for the symbiosis of the global city with the natural world" (Pyla 10). Within the Ekistics movement, striking a balance with nature was a value that became increasingly important in the theory and design of Ecumenopolis. The notion of the earth as a small planet and shared home is developed in this group statement made at Delos Ten:

> As we enter the global phase of social evolution, it becomes obvious that each one of us has two countries—his own and the planet earth. We cannot feel at home on earth if we do not continue to love and cultivate our own garden. And conversely, we can hardly feel comfortable in our garden if we do not care for the planet earth as our collective home. (quoted in Pyla 26)

This visionary anticipation of the concepts of environmental sustainability and ecological balance leads Pyla to conclude that the theorizing of Doxiadis is more than a "relic of [a] bygone era" and continues to become ever more current "as a new round of globalization is taking hold and as 'sustainable development' is fast becoming the favourite catchphrase of architectural (and other) circles" (29).

It cannot be said with certainty that McLuhan embraced the Ekistics enterprise as it was expounded in the 1970s, so he might not have agreed with the group's position on sustainable development. True to form in being a "dissident" thinker given to revising his views, McLuhan had pulled back from the group. At the tenth Delos Symposium in 1972, he even raised questions about formative concepts that had generated and shaped the movement by expressing resistance to the notion that the key to the city of the future was making invisible networks visible, arguing that physical configurations were becoming "redundant." Instead, he sketched out the position that James Joyce's *Ulysses* was "the greatest piece of city planning and building in this century" (quoted in Wigley 113), implying perhaps that we live in cities of the mind, even imaginary cities, rather than material and time-bound places. He began using the term "unsettlement" to describe a more mobile, less physical, environment.

Yet, even if McLuhan eventually challenged some of the stances taken by members of the Ekistics movement, the concept of "Ecumenopolis" stands as a synonymous term for his "global village." This village as McLuhan envisioned it was not entirely new—to take the place of the modernist city—but a throwback to a form of relatively unsophisticated community, a form usually understood as predating the modern city. By juxtaposing "village" with the relatively unknown term "global," McLuhan offered an example of his broader notion that the old is always made new again—in this case a return to a village unlike any village that our ancestors knew because of its size and networks. If we are currently being hurtled from city into global village, then it will not be long before this new village life in turn gives way to some returning form of city life. A similar dialectic is captured in the way that McLuhan moved from supporting to questioning and suggesting ways to reconfigure the global city of Doxiadis.

To the extent that McLuhan's theory of change indirectly postulates the eventual death of the global village and the return of a transformed city, McLuhan is in step with a strong current of urban theorizing that seeks to reassert the value of the local and material city. Doreen Massey's influential essay "A Global Sense of Place" emphasizes diversity and mobility as definitive of healthy urban communities and has prompted theoretical explorations of how the values of sustainability, diversity, and social justice play into current cosmopolitanism. Although the term "global village" remains an apt reference to how our lives are sourced by worldwide flows, there is increasing recognition that we go home to local neighbourhoods. Much of *Restless Cities: Essays in Metropolis in Perpetual Motion,* for example (a recent collection by British scholars and writers that explores the complexity, challenges, and creative potential of urban life; see Beaumont and Dart), ignores settled and suburban dwelling to link diversity and mobility to urban vigour. These contemporary arguments re-evaluating the liveliness and sustainability of local urban spaces as cornerstones of culture would not have surprised McLuhan, whose own cornerstone concept was that the old becomes new again but renewed in different ways.

MAKING (SOME) ROOM FOR NATURE AND LOCAL COMMUNITY IN McLUHAN'S URBANISM

I want to balance this discussion of McLuhan's view of urban life and change by noting that, while it is tied foremost to technology, McLuhan was nonetheless aware of the need for green space—that living space required cultivated gardens as well as built structures. I have already noted the pleasure that he took in the commodious nature of his Whychwood home and neighbourhood, as described in this letter: "The pond ripples outward into a heavily treed neighbourhood of twenty-two acres and fifty-four houses" (quoted in Gordon 233). His commitment to the Ekistics movement ensured that he was familiar with a view of balancing built development with green space. One of its central figures, Jaqueline Tyrwhitt, was a lifelong friend and associate of McLuhan, and she was noted for her scholarship on landscape and development of garden projects that contributed to horticulture and landscape architecture.

There was also an intriguing if brief connection between urban activist Jane Jacobs and McLuhan that needs to be noted since it has frequently been overlooked. Like McLuhan, Jacobs, his near contemporary, saw the city as an entity going through the process of death and rebirth, and she was deeply critical of the effects of car transportation. In one of her last books, *Dark Age Ahead*, Jacobs tells us how Fordism not only killed neighbourhoods by mis-shaping them with roads and gouging freeways but also derailed electric trolley systems and converted public transportation into combustion engine buses. As she tells the story of how car transportation hijacked other interests in the development of our cities, there is an ever-present tone of regret and often a call for action. McLuhan tells similar stories in his works, yet he speaks in a voice that is more deliberately neutral, his goal being to understand and explain. Rather than worrying that we will forget past gains and glories, he worries that we are unknowingly driven by the past so that we cannot see the present clearly enough to survive and plan for the future. He says outright that he is not interested in reaching "moralizers" who want things labelled as "a good thing or a bad thing" or those whom he refers to as "motivated somnambulists" in the "Author's Note" of *Culture Is Our Business* (8).

Despite taking different views of activism and of the influence of the past on our present urban dilemmas, Jacobs and McLuhan forged an alliance in 1970 to protest against the development of the proposed Spadina Expressway in Toronto. In the name of moving people more quickly through the growing city, the expressway was slated to cut through residential neighbourhoods and parks, dividing happy communities with a structure that McLuhan referred to as "a cement kimono" in a letter of protest to Premier Bill Davis (quoted in Gordon 269). He also warned against matching the mistakes of American cities—whose deaths Jacobs had outlined in her famous book—and pushed instead for a more productive move, asking that we "make" something new. As part of their activist efforts, Jacobs and McLuhan collaborated on a short film, *The Burning Would*, which had several screenings. Ultimately, they were on the winning side, and plans for the expressway were put on hold.

This incident of activism is important because it reveals several elements of McLuhan's character and beliefs often overlooked: his recognition of the value of saving communities and green spaces. Although we see protesting city plans for growth as entirely in keeping with the career of Jacobs, we are less inclined to think of McLuhan as an activist. It is true that his activism was motivated by self-interest in that he wanted to protect his home from the offending potential expressway. It is also true that such an engagement ran counter to the neutral voice and position that he typically cultivated in his writing, yet we need to remember that he hoped by this approach to provoke others to informed and improved actions. His passion for seeing the world fully and clearly is not without activist implications: only after we are awakened from our somnambulist ways are we able to see what needs to be done. In a late-stage book co-written with Kathryn Hutchon and Eric McLuhan, *City as Classroom: Understanding Language and Media,* his sense of mission is uncharacteristically visible as he encourages young people to avoid becoming alienated by becoming more alert to media changes in the environment. Exercises in the book train students to make sense of the urban life around them because "Understanding . . . enables us all to avoid that feeling of helplessness and frustration—that 'Stop the World I want to get off!'" (165).

Perhaps it is this sense of mission and the hope that it implies that leads his recent biographer Douglas Coupland—seldom considered an unbounded optimist—to refer to McLuhan as a figure who gives comfort by counselling the shelter of human community. He says that "Marshall gives comfort and helps us forward; Marshall lets us know that we are part of something long and grand, that we're not merely blips on a screen. . . . With Marshall's prodding we can choose community over self" (232). But apart from our taking comfort from McLuhan's vision of change and continuity in the human community, McLuhan himself would likely have wished that we take his advice to heart and become more aware of our urban environments to have some say in their design rather than simply following arranged patterns. We need to be producers rather than mere consumers of our environment, a concept that Richard Cavell notes was part of the non-determinist dynamic of McLuhan's thinking about material and social space: "This [potential to produce as well as consume] provides the basis for agency and resistance within the matrix of a totalized (or environmental) technology" (222).

Rather than simply pronouncing death to city worlds, then, McLuhan is more accurately understood as using dark and extreme words such as *obsolete* and *dissolve* to convey his sense of the depth and speed of urban change and to call our attention to such change. His emphasis on the link between transportation technologies and the physical and psychic landscapes that we inhabit argues that, far from being dismissive of human sociability and community, he saw linkages and networks as central organizing principles of human lives. The mechanical transportation technologies that shaped our modernist cities are no longer vital, he argued. Instead, McLuhan believed that human settlements need to be more responsive to invisible global networks. Eventually, he came to argue for the need to plan for unsettlement, invoking the concept of mobilities that currently dominates discussions of urban planning and living.

In sum, the most major change to human settlement that McLuhan envisioned, whether thinking about a futurist world city or thinking about life in the local community, was that physical connections such as roads and sidewalks should become less influential structural considerations; instead, we should be more aware of the growth of invisible networks affecting the entire ecology of place. McLuhan sought to release us from being overcommitted to conceptualizing and building concrete cities cemented in place, and to do this he joined forces over the course of his life with a variety of urban theorists and planners developing city imaginaries alive to mobility.

WORKS CITED

Amin, Ash, and Stephen Graham. "The Ordinary City." *Transactions of the Institute of British Geographers,* New Series, 22.4 (1997): 411–29. JStor. Web.

Augé, Marc. *Non-Places: Introduction to an Anthropology of Super-modernity.* London: Verso, 1995. Print.

Beaumont, Matthew, and Gregory Dart, eds. *Restless Cities: Essays in Metropolis in Perpetual Motion.* London: Verso, 2010. Print.

Cavell, Richard. *McLuhan in Space: A Cultural Geography.* Toronto: U of Toronto P, 2002. Print.

Coupland, Douglas. *Marshall McLuhan.* Toronto: Penguin, 2009. Print.

Cresswell, Tim. *On the Move: Mobility in the Modern Western World.* New York: Routledge, 2006. Print.

Dolan, Mathew. "Record Bankruptcy for Detroit." *Wall Street Journal* 19 July 2013: A1. Web.

Garvin, Rebecca Todd. "Responses to the Linguistic Landscape in Memphis, Tennessee: An Urban Space in Transition." *Linguistic Landscape in the City.* Ed. Elana Shohamy, Eliezer Ben-Rafael, and Monica Barni. Bristol: Multilingual Matters, 2010. Print.

Gordon, W. Terrence. "Introduction to the First Edition." McLuhan, *Understanding Media.*

Jacobs, Jane. *Dark Age Ahead.* Toronto: Random House, 2004. Print.

LeDuff, Charlie. *Detroit: An American Autopsy.* New York: Penguin, 2013. Print.

Massey, Doreen. "A Global Sense of Place." *Reading Human Geography.* Ed. Trevor Barnes and Derek Gregory. London: Arnold, 1997. 315–23. Print.

McLuhan, Marshall. *Culture Is Our Business.* New York: McGraw-Hill, 1970. Print.

——. *The Gutenberg Galaxy: The Making of Typographic Man.* Toronto: U of Toronto P, 1962. Print.

——. "Inside the Five Sense Sensorium." *Empire of the Senses: The Sensual Cultural Reader.* Ed. David Howes. Oxford: Berg, 2005. 43–52. Print.

———. *The Mechanical Bride: Folklore of Industrial Man.* New York: Vanguard, 1951. Print.

———. *Understanding Media: The Extensions of Man.* Critical ed. Ed. W. Terrence Gordon. 1964. Berkeley: Ginko, 2003. Print.

McLuhan, Marshall, Kathryn Hutchon, and Eric McLuhan. *City as Classroom: Understanding Language and Media.* Agincourt, ON: Book Society of Canada. 1977. Print.

McLuhan, Marshall, and Jane Jacobs. *The Burning Would.* Reason Association Productions. www.youtube.com/watch?v=GDzkjL-7r5zg. Film.

McLuhan, Marshall, and Barrington Nevitt. "The Argument: Causality in the Electric World." *Technology and Culture* 14.1 (1973): 1–16. Print.

McLuhan, Marshall, and Harley Parker. *Counterblast.* London: Rapp and Whiting, 1970. Print.

McLuhan, Marshall, and Bruce R. Powers. *The Global Village: Transformations in World Life and Media in the 21st Century.* New York: Oxford UP, 1989. Print.

Mumford, Lewis. *The Urban Prospect.* 1956. New York: Harcourt, Brace and World, 1968. Print.

Pyla, Panayiota. "Planetary Home and Garden: Ekistics and Environmental-Developmental Politics." *Grey Room* 36 (2009): 6–35. Web.

Solnit, Rebecca. "Detroit Arcadia: Exploring the Post-American Landscape." *Harpers* July 2007: n. pag. Web.

Wigley, Mark. "Network Fever." *Grey Room* 4 (2001): 82–122. Web.

CHAPTER 8

THE LIBRARY AS PLACE:
NEW MEDIA AND NEW DESIGNS
FOR CREATING COMMUNITY

Karen Brown and Mary Pat Fallon

Many words have been devoted in the past decade to pondering the future of libraries. The visions have ranged from utopian to fatalistic. Attention to this issue has been fuelled largely by the unprecedented shift from print to electronic resources, a shift that also captured the attention of Marshall McLuhan. Just a few excerpts from the library and information science literature highlight the range of perspectives that has emerged about the changing form and function of libraries. Community college librarian William Wisner recently proclaimed that "We must accept that the historic mission of libraries is finished, that our buildings will gradually disappear over the next one hundred years, and that the portable e-book, once perfected, will drive the last nail into our collective coffins" (quoted in Antell and Engel 537). In a similar vein, University of Illinois-Chicago librarian John Shuler says that "spending time in a library is merely a 'trip down nostalgia lane'" (quoted in

Antell and Engel 537). Harold Shill and Shawn Tonner, however, studied renovated and new academic library buildings that had been remodelled or built between 1995 and 2002 and found that these spaces "provide a vastly improved ambience that encourages use, rather than avoidance, of the library building" (quoted in Antell and Engel 538). Karen Antell and Debra Engel were also interested in the impacts of new information technologies on the function of an academic library within the academy and suspected that there might be a generation gap, with doctoral students favouring remote access to the library and faculty preferring the physical library. Published in 2006, their survey of doctoral students and faculty, however, revealed that the former, typically younger than the latter, valued library buildings because they are spaces conducive to scholarship and places where "scholarship happens" (536)—an acknowledgement, perhaps, that when form meets function McLuhan's ideas deserve serious reconsideration.

The allocation of public funds for building a new library or renovating an existing facility frequently sparks debate about the form and function of libraries. In 2006, Mark Hirschey, a resident of Lawrence, Kansas, wrote a letter to the editor of the local newspaper questioning the value of library buildings in the Internet age, as this passage conveys: "Rather than build an expensive new library downtown in the mistaken belief that such a monument to 19th century information technology will bring the community together, the city of Lawrence needs to consider the real advantages to bringing our entire community's information infrastructure into the 21st century" (n. pag.). Offering an opposing view, Helene Blowers, the digital strategy director at the Columbus, Ohio, Metropolitan Library, argues that "The library building isn't a warehouse for books. It's a community gathering center" (quoted in Sutter n. pag.).

Although much of the discussion has focused on notions of place in relation to physical libraries, there has also been consideration of digital or virtual libraries as *places*. Both physical and virtual libraries can be conceptualized as places where individuals come together and are provided with systematic access to a collection of resources. Physical libraries, for the most part, maintain collections of books, other tangible materials, and the technology necessary to access electronic information resources from within their walls. They also provide spaces for meeting and study. The virtual presence of the library, if it exists, is typically an extension of the physical structure. First there is the physical structure, and then the virtual library is added. Rarely is a virtual library created without the physical library as the initial foundation. Jeffrey Pomerantz and Gary Marchionini suggest, however, that it might not be long before we see the creation of digital libraries that are followed by the construction of physical branches.

These few examples present views that differ in significant ways, but the writers all agree on one thing: libraries are changing because the media of communication and information dissemination are changing. Libraries in the digital age cannot possibly be what they were in the print age. This is neither good nor bad in itself; it is simply a fact.

Wayne Wiegand, a professor of library and information science at Florida State University, urges us to consider the "library as place" from the perspective of "the library in the life of the user" (26), quite different from the more common approach that explores *the user in the life of the library.* His approach situates the development of libraries within an important and rich social and cultural context. By analyzing the history of libraries through this lens, Wiegand notes that libraries worldwide have been particularly influential in three important ways during the past century: "One, made information accessible to billions of people on many subjects; two, furnished billions of reading materials to billions of patrons; and three, provided hundreds of thousands of places where users have been able to meet formally as clubs or groups, or informally as citizens and students utilizing a civic institution and cultural agency" (76).

The ideas of McLuhan can contribute to discussions about the library as place by directing our attention to the impacts of media on notions of space and place. As he so aptly, and now famously, stated in *Understanding Media: The Extensions of Man,* "the medium is the message," and "the 'message' of any medium of technology is the change of scale or pace or pattern that it introduces into human affairs" (24). He was interested in the impact of the form of communication on our perceptions, ways of thinking, and patterns of interaction. His discussion of the impacts of two forms of communication media in particular—the printed word and electronic media—provides a framework for investigating changes in library design and use of space. These changes are more fundamental than simply altering how bricks and mortar are put together or how wireless networks are structured; they reflect significant shifts in our concept of libraries. More specifically, the dominant communication medium of a particular time has influenced how a society and culture defined the role and function of a library as well as notions of how knowledge is created, organized, and disseminated. In this chapter, we focus primarily on new and renovated libraries that have received recognition in the professional and popular press to highlight how McLuhan's ideas are reflected in emerging library spaces. These spaces say much about the shift from a typographic culture to an electronic culture.

Perhaps the most significant change in library structures over the past few decades has been the move away from secluded, dark spaces with endless rows of floor-to-ceiling shelving units interspersed with sequestered spots for quiet, individual study. These types of structures have been replaced with well-lit, open spaces of mixed media and designs that seek to promote civic engagement and collaborative learning. In fact, many new and existing libraries—for example, Brooklyn Public Library; Kraemer Library in Plain, Wisconsin; Spanish River Public Library in Boca Raton, Florida; Embudo Valley Library in Dixon, New Mexico; and many others—have defined or redefined themselves as community centres. Libraries, once cloisters of individual study, have become tribal spaces of ritualized behaviour. Library and information science scholar Cecelia Merkel notes that new libraries "perform functions in a ritualized way—much like churches" (422). The library profession refers to this shift as a change from the library as a warehouse to the library as an information and learning commons. Likewise, we think that McLuhan would characterize the shift as one from the fragmentation, specialization, and individualism of a typographic culture to the global embrace of a culture of generalized knowledge and tribalism, permeated with the values of electric technology: immediacy, feedback, fluidity, interaction, and convenience.

LIBRARIES IN A TYPOGRAPHIC CULTURE

Stewardship of the human record is one of the core values of the library profession, and thus the heart of a library is often considered to be its collection. Libraries have traditionally been buildings where a society's knowledge is assembled in one place and made available for study, learning, conversation, and civic engagement. Systematic organization of and access to a library collection are the hallmarks of a good library, and collections are arranged and maintained according to formalized cataloguing and classification practices, using familiar schemata such as Dewey and the Library of Congress. These cataloguing and classification standards, which have evolved and been perfected over the years and used with consistency by libraries around the world, emerged principally from the phenomenal growth of book collections and reflect McLuhan's perspective that in a Gutenberg culture there is "a place for everything and everything in its place" (156).

Historically, these library book collections have been developed and shaped by librarian-bibliographers typically assigned call number ranges that correspond with their areas of subject expertise. This practice mirrors the characteristics of specialization and fragmentation so prevalent in a typographic culture, in which taxonomies of knowledge are outlined in linear fashion. Librarians have relied on professional review sources to evaluate and select the materials added to a library collection. The reviewers of these materials are usually scholars, literary critics, or librarians with deep knowledge of a subject domain. Criteria such as reputation of the publisher, author expertise, and quality of referenced sources are important to the vetting process. McLuhan notes that the culture of the printed word gave rise to "the partial and specialized character of the viewpoint" (20), and in many ways the practices of collection development are dependent on the typographic cultural values of authoritative points of view and ordered evaluations.

Each library has also built a collection that is unique, by and large, to its community of users. The individuals of the community, whether an academic or civic community, identify with a particular library. So it is not unusual to hear one say, "My library is the River Forest Public Library" or "My library is at Dominican University." The members of the community see their library as the institution that stores and preserves the cultural heritage and knowledge of the community, and the library space is structured in such a way that attention to the organization and mainten-ance of the collection is showcased and dominates. The collection serves as the focal point for individual reference and study as well as public programs. Even though public gatherings occur, the li-brary from this perspective manifests the characteristics of a cul-ture steeped in the printed word. As McLuhan says, it is a culture in which "Separateness of the individual, continuity of space and of time, and uniformity of codes are the prime marks of literate and civilized societies" (86–87).

LIBRARIES IN THE ELECTRONIC AGE

Although these types of library spaces persist, new architectural structures with unique space designs are emerging, ones that seem to echo McLuhan's comments about the influence of electronic media on our social and psychic patterns. Library collections are no longer solely book collections. They integrate print, multimedia, and electronic resources, and increasingly this combination is in-tentionally designed to foster a synergy of sharing and content cre-ation. Individual study spaces are giving way to group study and collaborative meeting spaces. Even use of the term "library" is be-ing debated—known within the profession as the *L* word debate, conducted by scholars in the field such as Cronin, Germek, Intner, and Kennedy. Terms such as "information commons" and "learn-ing commons" are gaining popularity. For most library users, re-mote access to resources is a given, and library "apps" for mobile devices have been developed to provide 24/7 connection. In es-sence, the restrictions of time and space have been abolished. As McLuhan forecast as early as 1964, "Instant synchronization of numerous operations has ended the old mechanical pattern of set-ting up operations in lineal sequence" (302–03).

The Seattle Public Library, for example, has reinvented it-self and redefined the "public space" occupied by libraries. A glass-enclosed, diamond-shaped atrium joins information, reference, and reading functions with views of the city, public seating, and a café. In this redefined space, users are no longer "users" but an audience or groups of general and specialized audiences that include children, teens, and adults. Audiences use the physical space of the library to take classes, hear lectures, get homework help, learn Internet skills, and congregate and chat over coffee. Services have been decentralized from branch locations to the border-free digital space of the Internet: users can search, consult librarians, and access e-books and other digital media online. The book, while still present in this physical space, does not dominate it, moving from the centre to the periphery as it must in a hybrid physical and virtual space that has no definitive centre and is all peripheral.

Whereas a library's collection has traditionally been developed by librarians who have subject expertise and use well-established review sources in combination with a community needs assessment, there is a growing trend toward user-driven collection development. In other words, the collection is built as the interests and needs of library users are indicated electronically through online searches and user-centred assessment methods. The process of collection development is becoming decentralized rather than centralized.

Library collection organization schemata and access mechanisms are also increasingly user centred. For example, standardized cataloguing and classification practices are being replaced by user-generated tagging of collection item records creating folksonomies. "Discovery" searches that produce individualized, fluid word clouds and visual mappings are prevalent on library websites. The widespread use and growing acceptance of Wikipedia over traditional encyclopedias also reflect this trend and are evidence of the move away from a typographic culture. As McLuhan projected, electronic media compel "commitment and participation, quite regardless of any 'point of view.' The partial and specialized character of the viewpoint, however noble, will not serve at all in the electric age" (20). Social media applications also provide opportunities for library users to post reviews of books and movies on the library's website and to share their "favourites" with other users. The strict policies (and legislation) that protect a user's privacy are being challenged by the growing preference of users to connect and interact with others online. Again we see the words of McLuhan in *Understanding Media* as foreshadowing this dilemma: "Specialist technologies detribalize. The non-specialist electric technology retribalizes" (38).

At Ohio State University, the renovated Thompson Library has reduced its print collection by more than 25 percent, from over 2 million volumes to about 1.5 million volumes. Many of the remaining volumes in the print collection were transferred from the central library building to an off-site book depository. The space savings were dedicated to increased seating, study areas, an art gallery, food services, coffee bars, and other amenities. The uniform, linear, hot medium that was the book-based library has given way to the cooler, non-linear, shared spaces of electronic information.

Even the notion of a local library is waning in favour of a universal library in which collections and services can be accessed and used, regardless of the physical location of a library. The virtual spaces being created by libraries further amplify this trend. Library users like the local, the "village," but they want it to be "global." New library building designs have increased the role of libraries as centres for public dialogue and civic engagement, and virtual library spaces are providing opportunities for interaction and conversation.

Libraries such as the new Athenaeum at Goucher College in Maryland blur—if not eradicate entirely—the linear conceptual boundaries of the traditional, book-based, academic library. The Athenaeum is library, student centre, public square, recreation centre, restaurant, cultural hub, and health spa all in one—and open all twenty-four hours of the day. Taking its name from the ancient Roman institution of arts and learning, the Athenaeum was planned to be a postmodern *agora*, a town square where people are inclined to "bump into" each other. "I started doing research on the athenaeum of classical times," explained Goucher College president Sanford J. Ungar, "and it was a central gathering point where people came for a variety of purposes serious, frivolous, cultural, artistic, and social" (quoted in Carlson A17). The

Athenaeum's entrance, a wide-open space known as the Forum, is a four-storey-high atrium that cuts through the centre of the building. On one side of the Forum is an art gallery; on the other is a restaurant. On a balcony overlooking the Forum, one finds an exercise area with elliptical machines, stationary bikes, and rowing machines, served by unisex bathrooms with showers and lockers. There is also a commuter lounge complete with a kitchen.

After reading McLuhan, we can see how notions of the library as place reflect the influences of different forms of communication so well articulated by him. Four influences in particular are prominent:

1. Libraries of the typographic age emphasized fragmentation and specialization, whereas contemporary libraries embrace "organic interrelation" (McLuhan 306).
2. The Gutenberg technologies promoted "the typographic principles of uniformity, continuity, and lineality" (McLuhan 29) in library space and function, in contrast to the interrelated and circular characteristics fostered by electronic technologies.
3. Contemporary library designs and uses of space (both physical and virtual) promote the "village" over the individual.
4. And, finally, global is replacing local.

Libraries are increasingly *places* where knowledge is in a state of continuous creation and transformation. McLuhan refers to this process as one in which humans in the electric age "are suddenly nomadic gatherers of knowledge, nomadic as never before, informed as never before, free from fragmentary specialism as never before—but also involved in the total social process as never before; since with electricity we extend our central nervous system globally, instantly interrelating every human experience" (310–11). New library designs unite form and function in ways that embrace and foster the participatory, fluid, and organic characteristics inherent to electronic media.

WORKS CITED

Antell, Karen, and Debra Engel. "Conduciveness to Scholarship: The Essence of Academic Library as Place." *College and Research Libraries* 67.6 (2006): 536–60. Print.

Carlson, Scott. "Is It a Library? A Student Center? The Athenaeum Opens at Goucher College." *Chronicle of Higher Education* 56.4–5 (2009): A16–A17. Print.

Cronin, Blaise. "The Dreaded 'L' Word." *Library Journal* 126.5 (2001): 58. Print.

Germek, George. "Keep the 'L' Word." *Library Journal* 134.8 (2009): 10. Print.

Hirschey, Mark. "Libraries Are Limited, Obsolete." *Lawrence (KS) Journal-World* 2 Oct. 2006: n. pag. Web.

Intner, S. Sheila. "The 'L' Word versus the 'I' Word." *Technicalities* 28.3 (2008): 1–17. Print.

Kennedy, Shirley. "The 'L' Word." *Information Today* 24.8 (2007): 17–18. Print.

McLuhan, Marshall. *Understanding Media: The Extensions of Man.* New York: Mentor Book, 1964. Print.

Merkel, Cecelia. "Folkloristics of Educational Spaces: Material Lore in Classrooms with and without Walls." *Library Trends* 47.3 (1999): 417–38. Print.

Pomerantz, Jeffrey, and Gary Marchionini. "The Digital Library as Place." *Journal of Documentation* 63.4 (2007): 505–33. Print.

Sutter, John. "The Future of Libraries, with or without Books." *CNN Tech* 4 Sept. 2009: n. pag. Web.

Wiegand, Wayne. "Library as Place." *North Carolina Libraries* 63.3–4 (2005): 76–81. Print.

CHAPTER 9

THE MESSAGE IN MEDICAL IMAGING MEDIA:
AN ANALYSIS OF GE HEALTHCARE'S VSCAN™

Catherine Jenkins

arshall McLuhan died in 1980, on the brink of the technological revolution, but clearly he was a thinker ahead of his time. The changes that technologies have brought in the past thirty years have rapidly reshaped business, social life, education, entertainment, and even how physicians practise medicine. The rapidity of these changes leaves little time for critical reflection on their impacts. McLuhan provided us with tools for an in-depth analysis to consider how media and technologies alter our world and ourselves. Given the inescapable media noise in our environment and the plethora of technologies that facilitate our everyday lives, McLuhan's work seems to be even more relevant now than when it was first published. Offering an examination of a specific example, the advertising for General Electric (GE) Healthcare's Vscan™, as well as an analysis of the device itself, this chapter examines the relevance of McLuhan's work for assessing current media and technologies.

GE's Vscan™ is a battery-operated, hand-held, ultrasound device, a "pocket size visualization tool" that looks more like the popular iPod® than a medical instrument (GE Vscan). Similar to many electronic gadgets, it comes with accessories, including a docking station, a USB cable, a memory card, a protective carrying case, and a web portal for user support. Its industry debut was at the Web 2.0 Summit in San Francisco on 20 October 2009, with the commercial release on 15 February 2010, after the device had gained regulatory approval. While the dedicated website is targeted toward medical professionals, television advertising was aimed at the general public, potential patients who might suggest such a device to their practitioners.

"LET'S TAKE A LOOK"

Television advertisements for the Vscan™ were in heavy rotation during coverage of the Vancouver Winter Olympics (12–28 February 2010), garnering millions of viewing hits just as the product was being released. On 11 February 2010, GE uploaded the commercial to YouTube, where it received several thousand more viewings. The advertisement features physicians from different historical periods and cultures raising a boy's shirt to examine his abdomen while saying, "Let's take a look." The scene is replayed in ancient Mongolia, China, and Hungary, modern rural North America of the early 1900s, and finally a present-day hospital. Once the contemporary doctor comes onscreen, the voice-over states, "Doctors have been saying it forever, but they've never actually been able to do it like this. Vscan, from GE Healthcare: a pocket-sized imaging device that will help change the way doctors see patients."

In *The Mechanical Bride: Folklore of Industrial Man*, McLuhan critically analyzes a vortex of print advertisements seeking possible underlying meanings in their overt messages. As he writes in the book's preface, "Today the tyrant rules not by club or fist, but, disguised as a market researcher, he shepherds his flocks in the ways of utility and comfort" (n. pag.). What does an analysis of the Vscan™ advertisement reveal?

The cultural contexts in which early doctors appear are squalid and implicitly pre-Gutenberg; certainly, traditional Chinese medicine dates to before the Common Era. These practitioners are othered not only temporally but also culturally; they are neither North American nor European (although Hungary is now a member of the European Union, it has a culture and language unique in Europe). Although the technology itself might not have a moral valence, the advertising certainly does, effectively undermining any notion of a "global village" through its demeaning of other cultures. These early non-Euro-American "doctors" are portrayed as ineffective and ignorant, convening their practices outdoors in village squares or farmyards. When the boy's abdomen shows no obvious sign of trauma, having the appearance of any healthy belly, the "doctor" is puzzled and seemingly has no diagnosis or cure to offer.

First, this advertisement implies that pre-technological practitioners had no legitimate medical knowledge, diagnostic skills, or treatments, yet there are remedies and methods used today that trace their origins to archaic practices. In both ancient Greek and traditional Chinese medicine, those suffering from pain, swelling, or fever were prescribed willow bark. In the late 1820s, salicin, the active chemical ingredient in the bark, was isolated; after further experiments with buffering agents, acetylsalicylic acid was synthesized in 1893; it was first marketed as Aspirin® in 1899. Modern medicine thus confirmed that the ancients had correctly identified an effective analgesic with properties to reduce fever and inflammation (Bayer Health Care). Building on the humoral medicine of Hippocrates, Galen's knowledge and teachings dominated Western medicine for over a millennium through the hundreds of volumes of the *Galenic Corpus*. Although many of his anatomical findings were later dismissed as inaccurate, Galen must be lauded for his methodology of careful observation and rational prognosis. With this technique, he was able to determine which victims of the devastating Antonine plague of Rome in the 160s–80s were likely to survive and which ones were not. Those exhibiting only external lesions were likely to survive; those with internal lesions, as indicated by black stools caused by internal bleeding, were likely to perish. These are just two of many possible examples proving that ancient physicians had indeed developed some level of know-ledge, diagnostic skill, and treatment. Although much ancient knowledge has not been legitimated by modern science, some of it has been.

Second, the Vscan™ advertisement implies that all medical diagnostics rely solely on the visual sense, what McLuhan calls "the victory of the visual over the other senses" (*Gutenberg Galaxy* 56). Although the importance of observation has always been emphasized in medicine, from Galen to the present, and current trends in medical imaging further accentuate the visual, it is certainly not infallible and not the only sense used in the medical arts. The Vscan™ uses ultrasound technology, employing sound waves at frequencies above those audible to the human ear; however, helpful diagnostic sounds that are readily audible are omitted from the Vscan™ advertisement. Arguably, the most important sound in a medical encounter is the patient's voice. Since the late 1970s, numerous studies have proven the value of the patient's voice in medical diagnostics. Among these studies is "Clues to Patients' Explanations and Concerns about Their Illnesses: A Call for Active Listening," which concludes that, though patients generally do not disclose their own ideas about their symptoms, doctors who encourage their patients to talk and who actively listen to them are rewarded with stronger therapeutic alliances and superior patient compliance (Lang, Floyd, and Beine 227). GE's ultrasound technology ignores the relevance of the patient's narrative, the patient's illness experience, as an important diagnostic tool. When did the pain start? What kind of pain is it? Is it intermittent or constant? Does it radiate anywhere? These and other questions form the basis of knowing whether the boy in the commercial is suffering from mild nausea or acute appendicitis and help to determine the type and urgency of treatment. The answers to these questions are not available through ultrasound or any other type of medical imaging technology, only through the dialogue between patient and doctor. A primary argument of McLuhan's *The Gutenberg Galaxy: The Making of Typographic Man* is that, since the invention of type, the visual has become the predominant and most legitimized sense. The Vscan™ advertisement supports this perspective, completely dismissing what McLuhan calls in this book the "'primitive' or audile-tactile" as irrelevant (43).

"YOU'LL REALLY SEE YOUR PATIENTS NOW"

GE also launched a dedicated Vscan™ website and educational portal that includes a video announcement by Omar Ishrak, president and CEO of GE Healthcare; downloadable promotional brochures and press releases including quotations from American and European physicians; images of the device; and images taken using the device. According to the website, the Vscan™ "will be used by physicians, as well as, possibly, nurses, paramedics, or even medical students under the supervision/prescription of a physician" (GE Vscan). Although the site has a link to a patient page, clearly the online presence is focused on the professional market.

Ishrak's video announcement on YouTube reveals the excitement of the head of GE Healthcare about the Vscan™. Ishrak states that the device "is going to be a revolutionary product. It's got all the elements to make ultrasound into *the* tool for every physical exam and for every physician-patient interaction that is performed. I'm confident that sometime in the future . . . ultrasound *will* become *the* ubiquitous tool" (GE Healthcare). The message is clear that GE hopes to position the Vscan™ as an indispensable element of competently performed routine clinical exams; the device is not solely for use with specific indications or in emergency situations. A press release quotation from Dr. José Zamorano, the director of the Cardiovascular Institute University Clinic of San Carlos in Madrid, supports Ishrak's assertion about the usefulness of this tool in everyday examinations: "[W]e have experienced firsthand the value of adding such a tool to our clinical and physical examination, adding clinically relevant information in roughly one out of every four patients" (GE Vscan). The routine use of an ultrasound device was clinically relevant to 25 percent of patients in this clinic, but for 75 percent of patients it was not. Although ultrasound is generally considered a safe technology, there have been concerns about frequent use, especially on fetal development. Whether it is relevant, useful, and safe to incorporate ultrasound scanning into a routine physical examination has not been established.

The cover of the *Primary Care Online Brochure* features the slogan "You'll really see your patients now" (GE Vscan). The implication is that not using the GE Vscan™ means giving an inferior physical examination, one that does not meet optimal standards supported by current technology, or that without this technology the physician might not be fulfilling his or her responsibility to patients. Similar to Ishrak's video announcement, the brochure encourages doctors to "help redefine the physical examination" (GE Vscan). As well as allowing the doctor to "look inside your patients," the Vscan™ will help the doctor "connect more deeply with your patients for better care" (GE Vscan). Mildred Blaxter's "The Case of the Vanishing Patient? Image and Experience" offers a deep analysis of one patient's experience with diagnostic imaging technologies. Blaxter concludes that the patient found imaging technologies "informative and even reassuring" if also somewhat troubling (776). The patient voiced concern that doctors "privilege the image over the actual body and its experience" (762), the relevance of the patient and his or her narrative of perceptions of the lived experience of illness risks becoming lost in electronic images. Blaxter adds that "A picture provided by a machine carries with it a sense of objectivity and authority" lacking in the patient's voice (772). Although a deeper connection between doctors and their patients is clearly a desirable outcome, it might be difficult to prove that the Vscan™ will lead to such a connection. A 2001 study published in the *British Medical Journal* concluded that, though between 88 percent and 99 percent of patients indicated that they wanted strong patient-centred communication with their physicians, only 63 percent desired a physical examination (Little et al. 468). A meta-analysis of twenty-one studies over ten years on the therapeutic alliance between doctors and patients "demonstrated a correlation between effective physician-patient communication and improved patient health outcomes" (Stewart 1423). Such conclusions tend to support the idea that advanced communication skills, rather than the habitual use of advanced technologies, have the greatest impact on creating strong patient-doctor therapeutic alliances.

The Vscan™ brochure does more than support the notion of superior patient care; it also promotes the gadget's ability to "streamline care," "speed diagnoses," and "improve your workflow, for faster, more efficient patient care with fewer referrals" (GE Vscan). GE Healthcare recognizes that the contemporary clinic's priority might be efficient care; doctors who see more patients per day derive greater income. Increased efficiency is also supported by the quotation from Dr. Anthony DeMaria, a professor of medicine and the director of the Sulpizio Cardiovascular Center at the University of California, who states that "The handheld device should help physicians make treatment decisions more quickly" (GE Vscan). Speedy diagnostics also serve patients well, but they might inadvertently cause them to "feel like a piece of meat," pushed through an institutionalized process rather than genuinely cared for.

The website also includes animated images taken with the Vscan™. Viewing these images with an untrained eye underscores the skill required to interpret ultrasounds. Captions such as "Visualization of the gall bladder to evaluate the presence of stones" and "Visual inspection of the kidney to identify the presence of extra fluid" are neutral, giving the uninitiated viewer no sense of whether the images indicate pathological findings or whether the results are negative (GE Vscan). The final caption, "Visual inspection of liver size as adjunct to palpation and percussion," points to the manner in which the Vscan™ should ideally be used (GE Vscan). Whether it will be used as an adjunct or a primary tool in practice is anybody's guess. A rhetorical analysis is also revealing. In clinical practice, "visual inspection" refers to an external examination of the patient. Granting that a scan is not nearly as invasive as exploratory surgery, GE declares that the Vscan™ provides a "non-invasive method to help secure visual information about what is happening inside the body," but this is an overstatement (GE Vscan). This technology seems to be very invasive indeed.

"ONE MUST TALK WITH TWO VOICES"

McLuhan's breakthrough book of 1951, *The Mechanical Bride*, offers analyses of numerous print advertisements, including one for GE lightbulbs featuring puppet Charlie McCarthy and his ventriloquist master Edgar Bergen. One of the questions that McLuhan asks is "[M]ust [one] talk with two voices to be understood today?" (16). By targeting both potential patients and physicians, using appropriate media for each audience, GE effectively used two voices in its marketing strategy. McLuhan notes that Bergen, the puppet master, presents the "absent-minded technological world," while Charlie is "acutely sensitive and conscious" of his own lack of freedom, control, and authority (18). The position of a faceless, unconscious corporation such as GE, and the power of its media over the general public, are clear in this analysis. Practitioners and much of the public will accept Vscan's™ technology uncritically, recognizing it as another development of the "absent-minded technological world." McLuhan's consideration of Charlie as the "acutely sensitive and conscious" puppet can readily be equated with the patient, hyperconscious of his or her body, and the technological context of the hospital or clinical environment in which it is being considered. Physicians, with GE by their sides, master the situation, while patients might be intensely aware of their vulnerability to and dependence on medical technologies to halt their illnesses.

In *Understanding Media*, McLuhan defined the difference between "hot" and "cool" media: "A hot medium is one that extends one single sense in 'high definition,'" and "Any hot medium allows less participation than a cool one" (39–40). A cool medium is more stimulating; it requires greater participation and input from the consumer to fill in the necessary details in its low-definition output. Although McLuhan considered television a cool medium, new technologies seem to be extending the continuum's cool zone or shifting technologies that were previously perceived as cool into warmer climes. A computer is multisensorial and requires greater participation than a television does, making it an even cooler medium. A hand-held ultrasound device such as the Vscan™ with low-definition images necessitates even greater participation, requiring the stimulating synthesis, comprehension, and interpretation of diverse components.

GE's development of the Vscan™ launch campaign carefully considered the device's potential audiences, developing different aspects of the campaign for delivery through appropriate media based on the level of stimulation and participation required. The message to the general public was delivered through the cool medium of television using a forty-seven-second comical advertisement in high rotation during a period of peak viewership; the message to doctors, the professional users, and consumers of this technology was delivered via the even cooler medium of a website with a multiplicity of links to texts, images, and animations. Although a curious public might go to the website, parts of it—including pricing and ordering information—are accessible only to registered medical professionals. By talking in two voices and using media of appropriate coolness for each desired audience, GE ensured the capture of both public and professional audiences for its product launch.

VSCAN™ TECHNOLOGY AS AN EXTENSION OF HUMAN FACULTY

Although McLuhan focused on media, he was also concerned with the analysis of technology itself. In both *Understanding Media* and *The Medium Is the Massage: An Inventory of Effects* (McLuhan and Fiore), McLuhan inventories the pervasiveness of media technologies and their effects on our consciousness. He perceives that "All media are extensions of some human faculty," analyzes the dominance of the visual sense, and ultimately creates a method for analyzing complex technologies (McLuhan and Fiore 26).

Humans have used tools for millennia, and those tools have been extensions of ourselves, either physically or sensorially. The shovel extends the arm; the telescope extends the eye. For McLuhan, the advent of electricity changed the valence of these extensions: "[E]lectric circuitry . . . [is] an extension of the central nervous system" (McLuhan and Fiore 40). Although the Vscan™

effectively extends a doctor's visual faculty, allowing for "visual inspection" of a patient's interior, McLuhan would argue that it is doing something more.

> By putting our physical bodies inside our extended nervous systems, by means of electric media, we set up a dynamic by which all previous technologies that are mere extensions of hands and feet and teeth and bodily heat-controls—all such extensions of our bodies, including cities—will be translated into information systems. Electromagnetic technology requires utter human docility and quiescence of meditation such as befits an organism that now wears its brain outside its skull and its nerves outside its hide. Man must serve his electric technology with the same servo-mechanistic fidelity with which he served his coracle, his canoe, his typography, and all other extensions of his physical organs. But there is this difference, that previous technologies were partial and fragmentary, and the electric is total and inclusive. (*Understanding Media* 86)

Imaging technologies render the patient as flattened data without body or context; the Vscan™ turns the patient's body into information. "In this electric age," McLuhan notes, "we see ourselves being translated more and more into the form of information, moving toward the technological extension of consciousness" (*Understanding Media* 85). To extract this information, the technology requires a patient's docility. Blaxter's case study mentions that, during diagnostic imaging, the patient felt "responsible for remaining absolutely still, following positioning instructions exactly," and "[f]elt an enormous responsibility not to move, not to cough" (771). These are the actions (or inactions) of the acquiescent patient, the subject endeavouring to be the object to optimize precise technology. Such technologies do more than mediate the discourse between doctor and patient; they actually dominate this discourse. The physician's gaze extends into the patient's body, not by engaging directly with the patient, but by focusing on a small screen remote from the patient. Meanwhile, the patient is rendered inanimate while his or her interior landscape is exposed and examined. Nervous system meets nervous system on a small screen outside the hides of both patient and doctor. Little could be more invasive.

Vscan™ technology has global implications for extension as well. Its portability, long battery life, and price far below that of full-console ultrasound machines give it market appeal in remote locations and developing nations. GE Healthcare promotes this possibility as supportive of medical access to remote villages, for example in India. In March 2008, GE Healthcare launched its portable MAC 400 electrocardiogram unit with an advertisement filmed in rural India. Although GE's focus on expanding health care to those who might not otherwise receive it is laudable, it cannot be forgotten that GE is a profit-seeking corporation and that this marketing move could be construed as a form of neocolonialism. In an open letter to GE's president of South Asia, while speaking favourably of the capacity of portable health-care technologies to help rural people in India, Rajendra Pratap Gupta, the president and director of the Disease Management Association of India, pleaded that, "If the Vscan can identify the sex as in the case of the sonography machines, please do not launch the product in India." He was gravely concerned that, in a country where male children are more desirable than female children, the ability to determine sex *in utero* might have dire consequences for some fetuses. Regardless of such concerns by Indian residents, GE Healthcare launched the Vscan™ there and has since announced plans to focus on the country's growing market for portable medical technologies to service rural areas.

"THE VISUAL ORGANIZATION OF THE NON-VISUAL"

As previously noted, the Vscan™ uses ultrasound technology, controlled sound waves, to create visual images: "the visual organization of the non-visual" (*Gutenberg Galaxy* 138). McLuhan noted that, in a post-Gutenberg culture, audile-tactile senses are perceived as primitive, non-linear, and rebellious, while the visual sense observes rationally ordered linearity. Visual information is authentic and believable, so for something as important as medical diagnostics "We trust the eye, not the ear" ("Acoustic Space" 39). Even though the Vscan™ uses sound, its sound is transformed and fixed into images. The advantage of sound waves over some other forms of imaging is that they are *not* linear but effortlessly envelop organs and contours; such is the omnidirectional nature of sound. As McLuhan indicates, "The ear favors no particular 'point of view' . . . and creates a 'world of simultaneous relationships'" (McLuhan and Fiore 111). Given the fluid variability of the other senses, is it desirable to rely almost entirely on the visual, on imaging technologies, ignoring the utility of the other senses in medical diagnostics?

In a piece written for the *New Yorker* in 2004, Malcolm Gladwell cites two Canadian studies from the mid-1980s showing that clinical breast exams by palpation (the tactile) by experienced practitioners were just as effective as mammographic imaging for diagnosing breast cancer. As Gladwell writes, these studies underscore that "we should not automatically value what we see in a picture over what we learn from our other senses." Psychophysicist Mark Goldstein states that "There is nothing in science or technology that has even come close to the sensitivity of the human finger with respect to the range of stimuli it can pick up. It's a brilliant instrument. But we simply don't trust our tactile sense as much as our visual sense" (quoted in Gladwell). In the Vscan™ advertisement, all the doctors lift the boy's shirt to look at his abdomen, but none of them palpates his abdomen to check for tenderness or swelling. Setting aside the purely biomedical, touch also provides psycho-emotional comfort to patients. Although some doctors maintain that this kind of "touchy-feely" support is the purview of nurses, not doctors, patients might feel otherwise. Perhaps a patient with abdominal pain would prefer the touch of a practised physician palpating his or her abdomen to the touch of cold gel distributed by a hard, plastic ultrasound wand.

As well as touch, the Vscan™ ignores other senses commonly used in diagnostics by ancient and sometimes modern doctors. For instance, a patient's breath, body, or excrement can exude odours related to specific disease states, making the physician's olfactory sense a useful diagnostic tool. Gangrene is obvious by the smell of rotting flesh; fruity breath can indicate complications due to untreated diabetes; fishy breath might indicate kidney failure. Although many contemporary doctors scoff at the outdated practice of disease diagnostics through smell, research continues into the possible uses of olfactory disease detection. Dogs, with their advanced sense of smell, seem to have a natural affinity for detecting cancers, and several research studies have examined the potential use of trained dogs in cancer detection. A 2006 study of canine detection of lung cancer published in *Integrative Cancer Therapies* declared that the accuracy of olfactory results by trained dogs was a 99 percent match with the results of lung cancer confirmed by invasive biopsies (McCulloch et al. 30). Similarly, a subspecies of rat has been trained to sniff out tuberculosis. The results of a 2009 study published in the *American Society of Tropical Medicine and Hygiene* showed that African pouched rats increased the detection of tuberculosis in sputum samples to 44 percent; initial microscopic visual screening had detected just over 13 percent (Poling et al. 1308). HeroRATs trained by the humanitarian organization APOPO (Anti-Personnel Landmines Detection Product Development) are now being used to detect tuberculosis, as well as sniff out landmines, in developing countries where more expensive, and seemingly less effective, technologies are not readily available. Although electronic noses, such as Cyrano Science's Cyranose, boast how many sensors they have, thus far no human-made technology has matched the results of the natural noses of dogs and rats.

As has already been noted in the analysis of the Vscan™ advertisement, this technology seems to ignore the readily audible sound of the patient's voice in favour of ultrasound, frequencies beyond the range of human hearing that can be harnessed to create images. Other older, audible technologies can also be useful during a physical exam. Percussion is the art of tapping on the patient's body to listen for the variability in sound emitted. This old-school method helps the practised physician to determine the borders and sizes of internal organs as well as the presence of unwanted fluid in the body cavity. Auscultation, with the simple technology of a stethoscope used for nearly two centuries, can have diagnostic relevance by monitoring the presence, absence, or type of bowel sounds in an aching belly. At the Web 2.0 Summit in 2010, GE CEO Jeffrey Immelt said that the Vscan™ "could be the stethoscope of the twenty-first century" (quoted in Layne). The stethoscope, however, is limited to sound, whereas the Vscan™ uses sound to create images, perceived as more reliable and predictable sensory data, that dismiss the "'primitive' or audile-tactile" as irrelevant (*Gutenberg Galaxy* 43).

> Visual space, created by intensifying and separating that sense from interplay with the others, is an infinite container, linear and continuous, homogenous and uniform. Acoustic space, always penetrated by tactility and other senses, is spherical, discontinuous, non-homogenous resonant, and dynamic. Visual space is structured as static, abstract figure minus a ground; acoustic space is a flux in which figure and ground rub against and transform each other. (McLuhan and McLuhan 33)

The auditory and other senses must bow to the supposed superiority and rationality of the visual sense in the post-Gutenberg era. The Vscan™ and other medical imaging technologies support this perspective, but the question remains: how much are we missing by relying on only one sense? By dulling the other senses, we are effectively dumbing down, numbing, and reducing our potential sensory input. As McLuhan asserts, "Primitive and pre-alphabetic people integrate time and space as one and live in an acoustic, horizonless, boundless, olfactory space, rather than in visual space" (McLuhan and Fiore 57). This is not to say that the use of non-visual technologies is inferior; they are merely a different, more complex, and multivalenced way of perceiving the world and of diagnosing medical conditions.

A TETRADIC ANALYSIS OF GE'S VSCAN™

The marketing department of GE Healthcare has already told the public what the Vscan™ does, but what else does this technology do? In the posthumously published volume *The Global Village: Transformations in World Life and Media in the 21st Century,*

McLuhan, with co-author Bruce Powers, constructs an analytical and predictive tool called the "tetrad." Using this model, any technology can be assessed with these four questions:

1. What does any artifact enlarge or enhance?
2. What does it erode or obsolesce?
3. What does it retrieve that had been earlier obsolesced?
4. What does it reverse or flip into when pushed to the limits of its potential (chiasmus)? (9)

In *Laws of Media: The New Science,* another posthumously published volume that discusses tetrads in greater detail, McLuhan asserts that "Our laws of media [tetradic analysis] are intended to provide a ready means of identifying the properties of and actions exerted upon ourselves by our technologies and media and artefacts" (McLuhan and McLuhan 98). As a new technology, the Vscan™ is an appropriate object for tetradic analysis.

What does the Vscan™ enhance? As advertised, it enhances physicians' diagnostic powers by allowing the inspection of patients internally during routine physical exams. It provides an inexpensive and readily available alternative to console scanners for use in doctors' offices or busy hospitals. It also improves access to advanced diagnostic equipment in challenging circumstances. In the future, paramedics might perform scans at the scene of an accident and relay images to a hospital emergency room without having to move a traumatized patient and risk further injury. Care workers in seniors' residences might use the Vscan™ to assess elderly patients without the stress and inconvenience of transferring them to a hospital. The portability, long battery life, and comparatively low cost make the Vscan™ an ideal addition to practices in remote areas or developing nations.

What does the Vscan™ obsolesce? With ultrasound devices readily available to new users, the most obvious victim of obsolescence is the professionally trained sonographer. The Michener Institute, associated with the University of Toronto, offers a twenty-month Ultrasound Graduate Diploma available to registered health-care professionals or students with Bachelor of Science degrees. With courses in scanning techniques and simulations, recognizing normal and abnormal anatomy, writing technical reports, and more, this program helps students to fulfill the National Competency Profiles for both the Canadian Society of Diagnostic Medical Sonographers and the Canadian Association of Registered Diagnostic Ultrasound Professionals, enabling students to write exams for either the Canadian Association of Registered Ultrasound Professionals or the American Registry of Diagnostic Medical Sonographers (Michener Institute). Console scans usually require from fifteen minutes to an hour to perform, so the average two minutes per scan that GE suggests for the Vscan™ on its website will be a much more efficient use of time. Sonographers, along with their cumbersome, expensive console ultrasounds, and long waiting lists, will no longer be required, as every medical professional will have his or her own Vscan™. Given what has already been discussed about the inability of the untrained eye to assess ultrasound images, this seems to be unfortunate.

In time, the Vscan™ might also render doctors, or some elements of their practice, obsolete. According to the website, "Vscan is a prescription medical device and available for sale only to licensed physicians" (GE Vscan). With public access to websites such as eBay™, it seems to be only a matter of time before patients will own personal Vscans™. Accessibility to online health-care resources already supports patient education and self-diagnosis. Given market forces, at some point the potential for opening the market to an aging public with growing health concerns, coupled with increased stress on the medical system, might be too much of an enticement for GE Healthcare to ignore.

Additionally, the Vscan™ erodes the therapeutic alliance between patients and their doctors. By inserting a mediating tool between doctor and patient, the doctor allows his or her attention to focus on the device rather than the patient. The patient's narrative, an essential element of diagnostics, risks being silenced in favour of the image.

What does the Vscan™ retrieve? In spite of the concerns noted above, GE Healthcare advertises that the Vscan™ will actually improve patient-doctor relations, allowing physicians to "connect more deeply with your patients for better care" (GE Vscan). Although it might do so, this therapeutic relationship will be somewhat altered from that of the patient-centred model. The patient, flattened into onscreen data, will return to being the impersonal vessel for disease of the earlier biomedical model. The subjective patient of the patient-centred model will be lost, while the objectified anatomical patient of the biomedical model will re-emerge.

What does the Vscan™ reverse into when pushed to its limits? It becomes a toy, similar to the iPod®, which it resembles. In fact, this has already happened—and at the hands of GE itself. In December 2010, the GE Global Research website launched *Santa's Toy Lab*, hosted by Thomas the Elf. This online game encourages players to match GE technologies with children's toys to score points. One of the devices used in the game is the Vscan™. It gets paired with a children's play doctor kit. A link from the gaming site directs players to further information about the device with an article and video titled *Behind the Toy Technology: Vscan Ultrasound*. The text on this site admits that "In the future you may see it [the Vscan™] in a little child's toy doctors' kit."

Given this analysis, a tetradic diagram for the GE Vscan™ might look like this:

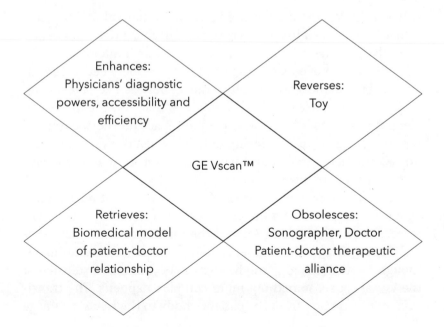

Enhances:
Physicians' diagnostic
powers, accessibility and
efficiency

Reverses:
Toy

GE Vscan™

Retrieves:
Biomedical model
of patient-doctor
relationship

Obsolesces:
Sonographer, Doctor
Patient-doctor therapeutic
alliance

CONCLUSION

In *Understanding Media*, McLuhan noted that "The effect of electric technology had at first been anxiety. Now it appears to create boredom. We have been through the three stages of alarm, resistance, and exhaustion that occur in every disease or stress in life, whether individual or collective" (43). If he perceived boredom in 1964, then by now, even with the perpetual reinvention of new technologies, that boredom has multiplied. In our culture, advanced technologies are normal and expected. A few years later a perhaps hopeful McLuhan asserted that "Electric circuitry is recreating in us the multidimensional space orientation of the 'primitive'" (McLuhan and Fiore 58). But his envisioned future is not what we are experiencing. Rather than reincorporating the audile-tactile senses, new technologies such as the Vscan™ further enhance the visual, ingraining it even more as our predominant sense.

The use of imaging technologies, such as the Vscan™, impacts patient-practitioner communication. An uncritical acceptance of such technologies disregards three key elements of medical communication. First is the subjective element introduced by a physician's sometimes imperfect interpretation of images, especially when the Vscan™ is advertised for use by general practitioners rather than trained image interpreters. Elizabeth Krupinski's meta-analysis of chest, bone, and mammographic radiological studies indicates an average false positive rate of between 2 percent and 15 percent and a false negative rate of between 20 percent and 30 percent (330). Her study also indicates that viewing images on computer monitors has a detrimental impact on the accuracy of reporting (332); consider the implications when the Vscan™'s monitor is only three and a half square inches rather than the twelve inches or more of most computer monitors.

Second is the patient's experience as an object of medical imaging. During real-time imaging, such as ultrasound, genomics researcher Maud Radstake found the images become more tangible to physicians than patients' living bodies (82). Additionally, though medical imaging might seem to be a benign extension of the visual sense, something more complex happens. The transition of information from the patient's body to the rendered image involves a computer-assisted series of algorithmic sequences or what Radstake calls "*black-boxing*" (27). Before becoming percept-ible images, ultrasound data are mathematically reconstructed "according to the capacities of computer-generated space," ren-dering the human body a purely informational, non-subjective, fragmented entity (Waldby 45). The medical gaze is concentrated not on the patient but on a simulacrum of the patient, a flattened, rationalized, less messy version. Sociologist Arthur Frank con-tends that "the image on the screen becomes the 'true' patient, of which the bedridden body is an imperfect replicant, less worthy of attention" (83). Although Radstake agrees that real-time imaging "alienates patients from their bodies" (6), she also suggests that a complex subject-object relationship occurs during real-time im-aging, such as ultrasound; while objectified, patients are simultan-eously aware of their subjectivity because of their communication with the physician or technician, their visual perception of the images, their haptic awareness of the process, their cooperation during imaging, and sometimes even their emotional attachments to the images (92). When image and patient conflate, however, re-search indicates that the objective image tends to trump the pa-tient's subjective experience for the physician and sometimes for the patient (Blaxter 762; Joyce 437–41; Waldby 97).

Third, and perhaps most pressing, is the way in which medical imaging technologies, such as the Vscan™, impact patient-practi-tioner communication. Physicians must respect patients not on-ly as objects on which images are based but also as subjects, as people. Doctors sometimes seem to be unaware that a mediat-ing technology can cause patients to feel objectified and there-fore struggle to assert their subjectivity. In Blaxter's case study, for instance, after a week of preparation, the patient's surgery was cancelled because of medical imaging that revealed what the pa-tient knew to be an old injury, irrelevant to the current diagno-sis. As Blaxter reports, "the world of the image and the world of the real body seemed to P to have existed in two separate spaces" (769). Seeing itself is not curative or diagnostic, and imaging— which can lead to physical modification through medical or sur-gical intervention—is certainly not a neutral activity (van Dijck 6–7; Waldby 27). Many imaging technologies require the body's physical transformation to function; in the case of ultrasound, high-frequency sound waves are introduced into the body, bouncing back from internal masses (Sawchuk 21). As communication specialist Kim Sawchuk notes, "this idea that representation can be without intervention is itself a wish, a fantasy" (21). Rather than struggling to keep up with technological advances, perhaps physicians would better serve their patients by building meaningful therapeutic relationships through improved communication.

Although McLuhan's work, in both media and technology assessment, provides many fruitful avenues for analysis, his hope for a multisensorial future through technology has not been realized. Arguably, his desire for a global village is slowly coming to fruition, though perhaps not smoothly, and more at the hands of profit-making corporations than governments and people. The spread of technologies such as the Vscan™ to remote regions of the globe is multivalenced. Although there are obvious concerns and problems, one hopes that this device will be used in positive ways to provide improved health care to a wider public.

WORKS CITED

APOPO. *Detection Rats Technology.* 2011. www.apopo.org/en/. Web.

Bayer Health Care. *Aspirin History on Bayer® Health Care.* 2009. www.bayer.com/en/history.aspx. Web.

Blaxter, Mildred. "The Case of the Vanishing Patient? Image and Experience." *Sociology of Health and Illness* 31.5 (2009): 762–78. Print.

Frank, Arthur. "Twin Nightmares of the Medical Simulacrum: Jean Baudrillard and David Cronenberg." *Jean Baudrillard: The Disappearance of Art and Politics.* Ed. William Stearns and William Chaloupka. New York: St. Martin's Press, 1992. 82–97. Print.

General Electric Company. Vscan Online Portal. 2010. www2.ge-healthcare.com/portal/site/vscan/aboutvscan/. Web.

GE Global Research, Edison's Desk. *Behind the Toy Technology: Vscan Ultrasound.* 2010. ge.geglobalresearch.com/blog/behind-the-toy-technology-vscan-ultrasound/. Web.

———. *Santa's Toy Lab.* 2010. ge.geglobalresearch.com/toylab/. Web.

GE Healthcare. *New Early Health Commercial—ECG MAC 400: 2008.* www.youtube.com/watch?v=yB47wx-b6sY. Web.

———. *Omar Ishrak, President and CEO Healthcare Systems: GE Healthcare Introduces Vscan.* 2010. www.youtube.com/watch?v=w3g-FpUY87E. Web.

GE Healthcare Vscan™ advertisement. 2010. www.youtube.com/watch?v=Gx4BEUChotM. Web.

GE Healthcare Vscan™ website. 2010. vscanultrasound.gehealthcare.com/pages/physicians. Web.

Gladwell, Malcolm. "Annals of Technology: The Picture Problem: Mammography, Air Power, and the Limits of Looking." *New Yorker* 13 Dec. 2004. www.gladwell.com/pdf/picture.pdf. Web.

Gupta, Rajendra Pratap. "A Common Man's Blog." Wordpress. 23 Mar. 2010. rajendragupta.wordpress.com/2010/03/23/250/. Web.

Joyce, Kelly. "Appealing Images: Magnetic Resonance Imaging and the Production of Authoritative Knowledge." *Social Studies of Science* 35.3 (2005): 437–62. DOI: 10.1177/0306312705050180.

Krupinski, Elizabeth A. "The Importance of Perception Research in Medical Imaging." *Radiation Medicine* 18.6 (2000): 329–34. Print.

Lang, Forrest, Michael Floyd, and Kathleen Beine. "Clues to Patients' Explanations and Concerns about Their Illnesses: A Call for Active Listening" *Archives of Family Medicine* 9 (2000): 222–27. Print.

Layne, Rachel. "GE Plans to Sell Phone-Size Ultrasound Device in 2010." *Bloomberg News* 20 Oct. 2009. www.bloomberg.com/apps/news?pid=newsarchive&sid=aVWwPivfTiMw#. Web.

Little, Paul, et al. "Preferences of Patients for Patient Centred Approach to Consultation in Primary Care: Observational Study." *British Medical Journal* 322 (2001): 468–74. Print.

McCulloch, Michael, et al. "Diagnostic Accuracy of Canine Scent Detection in Early- and Late-Stage Lung and Breast Cancers." *Integrative Cancer Therapies* 5.1 (2006): 30–39. Print.

McLuhan, Marshall. "Acoustic Space." *Media Research: Technology, Art, Communication.* Ed. Michael A. Moos. Amsterdam: G+B Arts International, 1997. 39–44. Print.

———. *The Gutenberg Galaxy: The Making of Typographic Man.* Toronto: U of Toronto P, 1962. Print.

———. *The Mechanical Bride: Folklore of Industrial Man.* New York: Vanguard, 1951. Print.

———. *Understanding Media: The Extensions of Man.* New York: McGraw-Hill, 1964. Print.

McLuhan, Marshall, and Quentin Fiore. *The Medium Is the Massage: An Inventory of Effects.* New York: Random House, 1967. Print.

McLuhan, Marshall, and Eric McLuhan. *Laws of Media: The New Science.* Toronto: U of Toronto P, 1988. Print.

McLuhan, Marshall, and Bruce R. Powers. *The Global Village: Transformations in World Life and Media in the 21st Century.* New York: Oxford UP, 1989. Print.

Michener Institute. N.d. www.michener.ca/ce/postdiploma/ultrasound.php?sub2=1. Web.

Poling, Alan, et al.. "Using Giant African Pouched Rats to Detect Tuberculosis in Human Sputum Samples: 2009 Findings." *American Society of Tropical Medicine and Hygiene* 83.6 (2009): 1308–10. Print.

Radstake, Maud. *Visions of Illness: An Endography of Real-Time Medical Imaging.* Delft, Netherlands: Eburon, 2007. Print.

Sawchuk, Kim. "Biotourism, *Fantastic Voyage,* and Sublime Inner Space." *Wild Science: Reading Feminism, Medicine, and the Media.* Ed. Janine Marchessault and Kim Sawchuk. London: Routledge, 2000. 9–23. Print.

Stewart, Moira A. "Effective Physician-Patient Communication and Health Outcomes: A Review." *Canadian Medical Association Journal* 152.9 (1995): 1423–33. Print.

van Dijck, José. *The Transparent Body: A Cultural Analysis of Medical Imaging.* Seattle: U of Washington P, 2005. Print.

Waldby, Catherine. *The Visible Human Project: Informatic Bodies and Posthuman Medicine.* New York: Routledge, 2000. Print.

POLITICS / SEX / RELIGION

CHAPTER 10

McLUHAN'S POLITICS

Allen Mills

Thee was a buzz of excitement about Marshall McLuhan and his ideas in Toronto in the late 1960s. I was a young immigrant to the city, just off the jet plane from that oral, tribal culture of Ireland. There the Catholic Church had regularly banned books, and this was one of the ways, presumably, in which Irish culture had remained immured in a preliterate, pre-typographical age. This was in spite of the great literary tradition of Jonathan Swift, Edmund Burke, William Butler Yeats, and George Bernard Shaw, but then they were all Protestants and rooted in Renaissance individualism, which perhaps proves McLuhan's point. McLuhan preferred James Joyce and his kaleidoscopic, surround vision. But he was a Catholic, which perhaps proves my eventual point.

I was filled with anticipation of what was for me the "brave new world" of literate, print-obsessed, fragmented, mechanical Canada—was it only English Canada in fact and not French Canada?—in the full apotheosis of its centennial year. Along with others of my generation, I had placed infinite hope in purposeful human action to overcome the inadequacies of traditional society. Something was up. History was running our way—and away with us—and technology might actually be recruited to our cause. Mc-Luhan we hardly understood, but, even though he looked like our parents with his fedora, suit and tie, and grammatically correct prose albeit larded with slang and the argot of the street and ghetto, he was cool and subversive, perhaps because of that alternative patois, and, though a Catholic, he was critical of many received ideas. There were those inner trips of the senses that he talked about—LSD was a lazy person's way of having the same experience as reading James Joyce's *Finnegans Wake,* he said (see www.youtube.com.watch?v=OMEC_HqW1BY). Of course, we were all lazy people. And then there was the intoxicating possibility that electronic technology might unite us all in a new, "global village." To boot, it was all happening in Toronto, *our* village and now the emerging centre of a universal consciousness. It was indeed the Age of Aquarius.

Politically, the times were exciting too. Pierre Elliott Trudeau had come upon us with the suddenness and brilliance of a shooting star. He was uncommonly different: French, articulate, unorthodox, mysterious in every way. Was he a communist? Unmarried at age forty-nine, was he gay? Conservatives, *sotto voce,* said that he was both, though they would have called him homosexual rather than gay and would have slurred the word *komyooneest.* Was he the Pied Piper leading callow youth astray and for his own partisan purposes at that? Women swooned and strewed flowers in his path. McLuhan and Trudeau—Catholics both—were attracted to each other from the outset. Trudeau intuitively grasped the implications of television, and he provided McLuhan with many examples of what McLuhan thought was charisma. Trudeau had a tribal persona, he said; he spoke to the re-emergence of an all-involving primitivism; he had an "Oriental" look to his face; somehow he was a universal person in an emerging global age; he looked like a lot of other people; he had Third World appeal; hippies liked him too. On another occasion, McLuhan saw something else in Trudeau: he wore "the perfect mask—a charismatic mask . . . the face of a North American Indian" (Zoomer 3). He was "the man in the mask," the Lone Ranger. There were yet more costumes that Trudeau wore:

> [Trudeau] is an actor, both emperor and clown. The clown is really the emperor's PR man, who keeps him in touch with the world that the emperor cannot reach. The clown interprets the emperor to his court or the public and indicates their mood. He tests the emperor's mood by teasing him, and in turn interpreting the whims of the crowd to the emperor. I've never heard of a politician who could fill both roles. Trudeau is unique. . . . Trudeau is aware of more than himself; he's not just trying to project an image. He is interpreting a whole process that he's involved in. So that when he slides down a banister or hops off a camel, it's not really a way of expressing what it feels like to be Trudeau; it's trying to express what sort of a hell of a hang-up he's in. He'll do anything to snap the tension. (Newman n. pag.)

Trudeau, then, knew how to wear an identity and put us on. We were happy to be among his army of Tontos, in a small way suddenly retribalized by the otherwise unthinkable act of voting for the Liberal Party.

McLuhan did not think of himself as being political. He was fond of the distinction between point of view, a characteristic of people in literate societies with their linear, causal logic and phonetic alphabets, and the perspective of those who, like himself, engaged in supposedly value-free "probes" of the new electric age of simultaneity, all-surroundedness, and intense involvement. Although McLuhan was intrigued by Trudeau, it is hard to classify him as a liberal, a social democrat, or indeed anything political. He said that he did not have a point of view. Douglas Coupland says that McLuhan had no practical, political, or religious position. He advanced no moral judgments: "Not only was Marshall politically neutral in public, but his work was intrinsically apolitical, in a short term sense" (186–87). He goes on to say that McLuhan was *political* only if the word is defined as presupposing the transformative, long-term changes in cognition that might take "decades . . . or hundreds or thousands of years to complete" (187).

This sense of politics as taking place within a world historical, stadal, and transformative process is consistent with one of McLuhan's earliest essays linking media and politics, "New Media as Political Forms," published in 1955. The central premise of the piece has to do with the radical effects of print technology on human consciousness leading to the triumph of mechanization and serial thinking. The onset of print was devastating to preliterate, manuscript, oral, and colloquial societies. But the new technologies of film and television in turn would be equally revolutionary, leading to the return of an all-surrounding, multiple, and instantaneous environment, already anticipated, as we know, by Joyce in *Finnegans Wake.* Joyce, says McLuhan, captured the "octophone" principle and the imagery of the new consciousness. Hazarding a political judgment of sorts, McLuhan observes that preliterate cultures such as India and China, "almost entirely oral and pictographic" in their consciousness, would have an advantage in the new age of film and television (see www.youtube.com. watch?v=OMEC_HqW1BY). McLuhan seems to have been saying that traditional societies could leap across the horrors of the individualistic print age and embrace the new electric order with greater abandon and immediacy. The West would die but be replaced by an East—how Orientalist this thinking is—that would reproduce a facsimile of pre-Renaissance Christian culture.

If we see politics, then, as existing within established normative and evaluative frameworks that have little to do with party partisanship or overt political engagement, then perhaps we can see McLuhan as political. This is the sense of politics that can loosely be called Gramscian, in which ideas and values are hegemonic and therefore "political" because they maintain or sanction a dominant system of power in which, most devilish of all, the dominated are somehow complicit in their subordination. But even within this perspective, there are several possible criticisms of McLuhan's political message. The principal delinquency in the view of left-wing critics was that McLuhan undercut the central claim of much of socialism about the priority of the economic and the ethical. Now and then he took potshots at Karl Marx, though Marx's account of class was an account of the role of technology as much as it was a theory of exploited labour. Recall his comment in *The Poverty of Philosophy* (1847) about how "The windmill gives you society with the feudal lord; the steam-mill, society with the industrial capitalist" (119), and so on. Actually, McLuhan did know this (*Understanding Media* 38).

He expatiated little on capitalism as such because his focus was on media. Consequently, he did not dwell on issues of distributive justice within different types of economies and societies. His tendency was to project a kind of universal uniformity of social life specific to particular, dominant technologies or media. Humanity was divided not so much between rich and poor as it was between the tribal and the individualistic, for example. However, McLuhan did talk a lot about the serious consequences of societies with very different types of consciousness interacting with each other in the new electronic age. Coupland concedes that McLuhan was "political" in regard to how painful transformative changes might be in the long run: "Marshall *did* foresee a long, painful process in which technology shifts would trigger massive identity collapses around the world, which would generate new and terrifying sources of disassociation between the reality of what was physically available to individuals and the unreality of a world depicted by electronic media. The result would be conflict, violence and war" (188–89). He also emphasizes that deep down McLuhan "liked" none of the technological changes that had come about since the Renaissance, which was when he believed that industrial, mechanical, individualistic, and fragmented print-based civilization had begun to take hold (146–48).

This fits with what Jonathan Miller says about another implicit political message in McLuhan's works that has to do with his partiality for a medieval, religious, rural, tribal synthesis that would repair the rupture brought about by scientific materialism and industrialism (5). Miller claims that his agrarian background gave McLuhan "a sense of the robust organic simplicities of village life" (20) and that he was moved by Catholic piety and the hope and expectation of "a new form of iconic symbolism through which the redemptive mysteries of God can be explained" (32). This was the role that electronic media would play.

Mention of McLuhan's religion and apparently rural roots raises the question of his personal history and how to make sense of the political impacts of the two most salient features of his background: his early years growing up on the prairies, particularly in Winnipeg, and his conversion to Catholicism at Cambridge University after his graduation from the University of Manitoba in 1934. McLuhan spoke of the influence of western Canadian perspectives:

> I think of the western skies as one of the most beautiful things about the West, and the western horizons. The Westerner does not have a point of view. He has a vast panorama; he has such tremendous space around him. . . . [H]e has at all times a total field of vision, and since he can take this total field at any time, he does not have to worry about goals. He can take his time about "making it." (McLuhan and Easterbrook 23–24)

There is more than a hint here of his approval of an organic, totalizing community. But he attaches himself to prairie vistas only by removing himself from the city, in this case Winnipeg, with its fragmentary, mechanical, industrial way of life, no doubt.

This privileging of organic unity affected McLuhan's expectations of the coming age of the electric world of contemporary media and the global village. His conversion to Catholicism, after a conventional Protestant religious upbringing, was no small matter at the time. Most conversions at Oxford and Cambridge in the late 1930s admittedly were radical rejections of a conventional, tepid Protestantism in favour of the Communist Party and perhaps even the Soviet KGB. To be sure, there were other converts to Catholicism at the time, notably Graham Greene and Evelyn Waugh, but they were still a small minority. In general, English society continued in its merry anti-Catholic ways. Such a startling decision by McLuhan, to leap into medieval religion, perhaps gives us a clue about how to understand his celebration of the electric age. Was it not in some way part of his imagining of how the mystical unity of the church and the body of Christ would be reborn in a coming age?

One other general point about "hidden" political messages in McLuhan's works is worth mentioning. There was his sympathetic identification with those who somehow did not fit into the age of print and mechanical technology, outsiders, misfits, liminal people. In the context of the 1960s, McLuhan had positive things to say about alienated youth, the "rebel without a cause," the dropout, the dope head, and, in his archaic language, the "Negro." Those in a minority or those who rebelled against the dominant worldview McLuhan celebrated as pioneers of new sensibilities. This might be thought of as a radical feature of his political thought. But if we follow the logic of his argument, such people in their ways were sort of fellow celebrants and Catholics *manqué*.

Nevertheless, McLuhan could hardly have been totally uninterested in politics, especially in the 1960s, that most political of decades, and he did comment frequently about the political juxtaposition of the medium and the message in the new television age. Nixon was too hot for television, and Trudeau was perfectly cool. McLuhan undertook an ongoing correspondence with Trudeau, who thought that McLuhan was a kind of guru or seer whose insights he might use to political advantage. Trudeau was profoundly curious about new ideas, but it did not follow that he understood McLuhan well. "Taking" to television came unconsciously to Trudeau, and of course there was a good deal of luck involved.

Trudeau had appeared on television from its beginning in Quebec in the early 1950s, and by the late 1960s he was well practised in its demands. In the 1968 federal election, when Trudeau was adored, his principal opponent was Robert Stanfield, the Progressive Conservative leader, who was not especially convincing on television and came across like some tongue-tied undertaker. Stanfield did not know that some things never work on television for a politician, one being that one should never be seen in public eating a banana. Another party leader at the time, Tommy Douglas of the New Democratic Party, also failed to communicate well but for other reasons. Douglas was, if anything, *too* alive; he was an over-earnest, hot fundamentalist preacher, too hot for a cool medium. Finally, there was Réal Caouette, the Créditiste leader, the frenetic—not to say frantic—car salesman from Témiscamingue, Quebec. He was so hot that he burned the television screen.

In Trudeau's personal papers is a copy of a "suggestion for research" that McLuhan sent to the Royal Commission on Bilingualism and Biculturalism in September 1963, a copy of which he
had presumably sent to Trudeau (McLuhan, "Effects"). Here at
least is one confirmed instance of McLuhan's interest in political
issues in his own time and society. McLuhan begins by making
some fundamental distinctions between states that were organized on the basis of maritime connections and space and those
that were land based. Maritime regimes, he said, tended to be decentralist, whereas land-based ones were centralizing. In the first
period of European settlement in Canada, in the seventeenth and
eighteenth centuries, politics was decentralist and multicentred.
But with the coming of the railway, Canada became more integrated: "A horizontal unity of [a] spatial kind was made possible
by the railway. Rail centres siphoned off products and populations
from the margins of the country. Areas like the maritimes that
had been centres now became margins" (2). Indeed, "[Confedera-
tion in 1867] was an event unthinkable apart from a railway system" (3). McLuhan invites the obvious conclusion that railways
in Canada produced a centralist polity and constitution, thereby
pulling together the two different cultures in Canada. In his view,
any friction between the two linguistic communities integrated by new railway technologies was not yet of any great political
consequence because change in the railway age proceeded slowly.
Only with the onset of electric technology did national unity become problematic. The telephone, airplane, radio, and television
brought the two cultures together more quickly and intensively
and led to political resistance by the subordinate society:

> The French-Canadian culture retains many features of
> oral structure that have marked it off from English-Can-
> ada from the first. The English settlers have been from a
> country that was more book-oriented than the French. No
> value judgments are implied here. An oral society stresses
> family structure and procedures in its economic and pol-
> itical life to a degree unfamiliar to the more individual-
> ist patterns of book cultures. The close cohesion of oral
> societies makes them resistant to the fragmenting and

specialist needs of industrialization and mechanization. But, paradoxically, the immensely cohesive force of electric technology (that is, of telephone and radio and TV) is very congenial to oral societies. French Canada has fended off mechanization with surly distaste, only to embrace technology in the electric age with enthusiasm. English Canada, book-oriented and industrialized, has, on the other hand, encountered the intrusion of electric forms with much bewilderment. Electric technology is an abrupt and all too pervasive a force to be congenial to a community based on the individualistic power of the book. Electric power engenders a tightness of social cohesion and involvement that amplifies all the forms of oral society, just as it corrodes the bonds of highly literate and industrialized communities. That is one face of separatism. (3)

McLuhan goes on to say that the Fathers of Confederation dealt with the bicultural reality of Canada through a policy of legal and political equality. This was an encouraging initiative, but the ongoing effects of radio, plane, and car, and the onset of an all-encompassing electric technology, intensified change, accentuated decentralist trends, and advanced the "advantages" of oral societies in an electric age. In the process, traditional politics became moribund, left high and dry as the tide of mechanical, industrial civilization receded, never to return, it seems. Electronic culture promoted involvement "in depth," "the interplay of several factors at once" (5). As McLuhan presciently puts it,

The actuality of very great participation in depth in the process of world affairs co-exists with archaic political arrangements built on the basis of slow communications and various [types of] participation by means of delegates and representatives. Today, the electorate participates in top decision-making sooner than its delegates can reach the political centre. In Washington it is called "government by news-leak." Actually it is government by direct involvement. It appears to threaten our party-system directly. (5)

McLuhan's proposals postulated the totality and homogeneity of an original, French Canadian, preliterate, preprint, pre-individualistic, and oral culture originating, presumably, in seventeenth-century Normandy, whence most immigrants to New France had come. French Canada resisted the specialization of industrialization and mechanization only to "make up" for its cultural lag and disadvantages under industrial conditions through its ability to enter the electric age feeling more at home with the new dominant media. French Canada, in other words, was rather like India and China.

It is not known what the estimable members of the commission thought of McLuhan's theorizing. For me, it is an example of that thrilling yet frustrating mixture of heuristic brilliance and empirical uncertainty that hovers over much of his prognostications. His proposals went far beyond the conventional idea that language, religion, and economics were at the bottom of what divided Canadians. According to McLuhan, there were technologically based identity reasons why the English and French could not get along. He was also incredibly prescient in anticipating the dissonance that develops when new media somehow confront established institutions, in this case those of Parliament and Congress. This insight anticipated by fifty years the effects on institutional politics of the televising of Parliament and the onset of the Internet, blogging, tweeting, and satellite television. Many political bodies now seem nakedly irrelevant as information swirls around them in such instantaneous and intense ways.

However, as with many of his stupendous insights, there is an uneasy sense that some of the building blocks of McLuhan's argument remain unexplained and unexplored. His thought was overly theoretical and overarching, perhaps untestable and unprovable. In this particular case, McLuhan recycled conventional English Canadian preconceptions of French Canadians, for example that they were a homogeneous culture inclined to tradition and resistant to industrialism and mechanical technology. In fact, Quebec and French Canada industrialized at precisely the same pace and time as English Canada, mainly Ontario. And, if it was the case—and it seems to be disputable—that print was alien to French Canada, was it because it was an oral culture, or was it because of other things: the role of the Catholic Church, perhaps, or the small size of its publishing market, and so on? It is well known that New France had no printing press at the moment of its conquest by the English in 1760. But it developed a distinguished tradition of literacy and literature by the mid-nineteenth century, so that by, say, 1960 Quebec had become as much a culture of the book as English Canada. Indeed, perhaps because of general French resistance to the digitalization of library holdings in the face of the urge to dominate of the anglophone digitalization projects of Google and Amazon, retention of the traditional book will perhaps be a greater priority in French Canada than in the rest of the country. And, anyway, where does the electronic book fit into McLuhan's scheme of things? Is it a continuation of Renaissance/Gutenberg individualism, or is it part of the all-surroundedness and immediacy of the electronic age? Is French Canada more cohesive because it is an oral culture or because it is a minority in a huge anglophone sea? Is English Canada more bewildered by the electronic age than Quebec? How would one even go about proving it? Differing suicide rates between the two groups? Divergent levels of mental illness? Differing birth rates and intensities of family and marriage breakdown?

Sometimes McLuhan also seemed to contradict himself. In some places, he claimed that nationalism was a construction of the print age and that electronic culture was more cohesive and underwrote a globalized order. Yet he also said that the electronic universe will be more fractious and conflict ridden: "When people get close to each other, they get more and more savage, impatient with each other. . . . [T]he global village is a place of very arduous interfaces and abrasive situations" (quoted in Coupland 186). So nationalism will not necessarily be overcome by the global village. Life on the electronic planet will be rancorous and perhaps genocidal. It is hard to see how this is much different from traditional nineteenth-century nationalism. There is perhaps too much speculative overreaching and overgeneralizing in McLuhan. It is hard to resist Miller's conclusion about his "[p]rocrustean tendency": "McLuhan conceives human development on such a grand scale that its component social details are often foreshortened to the point where they become indistinguishable. The unique elements that comprise the living character of communities are either ignored altogether or, where they seem to fit, subordinated to such enormous generalizations that they cease to be usefully recognizable" (43).

Both McLuhan and Trudeau were Catholics, the latter educated by Jesuits and the former probably wishing that he had been. McLuhan's Catholicism might be thought to hanker after the lost totality of the pre-Reformation Catholic Church. Trudeau embraced the more contemporary theological idiom of the existentialist personalism of Emmanuel Mounier and Pope John XXIII's Vatican Council of 1962. In Quebec, many Catholic critics thought that Trudeau was a Protestant. He read McLuhan's brief and made marks on the text, but unfortunately he made no remarks. But we do know about his response to separatism and the national unity crisis of the 1960s and 1970s in Canada. Trudeau believed that the independence of Quebec would be a tragedy and a defiance and betrayal of the pluralism that existed in Quebec itself. It was, for him, a general truth about territorially based societies that their populations were always drawn from many backgrounds and always socially intertwined and territorially overlapping so that the role and function of even a democratic state could not be based simply on a majoritarian principle but must instead take account of these multiple diversities under a common good. For Trudeau, the public-spirited state must be sensitive to minority and individual rights. What he proposed specifically was an advance beyond Confederation's dualistic bargain through the provision of greater bilingual rights to French and English minorities and a Charter of Rights and Freedoms for all persons. These rights, he emphasized, were to be enjoyed by individuals and not by collectivities such as provinces or peoples or nations, though some parts of the Charter spoke to collective rights of sorts for women, Aboriginals, multicultural Canadians, and, understood a certain way, French Canadians. In general, Trudeau's policies drew criticism for being overly dependent on the rights model of society and insufficiently sensitive to the claims of community and social rights in general. Such prescriptions seem to be alien to McLuhan's usual discourse. To McLuhan, the views of Trudeau would place him in the tradition of individualist liberalism with its dependence on print technology.

The oddity of the relationship between Trudeau and McLuhan was that the latter mainly assessed the former on the basis of his various political disguises, which became the foundation of some conclusions that he made about media. Trudeau was amenable to such comments and found them helpful in winning elections and holding on to power. But he was also a traditional politician who held to certain principles and had a point of view. By conviction, he was a social democrat who wanted a welfare state and the fulfillment of all individuals within a pluralistic, federal Canada. Implicitly, McLuhan held that these were notions derived from a print age and would become irrelevant as print was superseded.

Trudeau too was futurist enough to think about what the twenty-first century might look like. It was not the future of an electric age, though Trudeau was always open to understanding the role of technology in social change but not quite in McLuhan's way. His own sense of modernity emphasized the importance of federalism as a political arrangement that would take account of the twin forces of intensifying decentralization on the one hand and the expanding necessity of political integration on the other to deal with intersocietal matters in an increasingly globalized age. Electric technology was part of this globalization, but so were other forces and factors, none of which made redundant a belief in liberal democracy. As for McLuhan, he did not provide any explicit policy prescriptions in his paper. What he offered was a totalizing view of Quebec that so emphasized the singular character of the province that the two European peoples who made up modern Canada could hardly be imagined as co-habiting even a federal state for much longer. Separation was inevitable is what McLuhan seems to have been saying. The differences between English and French Canada were so polarized that it was inconceivable that French Canada would wish to have anything to do with liberal individualist modernity.

A consequence of McLuhan's thinking is that, in the impending electronic age, society will be so overwhelmingly communitarian and organic that social unity will be pre-eminent and the individual will fall away as a vestige of a dying age and its fading technology. This conclusion has parallels with the reasoning of Marxists in the early decades of the twentieth century in their imagining of a future communism devoid of the historically irrelevant impediments of bourgeois rights. What was justified in the Marxist view by the logic of history and the class struggle was justified by McLuhan in terms of the predominance of certain technological forms. What was explained by the Marxist as the reason of history was explained by McLuhan as somehow to do with the ways and reason of God. God was electricity, so to speak. In the end, we will return to where we began, before the Renaissance and the invention of print and the individual, and become again an organic people of God, his universal tribe. As with Marx, so with McLuhan: it will all work out in the end. We will return to the beginning and know the place for the first time.

WORKS CITED

Coupland, Douglas. *Marshall McLuhan*. Toronto: Penguin, 2009. Print.

Marx, Karl. *The Poverty of Philosophy*. 1847. Chicago: Kerr, 1913. Print.

McLuhan, Marshall. "The Effects of the Influence of Centralism and Decentralism in Canadian Society: Suggestions for Research by the Royal Commission on Bilingualism and Biculturalism." 30 Sept. 1963. Trudeau Papers, MG 26, series 02, volume 28. Print.

———. "New Media as Political Forms." 1955. *Marshall McLuhan Unbound 7*. Berkeley: Gingko, 2005. N. pag. Print.

———. *Understanding Media: The Extensions of Man*. New York: New American Library, 1964. Print.

McLuhan, Marshall, and Tom Easterbrook. "Marshall McLuhan and Tom Easterbrook." *Speaking of Winnipeg*. Ed. John Parr. Winnipeg: Queenston House, 1974. Print.

Miller, Jonathan. *Marshall McLuhan*. New York: Viking, 1971. Print.

Newman, Peter C. "The Lost Marshall McLuhan Tapes." *Maclean's* 16 July 2013. www.macleans.ca/society/life/the-lost-mcluhan-tapes-21. Web.

Zoomer. *Pierre Trudeau, Statesman: October 18, 1919–September 28, 2000*. everythingzoomer.com. Web.

CHAPTER 11

McLUHAN'S *PLAYBOY*—
PLAYBOY'S McLUHAN

David Linton

The centennial anniversary in 2011 of Marshall McLuhan's birth offered a propitious opportunity to reassess both his achievements as an individual and the cultural context in which McLuhan lived. I have chosen another *Übermensch* of the same era whose life and ideas also shaped the zeitgeist and whose presence provides an illuminating lens through which to view McLuhan: Hugh Hefner, one of the titans of twentieth-century publishing, a man whose grasp of the shifting media landscape demonstrates in pragmatic terms the concepts on which McLuhan built his theories.

Hefner and McLuhan were both reacting to a set of social conditions that led to stultifying regimentation and conformity, particularly in the area of gender identity and sexual mores. Both men came from traditional Methodist backgrounds and families with strong, even domineering, mothers, and both reacted against their backgrounds. McLuhan became a devout convert to Roman Catholicism and religiously orthodox; Hefner, on the other hand, challenged his religious upbringing by becoming notably unorthodox in his beliefs and practices.

Although McLuhan was more than a decade older than Hefner, their careers ran along parallel tracks. The works that brought both men to the attention of a wide audience were published within two years of each other: *The Mechanical Bride: Folklore of Industrial Man* in 1951 and the first issue of *Playboy* in 1953. The publications quickly established each man as a significant commentator on popular culture.

There is little in McLuhan's later work to suggest an interest in matters of sexuality and gender, but a look at his earliest forays into popular culture reveals a deep concern with the "proper" social roles of men and women. Those concerns are also reflected in his private correspondence, and, while they are similar to the feelings that also motivated Hefner, as we shall see, each man found different ways to work out these sexual anxieties. Both men were troubled by what they saw as the emasculation of the American male, and McLuhan was particularly disdainful in his views. He wrote about the sexual status of other men in the same way that he wrote about their media involvements, offering sweeping generalizations about their pathetic condition and their oblivion to their own lowly status. His posture was to suggest that somehow he himself had overcome the plight of the sexual and media victims whom he was writing about so that he hovered aloof and superior above the fray. In both his sexual and his media observations, there was always a strong taint of superiority.

This quality is evident in letters that McLuhan wrote to his mother, his brother, and the woman whom he was courting and soon to marry, Corinne Lewis. In 1939, shortly after a visit that McLuhan made to Fort Worth, Texas, to meet her family, he wrote to her and claimed that "the American male has an essential contempt for, as well as a fear of, women" (*Letters* 103). We can assume that he excluded himself from this generalization. A year later he wrote to his brother that "Texas men are incredibly infantile, and, of course, as tough outside as they are slushy inside" (124). A few months later he wrote to his mother to boast that he had finished an article titled "Fifty Million Mama's Boys," which described the doleful plight of other members of his gender. This essay has not survived, but its viewpoint found full expression a few years later in a published piece called "Dagwood's America" and again in *The Mechanical Bride*, which, according to Janine Marchessault, was originally "to have been [titled] Sixty Million Mama's Boys" (55). Apparently, in the ten years between the letter and the book, there was an increase of 10 million Mama's Boys.

Douglas Coupland has commented insightfully on the ironies in McLuhan's attacks on men for being dominated by their mothers and wives given how deeply in thrall McLuhan and his father were to his own mother. The special nature of McLuhan's relationship with his mother and how different it was from his relationship with his father are made dramatically clear by the collection of letters by McLuhan published in 1987. There are over forty long and intimate missives to Elise McLuhan and only one to Herbert McLuhan, and that a brief nine sentences written en route home from his wedding, which his father had not attended. But clearly McLuhan was determined not to emulate his father's fate, as his letters reveal. When he wrote to his mother about completing the essay about cry baby American men, a revealing detail was included: "A few moments ago I finished the 'Mama-Boy' article, which Corinne is typing" (quoted in Gordon 95). Note that revealing phrase: "which Corinne is typing." His wife was not about to go gallivanting across the country giving dramatic readings, stage performances, and elocution demonstrations, as his mother had, repeatedly abandoning her husband and family to do so. In fact, his own peripatetic career came to closely reflect that of his mother with frequent absences. McLuhan recapitulated on the lecture circuit the example that his mother had set as a peripatetic actress and travelling orator.

One of the clearest demonstrations of his notion of the ideal relationship with a woman is found in a long letter that McLuhan wrote to Corinne shortly after his courtship trip to Texas. In a condescending and pedantic letter of nearly 3,000 words, he lectures Corinne about the superiority of orthodox Roman Catholicism over her benighted Methodist faith: "One doesn't take the Protestant error very seriously after one has looked into a dozen or so similar heresies" (*Letters* 100). He goes on to patronize Martin Luther, calling him a heretic and liar, and he explains his own conversion to Catholicism as a result of his superior intellectual training: "Most converts tend to be intellectuals, people with special knowledge of history and philosophy" (100). He also puts in a cautious hedge about his own employment potential lest he not become the success that his mother has led him to expect: "I simply can't bring myself to curry favor among men who I consider inferior in ability" (103). It is also in this letter that McLuhan lays down the terms and conditions of his marriage proposal. They read like a spiritual prenuptial agreement: "You should know that, in the event of a 'mixed marriage,' the non-Catholic is obliged to receive a certain minimum of instruction about the Church, and to agree that the children, if any, shall be reared as Catholics" (102).

McLuhan's earliest published pronouncements about gender politics appeared seven years prior to *The Mechanical Bride*, in a 1944 article entitled "Dagwood's America" in *Columbia*, the magazine of the Knights of Columbus, a fraternal organization of Roman Catholic men. "Dagwood's America," on the surface, is an analysis of the popular cartoon strip about Dagwood Bumstead and his wife, Blondie. It is also a sweeping indictment of how "America has swung very far toward the feminine pole of the axis in recent years" (2). McLuhan claims that Dagwood's hair style, with its swept-up strands on either side of his head, represents the horns of a cuckold, the ultimate sign of a man's betrayal by a perfidious wife, though he does not blame Blondie for Dagwood's disgrace but his own failure to assert his rightful claim to control. The fact that Dagwood comes from a respectable family but has lost his wealth and respect by marrying a flapper showgirl is suggestive of McLuhan's unexpressed views of the marriage of his own mother and father.

Probably the best way to get a sense of how wrought up McLuhan was (and how insecure he might have been about his own masculinity) is to read a few representative passages from the essay.

> In ordinary society it is man who imposes his demands and standards on the conduct of the household. In traditional human relationships man imposes rational authority and order and purpose, receiving in return emotional support and security from his wife.... [Dagwood's] craving

for maternal affection is doomed, however. Blondie is efficiently masculine, purposive, egotistical and hard, just as Dagwood is ineffectually feminine, altruistic and sensitive. . . . Dagwood is absurd and pathetic, not in himself but because he reflects a widespread state of affairs in America today. Blondie and her children own America, control American business and entertainment, run hog wild in spreading maternalism into education and politics. (2)

Later in the essay, McLuhan continues exploring the theme of threats posed by gender difference:

[S]ince girls are more docile and industrious than boys, they easily outdo them in the classroom. This naturally encourages boys to abandon studies as effeminate. . . . American men seem to have been only too eager to throw the sponge of intellectual discipline to Mrs. Everyman. In so doing, they created a brand new human absurdity which exists today in a form so huge that it can no longer be taken in at a glance—the absurdity of boys being educated by women and in the same classroom as girls! (22)

Years later, in the 1969 *Playboy* interview, McLuhan claimed to have moved away from the moralizing, judgmental posture on display in early works such as this essay. By then, he contended, "I ceased being a moralist and became a student" (265). It might be worth noting that the single-sex school question continues to have occasional resonance as some educators, both conservative and liberal, ask whether the pressure to perform and uphold gender roles in the presence of "the other sex" sometimes impedes intellectual development and learning. In McLuhan's case, the question might embody both his gender rigidity and a humanistic impulse.

Hefner took a nearly opposite path. As McLuhan responded to the religious, sexual, social, and media upheaval of his times by becoming ardently orthodox and at times reactionary, Hefner became ardently heterodox, at least in social and sexual terms; in the economic realm, Hefner has always been a free-market capitalist. In fact, his approach to sex as expressed via the glossy display of women's bodies can be said to *embody* McLuhan's critique in *The Mechanical Bride,* as Marchessault suggests: "It is women's experiences that have disappeared in what McLuhan identifies as a drive to push the boundaries of physical experience beyond the body. . . . In post-war America, these bodies are advertised through 'glamour cake' postures and highly charged displays of affect and melodrama" (57).

In December 1962, the ninth anniversary of the first issue of the magazine and the same year that McLuhan published *The Gutenberg Galaxy: The Making of Typographic Man,* Hefner introduced a feature that was to continue for another four years and twenty-five installments, "The Playboy Philosophy." Although uninformed commentators might think that the philosophy was all about sex, in fact it was a wide-ranging exegesis of a huge variety of topics, including many that McLuhan covers in *The Mechanical Bride* and *The Gutenberg Galaxy.* Especially noteworthy are Hefner's discussion of film and other media, as well as religion, a topic that McLuhan assiduously avoided commenting publicly on, perhaps because his views tended to be so conservative that he feared his reputation would suffer. This might also explain his avoidance of remarks on the Vietnam War or even World War II, into which he had managed to avoid conscription.

Contrary to what one might expect from the publisher of what many called "a girlie magazine," the philosophy is quite erudite, well written, and cogently argued, steeped in solid scholarship and historical contexts. It regularly cites the views and arguments of critics of *Playboy* and refutes them artfully.

In the early instalments of "The Playboy Philosophy," Hefner is motivated in part by the same gender worries that show up in McLuhan's letters, in "Dagwood's America," and in some of the riffs in *The Mechanical Bride.* Time and again Hefner tells his readers that he is going to take up this crucial issue but then keeps putting it off. The January 1963 second instalment mistakenly states that the "third and final part of The Playboy Philosophy . . . discusses the Womanization of America and our drift towards an Asexual Society" ("Philosophy 2" 52). Part 3 does not get there, however, but we are promised that in Part 4 Hefner will address "the dangers he foresees in this drift towards an Asexual Society"

("Philosophy 3" 48). Yet Part 4 skips the topic, and Part 5 promises that future issues will include "a vivisection of Momism and the . . . effect Womanization has had on our manners and morals" ("Philosophy 5" 63).

Here Hefner does take a swipe at "the Vogue Woman," whom he finds "unfeminine, antisexual and competitive" ("Philosophy 5" 63), and then he moves on to what became his favourite topic and stalking horse, the anti-sexual, repressive nature of organized religion. After that, aside from one more fleeting mention of "our drift toward an asexual society" ("Philosophy 9" 71), he abandons the subject completely, and all instalments of "The Playboy Philosophy" stop abruptly after number twenty-five.

Along the way, however, it turns out that Hefner's interests sometimes echo McLuhan's, as in his observation in 1963 that "Science and technology have shrunk the earth to the size of a community" ("Philosophy 10" 68). McLuhan's global village was Hefner's community. Also like McLuhan, Hefner was cognizant of how twentieth-century media developments countered those that came to full flower in the sixteenth century. But, rather than bemoan the changes, as McLuhan did, Hefner celebrated them, claiming that "a more sophisticated time requires a more sophisticated faith" ("Philosophy 10" 68).

Yet, if Hefner's references to sixteenth-century media practices were made in passing, there is no questioning McLuhan's thoroughgoing understanding of that century, particularly as expressed by the sixteenth-century rhetorician, satirist, playwright, and pamphleteer Thomas Nashe, the subject of his doctoral dissertation. During Nashe's life, England was awash in raging debates about the place of printing, reading, and literacy in cultural life, with pamphleteers exchanging broadsides, lobbyists campaigning for patrons to get exclusive paper-making licences, and playwrights such as Shakespeare embedding wry critiques of literacy and publishing in their plays. England was experiencing the full impact of the printing press and all of the religious, social, and political upheaval that the press brought with it. The title of McLuhan's dissertation was "The Place of Thomas Nashe in the Learning of His Time," and it is remarkable that the place of Nashe in his time is so closely akin to the place of McLuhan in

ours. Nashe was to the media environment of his day what Mc-
Luhan is to ours: a discerning intellectual who fully grasped the
implications of his media milieu.

Nashe and McLuhan were both inordinately fond of wordplay, brilliant polymaths who employed all manner of classical allusions and name dropping. They were also at times misogynis-
tic, judgmental, arrogant, and, at their worst, pompous and smug.
And, when it came to responses to new media, both leaned in the
direction of the reactionary. Nashe compiled many of his concerns and criticisms in a long essay, perhaps better described as
a Jeremiad, printed in London in 1589. Its title, *The Anatomy of
Absurdity*, might have served for that of one of McLuhan's books,
perhaps *The Mechanical Bride*. It provides a similarly wide-ranging rant against all manner of wrong thinking.

Nashe's critique of the media practices of his day was a model
for McLuhan. Nashe took on the rhetorical styles and means of
production of the sixteenth century, just as McLuhan did in the
twentieth century, by pointing out the superiority of the classics
and their authors. Nashe also adopted the same casual dismissal of others and a sense of superiority that permeate McLuhan's
writings and public proclamations, including McLuhan's early literary criticism and his personal correspondence, especially
his letters to his mother. Both Nashe and McLuhan thought that
other men of their times were unmanly and that it behooved them
to point out their failings.

There are other areas of overlap between Nashe and McLuhan,
though the latter gives more subtle expression to shared themes
in keeping with twentieth-century literary conventions. For example, was McLuhan echoing Nashe in his disdain for popular
culture? Here is Nashe on his contemporaries: "[I]n their books
there is scarce to be found one precept pertaining to virtue, but
whole quires fraught with amorous discourse, kindling Venus'
flame in Vulcan's forge, carrying Cupid in triumph, alluring even
vowed vestals to tread awry, enchanting chaste minds and cor-
rupting the continen'st?" (4). Here is Nashe on what we might call
"new media": "Nothing is so great an enemy to a sound judgment
as the pride of a peevish conceit, which causeth a man both in life
and belief either to snatch up or hatch newfangles" (20). Another

close affinity between the two men was that both were adamant in their belief that their societies were becoming feminized. Nashe goes on for pages about women's inferiority and evil ways, as one typical example demonstrates:

> But what should I spend my ink, waste my paper, stub my pen in painting forth their ugly imperfections and perverse peevishness, when as how many hairs they have on their heads, so many snares they will find for a need to snare men in; how many voices all of them have, so many vices each one of them hath; how many tongues, so many tales; how many eyes, so many allurements. (7)

Clearly, McLuhan never expressed such resolute misogyny, yet this was the perspective of one of his most influential historical and theoretical forebears and provides a context for understanding McLuhan's attraction to the theme that men should at all costs avoid being feminized.

At first glance, it might appear that the oft-mentioned "objectification" of women in *Playboy*, with its hyper-sexualized images and adolescent sexual jokes and cartoons, is fully in sync with the perspectives that Nashe expressed four centuries previously. However, the "Playboy Man," with his shallow penchant for "the best" consumer goods in every realm, from whiskey to jazz to cars to women, and his anxiety about grooming, clothing, and general appearance, is not so different in the means of self-regard from the social role assigned to women. It was in the realm of ideas and aesthetics rather than more traditional macho posing that Hefner sought to distinguish himself from women (and from cruder men), and this explains the appeal that the likes of McLuhan and his intellectual, creative, and literary cohorts held for him. And *Playboy* clearly perceived McLuhan's intellectual celebrity cache.

From 1967 to 1969, *Playboy* published three pieces by or about McLuhan. His name first appears in the February 1967 issue. Consisting of a half-page report as part of a regular feature called "On the Scene," it includes a head shot in profile and refers to him as "the decade's most controversial intellectual." It opens with a quotation that refutes claims by some that McLuhan was an admirer of new media: "I find most pop culture monstrous and sickening. I study it for my own survival." The profile closes with McLuhan's thoughts about the *Playboy* playmates: "Nudity is basically a sculptural and plastic form. You're successful because you conform to a basic shift in our sensory life away from the visual to the tactile" (142).

Less than a year later, in the expanded Christmas 1968 issue, the magazine published a long article that continues for five typographically wonky pages and is titled "The Reversal of the Overheated Image." Here McLuhan lays out his ideas about "hot" and "cold" media and how new technologies cause older ones to flip into new forms.

Such a prominent place for McLuhan in the holiday issue is a sign that the editors caught on to his fame and importance, as further indicated by the description of him in the front of the magazine as "the messianic metaphysician of pop culture" and his essay as "a machine-gun analysis of how . . . new media create unforeseen problems that demand drastic new solutions" (3). A quip accompanies the article: "Mind your media, men, or you'll find yourselves catching a cold environment—and suffering from overexposure" ("Reversal" 131). Another sign of his status is found in the company that he was keeping. Among others, there are stories by Bill Cosby and Alberto Moravia, an essay by Norman Thomas, and a symposium on creativity featuring contributions by Truman Capote, Arthur Miller, LeRoi Jones, Henry Miller, Isaac Bashevis Singer, and John Updike, to name just some of the participants, and the interview that month was with Eldridge Cleaver. Further evidence of the editors' belief in McLuhan's power to sell copies is that his name is at the top of the long list of luminaries on the cover.

Then, just three months later, in the March 1969 issue, appeared the *Playboy* interview. The lengthy conversation, conducted by Eric Norden, a prolific interviewer and writer of episodes for television westerns, trails out for fifteen pages interspersed with facing page advertisements. Rising to the challenge to come up with yet another clever way of describing McLuhan, this time the editors settled on "the protean metaphysician of mass communications" ("Interview" 3). Indicating who else was of interest to the editors and, presumably, the readers of *Playboy*, some of the other interview subjects for that year included Lee Marvin, Allen Ginsberg, Gore Vidal, Rod Steiger, Ramsey Clark, Jesse Jackson, and Joe Namath.

Given his perceptiveness of and interest in the modes of expression of popular culture, it is surprising at first that McLuhan had relatively little to say about two of the most important social and technical developments of his time: the mainstreaming of explicit sexual material led by the creation of *Playboy* in 1953, followed by the FDA approval and the widespread marketing of birth control pills starting in 1960. His prim views of sex and proper gender roles in addition to his adherence to Roman Catholic dogma might have made it difficult for him to analyze insightfully the sexual revolution that, along with the media revolution, was sweeping across North America and finding expression most dramatically and commercially in *Playboy*.

One of the most interesting things about *Playboy* is how Hefner played off the elements of the media value systems against each other to gain publishing respectability and evade prosecution for the dissemination of pornography. It is almost as though he ingested, synthesized, and applied McLuhan's analyses with his own great pragmatic skill. *Playboy* was arguably the most literate and literary mainstream magazine of the 1960s. It published virtually every significant male novelist, essayist, short-story writer, public intellectual, and critic on the continent. The near absence of female writers is striking though unsurprising.

In each issue, embedded among pages of print and thousands of sentences, the essence of the print media culture whose passing McLuhan spent much of his life lamenting, were a few pages devoted to one of the media that he credited (or blamed) for the radical changes that he was cataloguing and critiquing: photography. It is probably true that many of those who bought the magazine did so for the few photos of naked women, but the social and political legitimacy of the magazine required that it present itself as a purveyor of print.

It took millions of words and the implicit endorsement of all those literary luminaries whose names graced the tables of contents to legitimize a couple of photos of semi-naked women. And then there was the "centerfold." In publishing parlance, these devices are called "gatefolds," and both terms have particularly apt meanings when it comes to *Playboy* and the shifting media environment. The centrefold was indeed at the physical and aesthetic centre of attention, both for regular subscribers and for those given to condemning the magazine. And it was the gatefold—that is, the gateway—that, when opened, ushered the reader into the sexual fantasies laid bare before him. Furthermore, it was the gateway to later generations of publications once there was no longer the requirement of costly literary offerings to excuse the nudity, not to mention the costly legal fees.

As mentioned above, McLuhan makes a brief comment about female nudity in his first *Playboy* appearance: "Nudity is basically a sculptural and plastic form. . . . [Y]ou conform to a basic shift . . . away from the visual to the tactile" ("Profile"142). If McLuhan had given attention to the design of the magazine, then he might have made much of the tactile experience of the layouts. It is noteworthy that the centrefold was usually arranged so that little of the playmate's naked body was visible. One had to open the folded page and turn it ninety degrees to see the full photo, thereby stripping the young woman of her covers: that is, undressing her. And one had the ever-present power to cover or uncover her at will or stand her upright or lay her back down and go on to other pages. Furthermore, the facing page, the one that had to be turned to gain full access to the naked woman, always contained black-and-white photos of mundane life. These photos gave subscribers the notion that these women were just like the girls next door as they saw them with their families, with their pets, or at their jobs.

Hefner's understanding of McLuhan's notion of the rise of tactility as a dominant sensory apparatus was brilliantly captured in 1970 when *Playboy* became the first "gentleman magazine" (as the genre was sometimes called) to be printed in a Braille version and funded by the Library of Congress. The Braille version includes all the written words but no pictorial representations. Congress cut off funding for this version in 1985, but U.S. District Court Judge Thomas Hogan reversed the decision on First Amendment grounds.

McLuhan had little to say about *Playboy* itself, aside from an observation in the December 1968 article: "The greatly improved photography of the Sixties has pushed the sex image all the way into non sex. The gatefold cuties in *Playboy* are sculptured and cool, as nudes must be" ("Reversal" 33). However, his chapter titled "The Photograph" in *Understanding Media: The Extensions of Man* in 1964 might well have been written with *Playboy* in mind. In an evocative phrase, the subtitle of the chapter says it all, calling photography "The Brothel without Walls." There, in four pithy words, McLuhan implicitly pins the label "whore master" or "pimp" on Hefner's mansion door.

The editorial mix of high-quality print and photography that Hefner used embodied McLuhan's idea expressed in the chapter on photography: "The step from the age of Typographic Man to the age of Graphic Man was taken with the invention of photography" (*Understanding Media* 171). Again, a few pages later, McLuhan expresses an insight that reflects exactly what the *Playboy* photo shoots set out to accomplish: "[T]he photograph is quite versatile in revealing and arresting posture and structure wherever it is used" (174).

It is also important to recall that McLuhan viewed with dismay the effects of photography on human values and relations. His views were held in common with other religious and social conservatives, though his rhetoric was more nuanced. Nonetheless, he maintains in *Understanding Media* that the camera "tend[s] to turn people into things" and that photography "cheapens and degrades" (170). Repeatedly, he likens photography to a brothel and photos to prostitutes, claiming at one point, in a strikingly crude phrase, that photographs of movie stars make them into "[d]reams that money can buy. They can be bought and hugged and thumbed more easily than public prostitutes" (170).

Although it is unlikely that Hefner was familiar with McLuhan's early literary essays, in practice his editorial vision embodied an idea that McLuhan laid out in a 1944 essay on Edgar Allan Poe and then again in *The Gutenberg Galaxy*: "It was Edgar Allan Poe who first worked out the rationale of this ultimate awareness of the poetic process and who saw that instead of directing the work to the reader, it was necessary to incorporate the reader in the work" (276).

Until *Playboy*, the dominant tradition in painting, sculpture, and photography of nude women, especially when the intention was to arouse erotic desire, was to invite a Peeping Tom response by making it seem either that the models were unaware of the ogling eye and merely caught at a disrobed moment or that they were demure and somewhat embarrassed at being watched. In art history, the posture is known as the "pudica pose," the contrivance by which the model's genitals are shielded by either a wisp of cloth, flowing hair, tree leaves, or an artfully placed hand. This pose is even enacted in pictures in which the narrative has the woman completely alone with no reason to be modest or shy. The prying eyes from which she is being shielded are those of the voyeuristic art patron. Her hair, garment, or hands are protecting us from her or, more precisely, from our own prurient desires, and, ironically, they actually draw attention to the shielded part of her body. In this presentation, the reader is both drawn into and shut out of the work.

The *Playboy* approach was radically different, wholly devoted to drawing in the reader. Although legal restrictions in the early years required that pubic hair be air-brushed out or hidden, every playmate model not only returned one's gaze but also seemed to be perfectly at ease with the attention that she received. Furthermore, in addition to the black-and-white photos mentioned earlier, there was always a brief written piece about the model's background, education, aspirations, hobbies, and other personal details. Again, this was part of the strategy to make the women seem like "the girl next door" rather than some unattainable model or actress.

Another idea of McLuhan's can be understood as illuminating a visual practice in *Playboy,* though again lines of influence remained unexamined by McLuhan himself. In 1962, the same year as the publication of *The Gutenberg Galaxy* and the first installment of "The Playboy Philosophy," another groundbreaking feature was added to *Playboy,* a feature that was to run sporadically for the next twenty-six years: the comic strip named "Little Annie Fanny." Eleven years earlier, in *The Mechanical Bride,* McLuhan had written about the original Little Orphan Annie as well as other comics, at one point stating that comics and television alike consisted of "iconic mosaic images." His discussion of Little Orphan Annie focused on her character and success: "Girded only with her own goodness, but menaced on every hand by human malice and stupidity, she wins through by shrewdness, luck and elusiveness" (66).

These were precisely the qualities that Hefner was both capturing and satirizing. In style, production, and content, Little Annie Fanny reflected the naive optimism of her predecessor as well as some of her physical attributes. Both were noted for their big eyes, big hair, and big smiles. But in production Annie Fanny applied McLuhan's idea of "the flip" to the comic strip genre.

Annie Fanny was the first fully painted feature in American comics. Every panel was painted in great detail, thereby emulating the high-gloss colour photographs of sexy women for which the magazine was famous. Unlike all preceding comics, Annie Fanny had the look of Kodachrome film or movie images. And in content the series performed a McLuhanish flip by both parodying and paying homage to the original Little Orphan Annie while simultaneously alluding to the crude underground pornographic genre known as Tijuana Bibles, which commonly depicted comic strip characters in acts of sexual debauchery.

Although there is no evidence that McLuhan and Hefner had any personal interaction with each other (requests to Hefner's office for an interview or comments about McLuhan were turned down), or that either was conscious of being influenced by the other, their shared space as two of the most influential figures in mid-twentieth-century media history cannot be overlooked. It is now more than thirty years since McLuhan's death and nearly fifty years since his last significant publication. Annie Fanny is a footnote in comic strip history. *Playboy*'s circulation, though still over 1 million, is a fraction of its 1972 peak of more than 7 million, and Hefner, thanks to Viagra, has the status of a horny octogenarian. Yet the legacies of both men linger. Together, a theorist and a practitioner, they informed and determined what we saw and how we saw. Their visions changed and challenged how we understand gender and technology as well as word and image.

WORKS CITED

Coupland, Douglas. *Marshall McLuhan*. Toronto: Penguin, 2009. Print.

Gordon, W. Terrence. *Marshall McLuhan: Escape into Understanding*. New York: Basic Books, 1997. Print.

Hefner, Hugh. "The Playboy Philosophy 2." *Playboy* Jan. 1963: various pages. Print.

——. "The Playboy Philosophy 3." *Playboy* Feb. 1963: various pages. Print.

——. "The Playboy Philosophy 5." *Playboy* Apr. 1963: various pages. Print.

——. "The Playboy Philosophy 9." *Playboy* Sept. 1963: various pages. Print.

——. "The Playboy Philosophy 10." *Playboy* Oct. 1963: various pages. Print.

Marchessault, Janine. *Marshall McLuhan: Cosmic Media*. London: SAGE, 2004. Print.

McLuhan, Marshall. "Dagwood's America" *Columbia* 33 (1944): 3+. Print.

——. *The Gutenberg Galaxy: The Making of Typographic Man*. Toronto: U of Toronto P, 1962. Print.

——. *Letters of Marshall McLuhan*. Ed. Matie Molinaro, Corinne McLuhan, and William Toye. New York: Oxford UP, 1987. Print.

——. *The Mechanical Bride: Folklore of Industrial Man*. New York: Vanguard, 1951. Print.

——. "The Place of Thomas Nashe in the Learning of His Time." PhD diss. Cambridge U, 1943. Print.

——. "The *Playboy* Interview—Marshall McLuhan." *Playboy* Mar. 1969: 53–74+. Print.

——. "The Reversal of the Overheated Image." *Playboy* Dec. 1968: 131–34+. Print.

——. *Understanding Media: The Extensions of Man*. New York: New American Library, 1964. Print.

Nashe, Thomas. *The Anatomy of Absurdity*. London: Thomas Hackett, 1589. Print.

"Profile." *Playboy* Feb. 1967: 142. Print.

CHAPTER 12

RECOVERING RELIGION FOR THE HISTORY AND THEORY OF RHETORIC:

LESSONS FROM MARSHALL McLUHAN

David Charles Gore and David Beard

> In Jesus Christ, . . . the medium and the message are fully one and the same. —MARSHALL McLUHAN, *The Medium and the Light* (103)

More than nearly any other thinker in the twentieth century, Marshall McLuhan used the media to advance his critical agenda. Appearing on television and in movies, and utilizing the most visual of print media, McLuhan was a savvy communicator, capable of careful and persuasive self-presentation. He presented a secularized version of his work, palatable for television news shows. In so doing, he erased the religious dimension of his thought, offering a secular theory for the analysis of secular media and technology. McLuhan appeared to the broadest public as a secular thinker to engage effectively a secular society.[1]

---

1   See Stearn for a representative sample of these popular accounts of McLuhan that are unaware of his Catholicism and treat him as a secular thinker.

His self-presentation among scholars was different; his works in literary criticism especially were inflected by his faith commitments. (For example, McLuhan published in the Catholic literary journal *Renascence* and delivered speeches at its symposia.[2]) As a result, it has been recognized that religion had a profound influence on him, but that Catholicism has not been integrated into the larger interpretation of his work (Kroker). This chapter begins a recovery of the faith-based dimensions, specifically his Catholicism, in the facets of his work that he elected to present as predominantly secular. In doing so, this chapter revises the popular understanding of McLuhan's theoretical and critical project among the public and among scholars of rhetorical and media theory.

Part of what we are building is a hermeneutic for reading McLuhan's work. We believe that each of his aphorisms and maxims works, in the end, much like a Trojan horse. There is an entirely secular way to interpret "the medium is the message" as a maxim, a flash of theoretical insight, and that flash has come to blind us to an alternative hermeneutic. You cannot read that maxim in quite the same way if you recognize that, for McLuhan, in Jesus Christ the medium and the message were one ("Religion" 103). (As we demonstrate below, it points toward the possibility of an unmediated experience of the sacred, an unexpected dimension for those familiar only with secular readings of McLuhan.) This revised understanding has implications for the reception of his work in rhetoric and media studies.

But more than that, by identifying the rich religious institutional and spiritual experience inherent in McLuhan's work, we hope to crack open a space for rhetoric and religion in twenty-first-century communication studies. Scholars of rhetoric operate within the secularized worldview that has come to typify our age; as a result, they have effaced the spiritual from the range of human experience open to rhetorical analysis. In the process of highlighting the sacred aspects of McLuhan's work, we aim to highlight the contemporary tendency to theorize communication and media from a secular point of view as well as to show the

---

2   See *Renascence* 64.1 (2011).

value that might be gained if media studies developed a capacity to toggle more easily between sacred and secular approaches.

By ignoring the influence of theology, communication and media studies risks misunderstanding its own history as well as its primary context within the secular age in which it was born and now thrives. Moreover, by not accounting for theology, rhetorical and media theory places untenable limitations on what it means to be human and how humanity might conceptualize communication in theory and practice. The reintegration of the religious dimension into McLuhan's intellectual project can be an exemplar for the broader reintegration of the religious dimension into rhetoric and communication studies.

OVERVIEW

To build this argument for multiple, non-contradictory readings of McLuhan, we build from what Richard Lanham calls "toggling." He uses this term to refer to the two different ways of looking at a text. We can look at the text, accepting its style and verbal surface, or we can choose to look through a text, getting to its essential substance. The skill that we need, however, is not one or the other mode of reading but an ability to switch back and forth between one mode and another to grasp a text's true social, political, and humanistic implications.[3] The ability to toggle between different hermeneutic frames, between philosophy and theology, between politics and religion, and between the sacred and the secular, is a windfall to intellectual and moral progress. To be denied the capacity to switch back and forth between different discourses limits the ability to see from different perspectives. We suspect that McLuhan himself was learning to toggle between the sacred and the secular as he presented facets of his work, and we believe that the fullest possible understanding of his work requires an ability to toggle in the same way.

---

3   The argument about toggling as the essential inheritance of rhetorical *paideia* is one that Lanham has been brewing for a long time over several works; see the entries in the Works Cited.

We believe that the secular interpretations are well established, and to establish the second perspective for toggling we rehearse the grounds for the religious interpretation through biography. In the second section of this chapter, we offer a narrative overview of McLuhan's discovery of Catholicism as an intellectual and a man of faith. This discovery, for McLuhan, was part and parcel of the recovery of the richest details of the intellectual tradition of the West. Catholicism became a lens that enriched his reading of the great works of philosophy and literature.

Then we read McLuhan's media theory in light of his religious commitments, which include the claim that the media environment has become an envelope that seals us away from God, revelation, and salvation. We are alienated from religious experience yet not without hope. McLuhan criticizes the church for failing to understand the consequences of media in the hope of encouraging a return to the unmediated experience of the divine. These dimensions of his reflections on media theory enable us to re-examine this theory as we have inherited it, to toggle between the secular media theorist and the media theologian.

We are not certain that a strictly secularist reading of McLuhan is a misreading. What we wish to assert is that it is, in fact, a *reading*, one conditioned by its historical and material circumstances. Most work on McLuhan is done from within the secular environment of state universities, where secularism is a dominant habit and state of mind. We think that this reading does not do justice to the profound influence of religion on McLuhan. His own scholarly research led him to question the tepid Protestantism in which he was raised and to convert to Catholicism. He wrote and spoke extensively about how religion could protect humanity from the instability created by new media technologies. Most secular readings miss that influence altogether, while others fail to appreciate more generally the impact that theology can play in media criticism and theory. At the same time, we acknowledge that a purely sacred reading is quite difficult to muster in the twenty-first century and might not lead to any better understanding of McLuhan's work or legacy. We seek not just to redescribe McLuhan as a religious thinker and to treat him in a long tradition of scholars stretching back through Aquinas to

Augustine. We respect the mutual validity and complementarity of the secular and religious readings of his work.

The implications of this argument are primarily for a better understanding of McLuhan's work, but there are larger possibilities for rhetorical and media studies. At the end of this chapter, we assess the state of communication studies in what Charles Taylor has called a "secular age." We argue that recognizing the rich dimensions of McLuhan's theory, when we account for his faith, can become a model for a richer engagement with the religious dimension of rhetorical culture, one that encourages the contemporary scholar of communication and media studies to toggle between the secular frame that we have inherited and the religious dimension of contemporary rhetorical culture.

TOGGLING: A HERMENEUTIC FOR RETHINKING McLUHAN'S RELATIONSHIP TO CATHOLICISM

It has been difficult to reconcile a Catholic image of McLuhan with the secular figure who became a pop culture icon. One approach to such reconciliation is to suggest that his ordinary and patient, daily and weekly, Catholicism was entirely separate from his work in media theory. This was the approach taken by Richard Kostelanetz in the *New York Times* in 1967:

> The major incongruity is that a man so intellectually adventurous should lead such a conservative life: the egocentric and passionately prophetic qualities of his books contrast with the personal modesty and pervasive confidence of a secure Catholic. What explains the paradox is that "Marshall McLuhan," the thinker, is different from H.M. McLuhan, "the man." The one writes books and delivers lectures; the other teaches school, heads a family and lists himself in the phone book. It was probably H.M. who made that often quoted remark about Marshall's theories: "I don't pretend to understand them. After all, my stuff is very difficult."
>
> And the private H.M. will say this about the technologies his public self has so brilliantly explored: "I wish none

225

of these had ever happened. They impress me as nothing but a disaster. They are for dissatisfied people. Why is man so unhappy he wants to change this world? I would never attempt to improve an environment—my personal preference, I suppose, would be a preliterate milieu, but I want to study change to gain power over it."

His books, he adds, are just "probes"—that is, he does not "believe" in his work as he believes in Catholicism. The latter is faith, the books are just thoughts. "You know faith differently from the way you 'understand' my books."

Kostelanetz paints a picture of two men who do not seem to understand one another. One is a Catholic who finds the changes of technology bewildering and mainly harmful. The other is a savvy media thinker who probes possibilities and reaches for understanding. One is fundamentally a conservative and wants to resist technology; the other is adventurous and egocentric.

We prefer the image of a whole person but are comfortable entertaining the possibility that this person is not without contradictions, perhaps even an internal capacity to toggle between enacting different characters and playing different roles.

The notion of toggling as a hermeneutic form derives from familiar contemporary technology, from the switches that operate our machines and control our computers. A toggle switch allows a user to move back and forth from one setting on a machine to another. Such a switch on my laptop controls whether my wi-fi is on or off or whether my computer records sounds from the internal microphone or from the external microphone that I plugged into a jack. The power and usefulness of the toggle switch is precisely in its reversibility: an "on" switch that cannot be turned off is useless; the user needs to be able to move back and forth between the two settings.

Lanham argues that rhetorical education is inherently structured around a kind of cognitive toggling:

Rhetoric is a method of literary education aimed to train its students to toggle back and forth between AT and THROUGH vision, alternately to realize how the illusion is created and then to fool oneself with it again. The literature such an education created—and this means most of Western literature until the nineteenth century—works the same way, by alternating speech and narrative, self-conscious and unselfconscious language. . . . To study Western literature is to master the particular binary oscillation between kinds of consciousness that each text advances. (*Electronic Word* 81)

A rhetorical education enables students to toggle between perspectives on a text, for example to toggle between the search for authorial intent and the mapping of reader response, to toggle between the search for the ways in which a text reflects the norms of its genre and the ways in which a text reflects its historical milieu. A rhetorical education "makes you comfortable with a bi-stable grasp of the world. Looking through experience and at it, first one then the other, comes to seem a natural way of seeing, a habit of perception. Such an oscillation will constitute your characteristic way of looking at the world" (Lanham, *Economics of {Attention}* 26–27). A hermeneutic grounded in toggling should be comfortable to an audience of scholars of rhetoric.

Like a literal toggle switch on my computer, which can simply be left in the "on" setting, rhetorical toggling can be left in one position. We can cease flipping the switch and view a text primarily from one perspective. Lanham describes the effects of this choice this way:

We can, if we like, shut the oscillation down and study, for example, only the rhetorical figuration, or only the philosophy. This, in fact, is how Western literature has been studied and taught for most of its history. We study "what Plato said," ignore the exquisitely wrought style that contradicts the "saying"—and miss entirely the ontological schizophrenia at the center of his being. (*Electronic Word* 81)

We believe that communication scholarship generally has operated with the switch "stuck" in the secular position as it has integrated McLuhan into disciplinary narratives. (These narratives themselves are often largely or entirely secular [see Park and Pooley; Rogers].) We hope to reopen the switch and enable multiple interpretations of McLuhan's work, including an explicitly Catholic interpretation.

McLUHAN'S DISCOVERY OF THE CATHOLIC TRADITION

> You see my "religion-hunting" began with a rather priggish "culture-hunting." . . . It was a long time before I finally perceived that the character of every society, its food, clothing, arts and amusements, are ultimately determined by its religion.—MARSHALL McLUHAN, *The Medium and the Light* (16)

The paths by which McLuhan became a scholar are already well documented. He completed an undergraduate degree and an MA degree in English literature at the University of Manitoba in Winnipeg before beginning study at Cambridge University in 1935. While at Cambridge, McLuhan completed an additional year of undergraduate work. He began graduate study but left in 1936 with a teaching appointment at the University of Wisconsin in Madison, returning to Cambridge in 1940 to complete his MA and begin his PhD, completed in 1943. His dissertation argued that the trivium was a necessary context for the writings of Thomas Nashe (*Classical Trivium*). As background, McLuhan traced the trivium at different moments in the cultural history of the West.

His readings in literary criticism introduced him to Christian apologetics and Catholic thinkers such as G.K. Chesterton. In Chesterton, McLuhan saw a side of religious experience that appealed to him, generative of the fruits of culture: "games and philosophy, and poetry and music and mirth and fellowship. . . . Catholic culture produced Chaucer and his merry story-telling pilgrims [along with] . . . Don Quixote and St. Francis and Rabelais" (*Medium* 15).[4] In a letter to Corinne Lewis reprinted in *The Medium and the*

---

4   In some ways, McLuhan learned from Chesterton what contemporary rhetorical and media theorists fail to recognize: that the products of culture can be fruitfully understood against the backdrop of religious experience.

Light: Reflections on Religion, McLuhan writes that "Clara Long-worth . . . produces an enormous amount of evidence to show how all of Shakespeare's friends were Catholics" and that Shakespeare was penalized by the Anglican Church, paying "about $2,000.00, in our money, to the local Anglican bishop for the privilege of being married by a priest" (27). McLuhan was convinced that literary history erased the Catholic influences on Shakespeare's works. In response, he sought to recover those influences.

For the non-religious reader of this volume, McLuhan's conversion from Protestantism to Catholicism might be hard to understand; they are both Christian faiths. But to understand this conversion as a switch in specific theological claims of faith is to misunderstand both the force of conversion and the nature of religious faith or at least to apply a limited way of thinking about religion. (For example, individuals do not elect to be a Protestant or Catholic based on whether they accept or reject the Assumption of the Virgin Mary; the selection is richer and more complex, a choice between one type of community and set of values and another.) The emphasis on statements of belief as the core of a religious experience, from McLuhan's perspective, is the reduction of religious experience to a game: "But insofar as it is a theoretical or intellectual construct, it is purely a game, though perhaps a very attractive game" (*Medium* 81). McLuhan understood religion as more than a game, and we need to give that understanding serious consideration as we assess the impact of religion on his work.

THE ROLE OF THE CHURCH AS AN
INSTITUTION IN THE MEDIA AGE

> Religion is veritably something which, if it could be presented in an image, would make your hair stand on end.—
> MARSHALL MCLUHAN, *The Medium and the Light* (18)

Having established in a skeletal way McLuhan's intellectual and personal discovery of Catholicism, we now demonstrate that McLuhan held a specific agenda for a Catholic media studies. His criticisms of the effects of media on society are blunted if understood only as secular critiques, and we lose a dimension of his work if we do not recognize that he was a critic of the media deployment of the Catholic Church as well as of the secular forms of advertising and mass communication.

In his criticism of the Catholic Church, McLuhan "felt like a man who has been arrested for arson because he turned in a fire alarm" (*Medium* 129). This feeling was magnified many times when it came to his efforts to convince the Catholic Church that it was in the middle of a media revolution the effects of which would surpass Gutenberg. McLuhan recognized that we live at a time when culture travels at the speed of light, "when we can live a century in ten years, when every day of our lives can pass through at least a hundred years of historical development" (*Medium* 46). Religious experiences and institutions offer stability in a time of change. As he claimed, "The Church, which offers to man and demands of him a constant change of heart, wrapped itself in a visual culture that placed static permanence above all other values" (*Medium* 49). As the culture accelerated through technological change, the church could play a role in grounding human experience.

While hopeful that Catholicism might play a cultural role, McLuhan was nonetheless critical of the Catholic Church in the electronic age. He worried about the church being oblivious to the speed of cultural change and (perhaps) even contributing to it. He was convinced that the church had missed the meaning of the communication revolution in the sixteenth century and was missing the meanings of the new revolutions of the twentieth century. Indeed, he raised a critical question—"Has the Church itself been responsible for much of the secular technology that has shaped the Western psyche?"—and wondered whether it might be complicit in the transformations of culture that now it must mediate (*Medium* 118). In raising these questions, McLuhan hoped to provoke the Catholic Church to respond to the problems created by new media forms. The church, in adapting to new technologies (from amplified sound to liturgies on television), was, in McLuhan's view, failing to confront the effects of these technologies on its ministries and parishioners (*Medium* 121–24). What McLuhan calls "the anarchy of contemporary experience" threatened secular social structures (*Medium* 124; "the city," as he talks about it in *Counterblast* [McLuhan and Parker]) as well as the church.

McLuhan believed that the Catholic Church's decisions inherent in Vatican II, including the move to vernacular-language mass instead of Latin, were short sighted. In his view, the church failed to recognize that "alteration or innovation strikes to the psychic core by the resonance of the auditory imagination" (*Medium* 125). In making the text of the mass accessible to local audiences, McLuhan contended, an important aspect of the ritual was lost, an aspect that made more than just the mass itself sacred. The mass lost the amplifying power of the interface between two tongues, a "dramatic tension far above either of them" (*Medium* 125). It was not the Latin of the mass that mattered but the presence of Latin in English, Spanish, Italian, and French that was magnified so many times over and captured the imaginations of Catholics prior to Vatican II. According to McLuhan, the language of the Latin mass infused the language of the everyday, and hearing Latin echoed in everyday speech encouraged Catholics to believe that the sacred infused the everyday as well. His rejection of the vernacular was not crotchety traditionalism; every bit of it was grounded in his theory of media.

THE TRANSFORMATIONS OF THE FAITHFUL IN THE MEDIA ENVIRONMENT

McLuhan was interested not only in the work of the Catholic Church as an institution in the media age but also in the experience of the faithful in the media environment. In *Understanding Media: The Extensions of Man,* he explains the relationship among the senses, the body, and media technologies. In the media environment, our consciousness is extended by the tools that we use. The wheel is an extension of the foot, the book is an extension of the eye, and clothing is an extension of the skin. These technologies develop at uneven paces: we developed the book into a form of mass communication long before we had a means to transmit the human voice. In their effects, McLuhan indicates, media result in an imbalance among the senses and a disorientation of human experience:

> [A]ny medium that singles out one sense, writing or radio for example, by that very fact causes an exceptional disturbance among the other senses.... We may be forced, in the interests of human equilibrium, to suppress various media as radio or movies for long periods of time, or until the social organism is in a state to sustain such violent lopsided stimulus. (*Understanding Media* 9)

Our experience of the world has been unbalanced by the web of technologies and media that we use.

Within this web of media technologies, our relationship to the world has changed. According to McLuhan, we are no longer "within the world" or "on the earth"; rather, we are located within "the satellite environment of the earth which for the first time makes the earth the content of a man-made container" (*Medium* 90). "Satellite environment" is McLuhan's term for the media-saturated environment in which we live, with no spot on the earth unsaturated by broadcast signals. Secular interpretations of McLuhan have summarized this experience in a cliché: goldfish cannot perceive the water in which they swim, and humans cannot perceive the satellite environment in which they live (McLuhan and Parker 22–23). But for him this satellite environment disrupts our relationship with God and obscures our experience of the divine: "The satellite environment has completely altered the organs of human perception and revealed the universal pollution" (*Medium* 81–82). Most city dwellers have no idea that light pollution obscures their ability to see the stars; contemporary humankind has no idea that the satellite environment obscures their ability to perceive the sacred.

The way to restore access to the sacred is to work toward an unmediated experience of the world, without microphones or television cameras, without screens or printed pages. In this, McLuhan was cribbing from Chesterton, who extolled "the sacramental sense of the life of earth and sea and sky, of tillage and growth, and of food and wine" (*Medium* 4). After all, "In Jesus

Christ, there is no distance or separation between the medium and the message: it is the one case where we can say that the medium and the message are fully one and the same" (*Medium* 103). In secular contexts, McLuhan claimed, the medium is the message, as if there were no access to the message independent of the experience of the medium. But, as a Catholic, he believed that we needed to break from media via prayer: "Today, personal prayer and liturgy (which are inseparable) are the only means of tuning in to the right wavelength, of listening to Christ, and of involving the whole person" (*Medium* 141). Read in the light of his religious beliefs, then, his claims about a satellite environment are more than descriptive claims; they contain an exhortation to seek another form of experience, possible if one embraces faith.

THE CONSEQUENCES OF EMBRACING McLUHAN AS BOTH A SECULAR AND A RELIGIOUS THINKER

We know that religion is an essential component of McLuhan's biography; if we have demonstrated that religion essentially reframes his critical and theoretical work, then we have made a modest contribution to McLuhan studies. In making these claims, we do not seek to supplant the secular readings of McLuhan; we do not wish his appearance in *Annie Hall* to be rewritten as a subtle form of proselytizing; we are not authorizing a reading of *The Mechanical Bride: Folklore of Industrial Man* as a subtle play on the idea that the church is the bride of Christ. Our claim does not overwrite the secular interpretations of McLuhan's work. Rather, we hope to augment those readings, and we hope to use this perspective to demonstrate that communication studies must be open to religion as a dimension of the history of rhetoric and of contemporary communication criticism.

McLuhan himself, we believe, was toggling, capable of foregrounding some dimensions of his work, for some audiences, in a way that never (or rarely) contradicted his other (religious) commitments. He was a secular thinker, and he was a religious thinker. He was both. Perhaps that dualism was inevitable given the world in which he wrote (an increasingly secular society). Much overtly religious work was published in places that would reach specifically Catholic audiences, while his more secular writings grabbed the attention of wider audiences. McLuhan eschewed the label of theologian, but his thought was religiously inflected.[5] Because religious belief has shifted so radically in modernity, the prospect of a happy marriage between philosophy and theology has been considerably diminished (Caputo 11). One avenue open to religiously motivated thinkers is to toggle consciously. Our work in encouraging scholars to toggle in their interpretations of McLuhan might only be asking them to mimic his decisions as a rhetor to toggle himself. But as scholars, it is imperative that we take a more complex view, and we contend that this means sustaining the secular McLuhan as well as the Catholic McLuhan as we advance our understanding of his work.

McLuhan is not, we believe, an outlier in the history of the communication discipline. His religious turn was not idiosyncratic but part of an overlooked tradition that provides a corrective to a secularizing turn that has defined rhetorical studies for more than 100 years. The relationship between rhetoric and religion is not just undertheorized in disciplinary scholarship but also, we think, repressed.

We can offer an example, drawn from our pedagogy, of the ways that the history and theory of media have been secularized in the history of the field, even while teaching McLuhan's work. In teaching a course in the history of literacy, David Beard uses a combination of books, including Henry Petroski's *The Book on the Bookshelf* and Marshall McLuhan's *The Gutenberg Galaxy: The Making of Typographic Man*. The class begins by distinguishing oral, manuscript, and print cultures. A manuscript culture, the culture of the monasteries as they preserved scripture and other texts through hundreds of years, involved a complex web of practices: manuscript copying, commentary, and illumination. An entire form of life, from the raising of sheep whose flesh would serve as paper, to the collection of precious gems and metals for binding, to the chaining of books to carrels to prevent theft, arose to

---

5   McLuhan wanted to leave theology to the professionals, so to speak; see Higgins.

support the creation of books. The moment of revelation for Beard came from an earnest question from a student: "When will we discuss the contents of the books?" In teaching about the history of literacy as a set of practices and technologies, Beard had erased the reason that monks had devoted their lives to their work. In the narrative of his class, they could just as easily have been transcribing baseball statistics or recipes. That these monks believed they were transcribing religious truth was an inconvenient detail that Beard had omitted from the class narrative. Sometimes scholars of rhetoric simply erase religion from the history of the field.

And sometimes religion is reinvented or translated so that it becomes a topic that we are more comfortable discussing. For example, scholars of rhetoric have written over the relationship between rhetoric and religion, palimpsestically, with the relationship between rhetoric and philosophy. As a result, it is Plato's epistemology that interests them, not his cosmogony. When we speak of the relationship between truth and rhetoric, we speak of a philosophical conception of truth (whether a priori truths or experimental truths or logically deduced truths) in opposition to rhetoric. We overwrite questions of revealed (or religious) truth with philosophical problems.

When we address religion, we do so awkwardly. We define homiletics along a spectrum of rhetorical genres. We define scriptures along a spectrum of texts. We define churches along a spectrum of human social institutions.

The impulse to erase or efface religious experience is not unique to scholars of communication as they write the history of the field; it is common in contemporary culture. Charles Taylor's *A Secular Age* traces the development of secularism. Where McLuhan's historical research was dictated by transformations in technology, Taylor is driven by transformations in theology, including religious practices and beliefs. He notes that modern secular thinkers adopt a purely instrumental reason. Following Bacon, modern secularists appropriate Aristotle's four causes by simply dropping final causation so that "efficient causation alone remains" (98). What comes with instrumental reason is a scientific view of truth, and before long one envisions the world as existing to be managed and controlled.

Whereas earlier humans were enchanted by a wonderful and sacred world and deeply embedded in practices, rituals, songs, and work that allowed them to participate in creation, modern humans under secularism quickly reimagined their circumstances. What was once an ordered whole lost all normative hold on the imagination. Instead of a world that exhibited patterns on which humans should model themselves, the world became "a vast field of mutually affecting parts" supposed "to work in certain ways, that is, to produce certain results" (Taylor 98). Rather than stand in awe at the signs of an awesome creation, we moderns developed an instrumental relationship with nature.

Gradually, according to Taylor, the West slipped into ever-increasing visions of secular order. This order disembedded Western humans from their religious traditions and gradually disenchanted the world. With disembedding and disenchantment came the rise of modern bureaucracies based on rationality and rules (133–34). This disengaged, disciplined, buffered self has become part of the essential defining repertoire of the modern identity. The new disembedded and disenchanted social order was coherent and uncompromising. It brought a new uniformity of purpose and principle. It tended toward individualism rather than collectivism, and it created distance between us and our emotions (139).

When the ground shifts so dramatically under our feet, it is necessary to establish new ways of arranging society and new methods of ordering knowledge. Gradually, we come to obscure the theological and religious aspects of our nature, precisely because these aspects seem to serve so little instrumental purpose. Thus, in such a context, it becomes easy to read McLuhan only as a secular thinker, partly because he wrote in a way that sometimes obscured his moral and religious opinions, beliefs, and judgments, partly because our secular age is tilted toward such misreadings. Twenty-first-century rhetorical theory in Western universities is slanted toward non-religious readings of key texts. It seems that we have (almost) no Augustine and want no Augustine. Thus, current theories of rhetoric ignore the religious dimensions of historical rhetorical theory, preferring to emphasize the secular, the dominant disciplinary mode of our times.

Taylor's work suggests that we adopt a new mode of theorizing the sacred and the secular by stressing the need to be more conscious of our historical moment. It might be obvious to say that one kind of secular rhetorician might see in rhetoric's conversation evidence that faith in God is simply self-deception. A Christian thinker might see in a secular approach to rhetoric's story some blindness to what has been given. Another Christian thinker might decide to conceive of rhetoric's grand conversation in terms of a religious worldview or religious explanation. Somehow our conversations about rhetoric need to accommodate these different approaches and to understand the plural dynamics of belief as we struggle to understand rhetoric's role in transforming, sustaining, and manifesting belief.

We have to be careful to avoid saying that there are two clearly drawn sides to rhetoric's conversation on questions of faith—that of believers and that of unbelievers. The works of George Kennedy and Martin Medhurst do not make the mistake of thinking in binary terms, but they do exemplify the evolution of rhetorical theory in the past few decades toward appreciating the sacred in a situation in which secularism is the dominant mode of inquiry. Kennedy is much too careful a scholar to suggest this, but the title of his important introduction to the history of rhetoric, *Classical Rhetoric and Its Christian and Secular Tradition from Ancient to Modern Times*, is somewhat misleading. Moreover, the work undertheorizes the "secular." For example, the approach adopted in his text appears to weave together two traditions in the story of rhetoric. One tradition, in the West, was the secular tendency to view rhetoric in terms of political questions. The other tradition, Christian, viewed rhetoric as a tool for promoting and defending faith. Of course, the traditions share the tendency to puzzle over just what it means to persuade and how persuasion has been tied up with things transcendent, sacred, or ultimate. Kennedy points to some of the difficulties in distinguishing these two traditions when he speaks of Augustine:

> Although Christian rhetoric as described by Augustine has a distinct subject matter, he does not distinguish it as an art from secular rhetoric. . . . In *The City of God,* even

the Roman Empire is so treated, and Augustine's writings on grammar, dialectic, music, rhetoric, and other subjects equally show his effort to make them religiously neutral, capable of utilization by a Christian for a Christian purpose. (181)

It is hard to imagine that stripping an art of its pagan associations does not in important ways transform the art in question, if not distinguish some new art. In any case, Augustine was successful in converting the conversation of rhetoric from a pagan one to a predominantly Christian one for many centuries, at least in the West. Regardless, what Kennedy shows is that unravelling the sacred and the secular strands of rhetoric's great conversation is not so easily done. Some religious voices in the conversation differ about whether rhetoric can bear sacred qualities or whether it is at best a neutral tool or something more sinister. The recognition of diversity among thinkers informed by religion—whether of the same faith or of different faiths—is one step toward acknowledging the highly problematic nature of dealing in concepts such as "Christian" and "secular" traditions.[6]

Kennedy is one of many historians and theorists of rhetoric who have underestimated the rich relationship between major figures in rhetoric's history and a great diversity of religious beliefs. McLuhan is one of a handful of major thinkers of rhetoric who understood the power of religion (specifically the Christian tradition) as an integral component of understanding human experience and the rhetorical tradition, even if he was reluctant to accept the label of theologian. If we are to think our way through these questions, then we might turn to him first. His religious worldview allows us not only to reconceptualize but also to revitalize our understanding of our historical traditions and, perhaps more importantly, rejuvenate our experience of the divine.

However, the work of both McLuhan and Kennedy came at a moment when our discipline did not have the rich vocabulary and

---

6   McLuhan's own transformation in his conversion to Catholicism shows that a diversity of perspectives can exist within a single thinker in the rhetorical tradition.

understanding of our secular age to fully appreciate the many dimensions of how the sacred and the secular interact. A special issue of *Rhetoric and Public Affairs* on rhetorical invention and religion exemplifies the problematic nature of thinking about the sacred in a secular age. The journal devoted its winter 2004 issue to *Religious and Theological Traditions as Sources of Rhetorical Invention.* The issue is special precisely because it draws attention to the aspect of the field so often suppressed. Editor Martin Medhurst called on an array of scholars "to reflect on how their own individual traditions inform and shape their own rhetorical invention as scholars" ("Introduction" 446). In his own essay in the special issue, he goes on to claim that his professional work as a rhetorical critic is a religious act of devotion:

> If my work is a prayer, then regular scholarly activity becomes a way to fulfill the biblical mandate to "pray without ceasing" and to "work" before the night comes. As a critic, I am, in a sense, petitioning the reader to draw near, to hear my plea, to affirm my being by recognizing in my writings even a glimmer of the truths whose ultimate ground is Truth itself. It is not divine discourse, but it may be discourse that reflects the divine impulse of reaching out in love to the Other—discourse in which author and reader discover a transcendent ground upon which both can stand. How does that happen? Only by the Spirit. ("Filled" 570)

His claim that critical discourse can offer "transcendent ground" seems to be overstated, however. Reading his scholarship as an act of love and faith grounded in his Pentecostal experience is discouraged by the lengthy peer review and editing processes that take place between writing and publication. What remains, by and large, for the reader is the presumption of the disengaged and disciplined scholar engaged in critique of the disenchanted social order, as Taylor has described it. That religion is the theme of a special issue of a secular journal, which then returns to the mode of secular inquiry, implies that religion can best be approached in terms of a toggle whereby it is turned on or off.

The special issue itself, however, creates exactly the kind of space that we think communication theory needs for theorizing the sacred, and we argue that our discipline would be enriched if the sacred/secular toggle is seen as more central and essential. The historical conversation about rhetoric has benefited from the participation of many religious voices persuaded of various religious truths. However, understanding the contributions of these religious voices and the effects of their claims on our understanding of rhetoric has not always been easy, partly because the religious voices in the conversation have not always agreed with one another. Voices that have long been assumed to be "secular" often speak to us from a place and time where gods, heavenly signs, and cults or sects held sway over the imagination in ways that we scarcely acknowledge. It has also not been easy to acknowledge and scope the relationship between religion and rhetoric because most of our discussions take place in a secular age wherein the taken-for-granted place of religious belief is on new ground.

If we restore religious history to a central place in creating our best histories of rhetorical theory, pedagogy, public address, and print culture, then we will produce richer histories attuned to resonances that we never felt before. If we rethink contemporary religious experience as a means of perceiving the world and of apprehending the transcendent within the world, then we will enter a far richer conversation and acknowledge the importance of different kinds of voices and different ways of seeing. This is not only to argue for the tolerance that should prevail in all conversations but also to argue in favour of acknowledging the complexities involved in human relationships and human ways of knowing. It is to call for an appreciation of a richer picture of what it means to be human without doing away with a conversation because of its inability to be reduced to the language of markets, bureaucrats, and mere secularization.

It is our contention that, if rhetorical and media studies were to develop an approach to the problems that it seeks to address that could make room for acknowledging problems addressed through theology, then it would be better for it. Rhetorical and media studies would be more capable of seeing human beings as whole persons, captivated by the cacophony of voices in our modern, liberal, mediated environments but also still searching for a voice more meaningful than them all.

Our attempt to reclaim elements of McLuhan's religious conversion raises more questions than it answers about rhetoric. What does sacred rhetoric mean in a secular age? How should religious voices participate in conversations about rhetoric? To what extent should the rhetorical tradition be understood as having separate or distinct secular and religious traditions? Can there be a postsecular rhetorical theory? Are there postreligious rhetorical theories? Without reflecting on more of these questions, our conversations about rhetoric will likely not keep up with emerging conversations in philosophy, history, and economics about the role of religion and belief in our secular age. Indeed, rhetoric has a crucial part to play in these larger conversations.

One way for it to fulfill that part is to move into a greater understanding of just what "secular" and "religious" mean in its own story and in terms of that story's interactions with wider worlds. By recovering the religious dimensions of McLuhan's thought, we have argued that our discipline can enrich its hermeneutic approach by being more attuned to the influence of the sacred. Just as McLuhan learned to toggle between sacred and secular explanations of our media environment, so too we must learn to toggle between sacred and secular dimensions of communication theory and practice. In the end, however, it is not a child's game of flipping on and off a light switch that will illuminate our understanding. What we need, instead, is a better way to avoid our tendency to undertheorize the sacred, not by undertheorizing the secular, but by exploring their points of contact and the wealth of their interactions. This seems to us to be something that McLuhan saw clearly.

WORKS CITED

Caputo, John D. *Philosophy and Theology*. Nashville: Abingdon, 2006. Print.

Higgins, Michael W. "Prophet of the Electric Age: Marshall Mc-Luhan'sPost-Curial Catholicism." Commonweal 26 Sept. 2011. www.commonwealmagazine.org/prophet-electric-age. Web.

Kennedy, George. *Classical Rhetoric and Its Christian and Secular Tradition from Ancient to Modern Times*. Chapel Hill: U of North Carolina P, 1980. Print.

Kostelanetz, Richard. "Understanding McLuhan (in Part)." *New York Times* 29 Jan. 1967. www.nytimes.com/books/97/11/02/home/mcluhan-magazine.html. Web.

Kroker, Arthur. *Technology and the Canadian Mind: Innis/McLuhan/Grant*. Montreal: New World Perspectives, 1984. Print.

Lanham, Richard A. *The Economics of {Attention}: Style and Substance in the Age of Information*. Chicago: U of Chicago P, 2006. Print.

———. *The Electronic Word: Democracy, Technology, and the Arts*. Chicago: U of Chicago P, 1993. Print.

———. *The Motives of Eloquence: Literary Rhetoric in the Renaissance*. New Haven: Yale UP, 1976. Print.

McLuhan, Marshall. *The Classical Trivium: The Place of Thomas Nashe in the Learning of His Time*. Corte Madera, CA: Gingko, 2006. Print.

———. *The Gutenberg Galaxy: The Making of Typographic Man*. Toronto: U of Toronto P, 1962. Print.

———. *The Mechanical Bride: Folklore of Industrial Man*. London: Routledge and Kegan Paul, 1967. Print.

———. *The Medium and the Light: Reflections on Religion*. Ed. Eric McLuhan and Jacek Szklarek. Eugene, OR: Wipf and Stock, 1999. Print.

———. *Understanding Media: The Extensions of Man*. New York: McGraw-Hill, 1964. Print.

McLuhan, Marshall, and Harley Parker. *Counterblast*. New York: Harcourt, Brace and World, 1969. Print.

Medhurst, Martin J. "Filled with the Spirit: Rhetorical Invention and the Pentecostal Tradition." *Religious and Theological*

Traditions as Sources of Rhetorical Invention. Ed. Medhurst. Spec. issue of *Rhetoric and Public Affairs* 7.4 (2004): 555–72. Print.

———. "Introduction: Religious and Theological Traditions as Sources of Rhetorical Invention." *Religious and Theological Traditions as Sources of Rhetorical Invention.* Ed. Medhurst. Spec. issue of *Rhetoric and Public Affairs* 7.4 (2004): 445–48. Print.

Park, David W., and Jefferson Pooley. *The History of Media and Communication Research: Contested Memories.* New York: Peter Lang, 2008. Print.

Petroski, Henry. *The Book on the Bookshelf.* New York: Vintage, 2000. Print.

Rogers, Everett M. *A History of Communication Study: A Biographical Approach.* New York: Free, 1997. Print.

Stearn, Gerald, ed. *McLuhan: Hot and Cool, a Critical Symposium.* New York: Dial, 1967. Print.

Taylor, Charles. *A Secular Age.* Cambridge, MA: Belknap, Harvard UP, 2007. Print.

LEGACY / MEMORY / IMAGINATION

CONDUCTING THE INTERVIEWS:
LEGACY / MEMORY / IMAGINATION

Jaqueline McLeod Rogers

T he following interviews have different textures in keeping with the varying circumstances under which I conducted them. I spent several hours interviewing Michael McLuhan in person and collected pages of transcript. In the interview that follows, I have tried to distill the most interesting insights that emerged from that conversation as well as comments with resonance in the other interviews. My interview with Eric McLuhan was much briefer though still conducted in person. When I wrote up our conversation, I was struck by how his responses differed from Michael's to the same questions. It was not so much that Marshall McLuhan's sons presented conflicting facts about their father but that each was interested in and knowledgeable about different aspects of his life and so told different stories.

I interviewed Douglas Coupland in a seventy-five-minute phone conversation. What most intrigued me was that he described empathy and respect as governing his biographical project despite what I have come to see in retrospect as my attempts to draw him into defining a sort of "new biography" built like new journalism on subjectivity and interpretation. Coupland was less inclined to worry about the limits of knowing than about the biographer's need to work within self-imposed limits. The challenge that he spoke of was attempting to tell about another's life without rummaging into things that should be left, settled, in the past.

Perhaps it is not surprising that this triad of voices illustrates that knowing is positional and interpretive—shaded by standpoint, sensitive to both place and time. The wording of the title to this introduction to the interviews attempts to capture the distinct thematic core of each: Michael was concerned with "legacy," Eric with "memory" (remembering and extending the concepts), and Coupland with "imagination," particularly with the responsibilities of imaginative knowing. Although each was connected to the figure of McLuhan in different ways, no one emerged as having special purchase on knowing the man.

More unexpected was the diversity of ethical positions that emerged in relation to issues of representation and disclosure. Although this outcome—this "inability to agree with one another"—might have been predicted by communication ethicists Arnett, Harden Fritz, and Bell, who define our era as challenging "the assumption that there is only one form of reasoning and one understanding of the right and good" (13), it struck me as interesting that the central issue in dispute centred on conflicting conceptions of generic form, specifically on defining good biography and sound biographical practice. For Michael, family members might be said to have known their father best, for they had personal contact with him; a biographer should privilege family knowledge and leave no stone unturned in uncovering the life history of the subject. For Michael, Coupland did not ask enough people enough questions and instead tells "Marshall" through himself in ways that obscure and even damage the subject. For Eric, Coupland made sensible rhetorical decisions, introducing McLuhan to a generation of readers who follow Coupland but who might not have been born when McLuhan lived. For Coupland, writing about McLuhan required empathy and even acts of acceptance; this was no easy impersonation but creative portraiture.

Each of the men interviewed shed light on the life of McLuhan that helps to inform our scholarly reading: Michael was committed to upholding the best parts of the legacy, Eric to continuing to explore and extend his father's ideas, and Coupland to imagining and recreating the life of "Marshall." As David Linton notes in the penultimate chapter of this volume through his exploration of McLuhan and Hefner, we have reached a propitious moment in which "to reassess both his achievements as an individual and the cultural context in which he lived" with the recent centennial of McLuhan's birth. Equally, the interviews are responsive to influential strands of postmodern reading theory that implicate the reader in the production of meaning, amplifying the need to consult "what is known of the author [him- or] herself" (Warhol 39).

WORKS CITED

Arnett, Ronald C., Janie M. Harden Fritz, and Leanne M. Bell. *Communications Ethics Literacy: Dialogue and Difference.* Los Angeles: Sage, 2009. Print.

Warhol, Robyn. "Authors, Narrators, Narration." *Narrative Theory: Core Concepts and Debates.* Ed. David Herman et al.. Columbus: Ohio State UP, 2012. Print.

MICHAEL McLUHAN:
PROTECTING THE LEGACY

interviewed Michael McLuhan for several hours in the living room of his home north of Toronto, late in the afternoon of 22 February 2012. Marshall McLuhan's youngest son, born in 1952, lives with his wife and two large ginger cats on a large stretch of land close to Georgian Bay, where he works as a photographer and spends considerable time pursuing contract and royalty agreements in his role as executor of the McLuhan estate. (Marshall McLuhan died in 1980; Corinne McLuhan died in 2008.) Michael describes his work as executor as both time consuming and interesting. His father was a prolific writer, and because many of his books were published at least forty years ago, contracts and royalties need to be renegotiated. There is also the job of tracking publication and distribution of McLuhan materials outside Canada, particularly in European countries, where interest in his work is vibrant. Photographs and films also require restoration work, some of which, if put on public display, might reveal aspects of McLuhan's life never before or seldom seen.

When I approached Michael for an interview, my primary goal was to capture a son's memories of his famous father, perhaps of private or personal habits that might affect habits of mind. In this regard, it was interesting to learn from the interview that McLuhan never cut the grass or shovelled snow—and certainly never followed any exercise or fitness program. Photographs capture his muscular physique during his Cambridge University years (McLuhan was a dedicated member of the rowing team), yet once he returned to North America he became more lean and wiry. Michael noted that this changed physical appearance fit McLuhan's desired image of the scholar-professor. Although this supports observations often made about McLuhan's penchant for self-dramatization, Michael provided another way of understanding it as more integrated and embodied by referring several times to the fact that his father loved being an intellectual, pursuing his work and studies with passion, so that "he was who he wanted to be."

In other memories of home, we have McLuhan, every evening after work, reclining on the couch in the living room, drinking a beer, and reading. But he was not solitary, standoffish, or demanding of silence. He would often join family members to watch television programs such as *Have Gun Will Travel* and *Car 54, Where Are You?* He loved *Perry Mason,* especially for starring Canadian actor Raymond Burr. Michael remembered his father directing and monopolizing talk at the dinner table, certainly "never part of the wallpaper," encouraging his children to vie for attention and even for position as favourite. Michael also remembered driving with his father at the wheel as "an absolute horror show," for the elder McLuhan—despite ruminating about the snug relationship between car and driver—never mastered the multitasking that driving implies. According to Michael, "You wouldn't want to drive with him."

When I asked Michael for an interview, he wanted to find a space in which to express strong objections to troublesome academic practices that he perceived as threatening to his father's reputation. He was particularly skeptical about the scholarly distortions and inaccuracies of studies focused, exposé style, on revealing McLuhan's tendency to borrow from others without acknowledging the intellectual debt. Michael pointed out, for example, that, despite the allegation that McLuhan raided the work of Harold Innis without attribution, throughout his career he actively acknowledged the influence of Innis's innovative thinking on his own. Michael also had reservations about recent scholarly speculations supposing that McLuhan and Ted Carpenter parted ways over a dispute about the authorship of *Understanding Media: The Extensions of Man.* Michael countered that it can be otherwise documented that the pair maintained—in letters and in person—a lifelong friendship: Marshall and Corinne last visiting Ted and Addie de Menil at their place on Long Island in September 1980 prior to his death.

Douglas Coupland's recent biography of McLuhan presented another concern for Michael, especially its suggestion that McLuhan's genius and personality can be understood as an expression of autism or disability. In an email to me, Michael expressed interest in talking to me if only to "counter some of the misapprehensions that Coupland has been laying about the McLuhan landscape." I understood his concern, having recently attended a conference session in which a presenter evaluated McLuhan's artistry in relation to autism, referring as she spoke to a slide copied from Coupland's biography that portrays the scale of autism (68–71). What Coupland had offered as speculation—McLuhan's autistic tendencies—was adopted by this scholar as probable fact on which to form further speculation. While it struck me that this scholar should have been more judicious in drawing from and applying source materials, I also began wondering whether Coupland's speculative and imaginative book might be better understood if reclassified as something other than biography, if we commonly understand biography as a genre that provides a factual rendering of a life.

In his *Marshall McLuhan,* Coupland exercises the embodied and ethical empathy that anthropologist Ruth Behar describes in *The Vulnerable Observer: Anthropology that Breaks Your Heart* as a postmodern stance for writing about others that is suitable whenever humans observe other humans. The sort of "tenderminded toughmindedness" that she recommends—by which writers make "the most of their own emotional involvement with their material" (6)—is exactly the sort of relationship that Coupland establishes with his subject "Marshall." There is often little space between self and other/subject. In describing McLuhan's media presence, Coupland remembers his own fast fame with the publication of *Generation X* and notes the "definite parallels between us" (24); later he observes that reading McLuhan family history is like "staring at a genetic and ancestral mirror" (238).

Yet this sense of kinship was not felt by Michael, who resented the traffic and transfer between biographer and subject that he thought resulted in inaccuracies. As it currently stands, Coupland's book is brilliant, yet Michael felt offended by its imaginative licence. Before our interview, he encouraged me to read the authorized biography by W. Terrence Gordon, recommending him as an author who "really got my dad." Detailed and well written, Gordon's book provides what might be described as an intellectual biography, or a biography of ideas, for it concentrates on tracing the growth of McLuhan's thinking. Gordon trades in triangulated facts, not hermeneutical constructions and empathic hunches, and a scholar can turn with some confidence to this source for information. Making a similar turn to Coupland is ill advised, for his biography resonates with the claim that "there are definite parallels between us." Perhaps, if both books did not fall into the single category of "biography," it would be easier to groom our expectations. Coupland's book is better understood alongside other postmodern biographies and ethnographies whose perspectives are more interpretive than objectively voiced and fact driven, written about both self and other.

As I left the interview, Michael thanked me for trying to get at the truth. I was startled, a bit flattered, and then aware of the impossibility of any such undertaking, at least in any absolute terms. Ahead is my somewhat edited recording of what Michael remembered about his father.

Can you describe some of your first (or early) memories of your "dad" and your family home?

I was born in 1952, and we moved to Wells Hill in 1955 [in an area just north of the University of Toronto]—not a "smart" area at the time but vibrant and ethnically mixed. We bought our first television, black-and-white of course, used, from neighbours a few houses down. We all attended Catholic primary schools. I went to public high school. I was the youngest of six, so I think mom and dad had mellowed in some of their expectations about what we [kids] needed to do.

Later, when I was fourteen, we moved to New York and lived in Bronxville when dad taught at Fordham. Here there was more money—even some celebrity neighbours, like Jack Parr, first host of *The Tonight Show*. But I only lasted with them for a short time—I left home for about a year and a half when I was fifteen. Of course, it made my parents frantic. Of course, I was thoughtless, terribly selfish. I was young, and it was the '60s. I wasn't the only one of the kids in the family to leave early—Eric left when he was seventeen in 1959 to join the USAF, Strategic Air Command, in Great Falls, Montana. Eventually, he ended up being a lot like dad, the only one of us six kids who is a practising Catholic. We all moved out to live our own lives at a fairly young age.

Do you remember your dad giving you advice? He expressed particular interest in waking somnambulant youth—in getting in the way of "stop the world, I want to get off" attitudes, to borrow a phrase he used in City as Classroom. *Did some of this sense of mission or purpose rub off in his conversation?*

At dinner, my dad would talk and talk non-stop. It was his habit to pontificate. He was never part of the wallpaper.

Was this oppressive?

Actually, no, he was a hilarious guy. He would tell funny stories and say funny things. It's just who he was. And because we grew up with him that way we never really thought there were other ways to be.

When he wanted to, he had a way of making people believe they were most important to him. He could be very charismatic. I think he had each of my sisters convinced that they were his favourite. Maybe there's something a bit dark or manipulative in that, maybe it was just good, honest parenting. The result was they all felt close to him.

When I was young, we had a family game for a while. We were supposed to look up important quotes and explain why we liked them. But it only lasted a few months. I remember he was irritated with me because he thought I was being lazy by bringing quotes from the same source, Edmund Burke, I think. He wouldn't believe I actually liked this writer.

There have been several readings of your father's references to men in North America falling into the trap of behaving like Dagwood—ineffective, feminized. What do you think he meant by this connection?

I think he was critical of North American male attitudes— maybe more in the States than Canada. But I think it should also be understood as a phase that kind of went along with his being young at the time. Most young men are interested in what it means to be a good man. This was, after all, during World War II.

As I was growing up, I remember him reading and liking some of the comics. He liked *Blondie*. And Al Capp—his *L'il Abner* was smart, even though Capp was a racist. And *Pogo*—maybe that was dad's favourite.

Did he see Canada and America as different social milieus?

He was comfortable in Canada, I think. But I'm pretty sure a big reason he left the States (in 1968) and came back was because he was intrigued by—maybe even passionately hopeful about—Trudeau. He thought Trudeau could change Canada and make things better. I think he could comfortably have been a Liberal, especially during the Trudeau years. I think, if he had been politically active, he would have followed a social activist platform. Maybe I just like to believe this because I am socially inclined.

But I do know that Trudeau was important to him. I think he might have had party affiliation, but his views about abortion probably kept him out. He was very conservative about morality and sexuality—he was straight laced, but many were at the time. I know my mom and dad weren't wealthy people, but when I told them about some people I knew who really needed financial help they listened, and in the end he said, "How much?" I know this kind of charity is out of step with activism and promoting real equality, but it always touched me as an act of generosity and goodness.

A bit later in his life he did become an activist against urban development. He took an interest in the state of the city and struck up a partnership with Jane Jacobs. It resulted in their co-writing a short film against the Spadina Expressway, *The Burning Would*. My dad argued against the proposed expressway [which he called "a cement kimono" in a letter to Premier Bill Davis (quoted in Gordon 469)]. The expressway plans were eventually cancelled, and I think he helped influence the vote against this expansion.

To continue with the issue of politics, some feminists have been uncomfortable with McLuhan. They claim he had a masculine perspective, dismissive of women or at least relegating them to traditional roles. Did you see any of this play out in your family, say in his expectations of what your mother should do or of career paths for your sisters?

His mother [Elsie McLuhan] was a successful career woman, so driven she left the family. Granddad raised the boys. I'm not saying dad liked this. But he was raised with the model of a strong, independent woman. My mom was strong too, although she took on the role of running the house and us kids. My sisters are successful career women.

My dad was friends with and admired many academic women he met: Margaret Mead, Jaqueline Tyrwhitt and Jane

Jacobs, and Sheila Watson. You need to remember that there weren't many women in his milieu as colleagues in the '40s and '50s.[1]

But that said, my dad was a very conservative guy in his views about morality. He might have had an interview published in *Playboy*, but there's no way a magazine like that would be on display in our house. If you remember the '60s, you'd remember that magazines like that weren't kept around the house.

What can you tell me about Harley Parker?

He was an artist, teacher at OCA [Ontario Arts Council], exhibit designer at the ROM [Royal Ontario Museum], and I know my dad worked closely with him for several years. He did wonderful paintings. I particularly remember one called *Children Flying*. He didn't come around our house too much, maybe because he smoked and drank a lot, and probably my mom didn't like that. The short film *Picnic in Space* captures their relationship, showing dad as the boss and Harley as his sidekick. There was a recent article on Harley in *Hunter and Cook* [a now defunct Toronto publication; see Lauder] that was excellent. I think after he ended his affiliation with dad he went on to some other successful work. I always thought he was a really neat guy. He always took time to chat with me.

You have mentioned being irritated by Douglas Coupland's biography, for his self-involvement and his interpretive approach. Can you comment?

Apart from some of the smaller faults, like putting passages of his own creative writing in the biography, I really resent him implying dad was autistic. This was a guy who knew how to communicate—who had an active professional and

---

1   Michael recalled Tyrwhitt as often coming to the McLuhan home and as someone whom his father admired.

teaching life, a media personality, and a busy social life: engaged, humorous, and gregarious. So it's bullshit.

And it's the sort of thing that can hurt family members. I get irritated by the implication that there has to be some sort of aberration for someone to think like dad. It enables one to dismiss his achievements.

Let me read a passage about the difficulty of writing biography that comes at the end of Coupland's book. After I read it, please comment/respond.

Life is cruel. Writing a biography feels cruel. The writer knows when the subject entered the world, what he or she did, and when he or she died. The subject didn't have the same luxury. What may have felt to a biography's subject like a regular patch of life while it was happening turns out to have been a poignant phase of say, lost options, eroding friendships, dwindling brain capacity, unmet goals, irretrievable lost loves. (230)

What do you think?

I think that part is good. I think he can get some good passages off. But I can't get over resenting his portrait of dad.

Your father had a history of strokes, yet it strikes me that some who write about him and his ideas may overlook the reality or effects of suffering and convalescence in his life—how much energy it takes and how it necessarily changes people. Your dad had his first stroke in 1967. Did he prefer not to dwell on his health, or did he worry about impending strokes and take precautions? When did you start to think of him as a vulnerable person, someone who needed to watch his health?

I believe that it is now thought that he had started having mini-strokes in the late '50s. He was misdiagnosed for several conditions. I remember that he had a spinal tap, due to symptoms of his brain tumour. He had an immense distrust of doctors and the medical system. He hated it and what they did to him. He felt that they were worse than medieval torturers. So he definitely had pain. He hated slowing down or appearing vulnerable. I think he felt that barging ahead and ignoring issues of health was the best course. I started to think of him as vulnerable in 1979. He was a dynamo before then.

We all know the "sadder but wiser" adage "If I only knew then what I know now." With this phrase in mind, can you comment on some aspects of your relationship with your dad?

For many years, I regretted not having someone to throw a ball with—no sports—so I was not raised to be athletic. I had four sisters and a much older brother. When he was younger, dad had a real love of rowing and sailing, but a boat turned over in Lake Ontario—I think the story was that Eric fell in—and he quit all that.

More recently, I have been thinking about some of the opportunities to meet famous people that I had with dad. When I was a young teen, I went on a ten-day boat cruise in the Aegean—the Doxiadis cruise [organized by Greek architect Constantine Doxiadis] bringing together important thinkers to pool ideas on improving cities and the environment. Jacky [Jaqueline] Tyrwhitt helped plan and organize it, and I was lucky enough to be at the dinner party when dad was invited, and I was asked to come along too.

The idea was to get a group of intellectuals together to think about the state of city and city development by day. They talked and theorized in the mornings and then at night toured the sights and partied.

For me to have gone along was really the opportunity of a lifetime—there were brilliant academics, many public figures, the sort of people we went on to read in our university courses. Probably most of them are still important today. There was Bucky [Buckminster] Fuller, Arnold Toynbee, and Margaret Mead, for example. Of them all, Toynbee stands out as being my dad's equal in being able to spontaneously and engagingly expound on theory. I remember him standing across from the Acropolis and talking about the Indian caste system, Greek democracy, and the British public school system, tying them all together as an evolutionary continuum—rather mind blowing to a nineteen year old. Don't know if his reputation has held, but he was brilliant in conversation or monologue!

Of course, there were some younger people along for the cruise too, so it was possible to slip away and have a good time. But it was set up to be a meeting of great minds.

What about his iconic appearance in Woody Allen's
Annie Hall—*for you, was your dad the epitome of*
"cool" (in the sense of hip), or was it all a bit much?

The whole *Annie Hall* thing was extraordinary. More people have commented on that singular appearance than on anything else about Marshall to me over the years. The coolest thing for me was meeting John Lennon and Yoko Ono Lennon, who came to the centre. Actually, lots of prominent Canadians came to the centre, but for me that was the coolest. He was in Canada for his "bed-in" and was to be interviewed by dad for CBS. My sister Liz and I spent a fair amount of time with him while they were getting ready. He was extremely generous and passionate about peace.

We've talked about ways of remembering your father
and his ideas that you find unhelpful. What do
you think people should know or remember about
your dad—something that tends to be overlooked?

I have collected and am restoring many family photos, and I think they reveal a lot. One thing that is clear when you look at photos of mom and dad is that they kept up an active social life. You notice they went out to dinners and events a lot and that they put effort into looking the part—in many, they are dressed up and glamorous, for going out in style. My mom often wears evening gowns, and my dad is in formal dinner dress. My point is my dad didn't live like a recluse, not a quiet, contemplative life, but was very sociable and jovial. I don't think this is the sort of life we imagine for an autistic guy who is oversensitive to noise. If you look at these photos, it's pretty clear they looked forward to parties and socializing and had fun. [*What I observe is his mother's "stunning beauty" and his father's handsome appearance. Both conform to what we have learned to call in cultural studies "beauty standards." Gordon furnishes a positive comment on the appearance of McLuhan by noting that a female student "confessed in a footnote that she thought he looked just like the movie actor Frederick March" (71).*]

These pictures tell a different but very real story about my dad. He had a loving relationship and an active social life. Again, I want to emphasize this against some trumped-up picture of him as a stumbling or struggling person with personality problems or mental troubles. These pictures tell the story of a busy, happy, successful guy. As I said earlier, being an academic was entirely what he wanted to be.

WORKS CITED

Behar, Ruth. *The Vulnerable Observer: Anthropology that Breaks Your Heart.* Boston: Beacon, 1996. Print.

Coupland, Douglas. *Marshall McLuhan.* Toronto: Penguin, 2009. Print.

Gordon, W. Terrence. *Marshall McLuhan: Escape into Understanding.* Berkeley: Ginko, 1997. Print.

Lauder, Adam. "Harley Parker: Design for 'A New Ordering.'" *Hunter and Cook* 9 (2011): 52–57. Print.

McLuhan, Marshall, and Jane Jacobs. *The Burning Would.* Reason Association Productions. www.youtube.com/watch?v=GDzkjL-7r5zg. Film.

McLuhan, Marshall, Eric McLuhan, and Kathryn Hutchon. *City as Classroom: Understanding Language and Media.* Toronto: Book Society of Canada, 1977. Print.

McLuhan, Marshall, and Harley Parker. *Picnic in Space.* www.youtube.com/watch?v=2HwmdSSrvfQ. Film.

ERIC McLUHAN:
LIVING THE LEGACY

O
n a muggy May morning in 2012, I took a street-car up Gerrard Street to a house in Toronto's Upper Beaches to meet with Eric McLuhan to discuss his recollections of his father and his continuing engagement with his father's work. I knew that Eric (just turned seventy, as he told me) had recently published three books. According to his description, one of them, *The Human Equation: The Constant in Human Development from Pre-Literacy to Post-Literacy*, is the first instalment of an intended series. Co-written with a mime ("who better to understand the rhythms and actions of the body," Eric noted; see McLuhan and Constantineau), it explores four essential embodied patterns of human behaviour. His example of how the equation works is intriguing. He asked me to name the four main tools that we use to eat—our cutlery options, as it were—and I listed spoon, fork, knife, and chopsticks. "Exactly," he said. "Two to use with the plate and two for the bowl. This is an illustration that extends to all human invention. Innovation always comes in

groups of four." For me, this exchange about the significance of patterns revealed to those who pay attention is emblematic of his engagement with the difficulties and rewards of perception: many of his ideas presented variants of the theme that pattern recognition is the reward for coming to our senses, yet there can be loneliness in knowing what others have yet to grasp.

The other two books undertake a fresh articulation of core elements of Marshall McLuhan's thinking. Eric described the attachment to spatiality of *Media and Formal Cause* in this way:

> Formal cause has been misunderstood since the middle ages; it is environmental cause, not linear causality, and we switched to linear (efficient) cause as a mode of science about a thousand years ago. All our modern media exert their causal powers via the environment, so our established modes of study are helpless to understand them. Needless to say, formal cause is the principle mode of my father's approach to media—which explains why people find him baffling.

Eric described *Theories of Communication* as "co-authored with my father" and "pure rhetoric from top to bottom." In our conversation, he made an emphatic distinction between Aristotelian rhetoric and Ciceronian rhetoric, arguing for the superiority of the latter in understanding the meaning of rhetoric: "Academics start with Aristotelian rhetoric, but Aristotle was all philosopher, interested in truths and proofs, and not really interested in rhetoric at all. All his works, no matter the topic, are written in similar style, making no attempt to employ rhetorical patterns to engage or persuade." Without blinking, he connected the opposing views of these classical scholars to the goals of ad men in modern times: "The marketing men are Ciceronian—they want you to change your mind and be persuaded by their arguments of the superiority of their products. They want to change you from non-buyer to buyer. The agency or PR men are more Aristotelian; they want to change your mind about the company, so that you have a more favourable opinion of it."

Eric currently teaches at the Harris Institute for the Arts, a private school that has a "state-of-the-art recording studio." He teaches what he refers to as a "propadeutics" course, providing a general introduction to and an intellectual background in the theory of sound, drawing some of his central theory from R. Murray Schafer. Despite his conservative and scholarly appearance, I know from having read *City as Classroom: Understanding Language and Media* (a text that Eric co-authored in the 1970s, currently out of print; see McLuhan, McLuhan, and Hutchon) that he is given to innovative pedagogical experimentation. The book, now over thirty years old, anticipated current academic interest in community-engaged learning and local culture. Exercise questions prompt students to denaturalize their walks through the world—to see more clearly, to sense more fully, and to imagine what can be changed. Eric acknowledged the strengths of the book but thought that, beyond promoting change in terms of seeing and thinking, it should also foster critical media literacy to earn republication: "To address today's world, I'd add a section asking students to put the Internet on trial—to do it in an authentic way that could help them learn something about the law as well as about media environment[s] and effects."

Eric was adamant that the role of education is to train perception toward building synesthetic awareness:

> Most of us ignore our potential. I have taken a class of students on a field trip, all of them blindfolded. It was winter time, and when we got into a snowball fight, blindfolds in place, all of the students could still hit me dead on. Do you know why? Without being able to see, they developed 360-degree vision. I mean this quite literally: they could see forward, to the sides, and right around to the back, once they got adjusted to being stripped of regular sightedness. One of the boys was standing on a balcony looking forward, yet when I came into the room behind him he immediately put up his hand and waved hello. He could see me—literally, eyes in the back of his head.

When I ventured that many people would dispute this claim, he agreed wholeheartedly: "They'd say I'm crazy. But the truth is I've seen the heightening of perceptual acuity many times. When you take away a sense, not only do others come on stronger, but the lost sense returns in different form." He was ready for me when I asked why the blind don't say they see:

> The blind don't develop this sort of sight because all their energy is focused on seeing with their eyes. It's worse still for the sight impaired. They cherish what sight they have—are terrified to let it go. I once suggested to a vision-impaired friend that he stop wearing corrective glasses and try to develop 360-degree sight. Of course, he refused. He was terrified by the idea and would never give up what he had and knew. Worst of all is when the blind use a cane. In this case, they depend on a dead stick of wood rather than develop their own senses.

It's hard to imagine anyone as well positioned as Eric to fully comprehend Marshall McLuhan's thinking. I came to the interview equipped with a sheet of prepared questions, many of them aimed at combing through the past and asking about childhood and family memories. But talking to someone so completely versed in McLuhan's worldview and devoted to applying it to contemporary contexts led me to set the script aside. Eric's passionate lucidity made my visit a rich intellectual and human experience, some of which is captured in the following excerpts of our conversation.

What do you remember about the
early years, growing up?

> I don't spend a lot of time thinking far back. You know, I just turned seventy, and I have about ten books that still need to get written and come out. So I am consumed with getting on with work that still needs to be done. Some of it involves extending projects my father started, and some of it [is] my own.

*Would you highlight something in particular
as a formative experience or event?*

I spent four years in [the] U.S. Air Force. Because I had U.S. citizenship (born in St. Louis), I would have been drafted and sent to Vietnam, so I decided to enlist so I could choose the Air Force rather than being thrown into foot patrols as gun fodder. As it was, I spent the time at a desk as a supply clerk, somewhere in Montana. I hated it—it was a really tough four years. I probably saw enough damn stupidity to last a lifetime. I don't think it's entirely a matter of having been in the U.S. military—the Canadian military is likely about the same. Once you are in, you stay till you've done your time. After four years, I was out of there. If I'd stayed, I would have been sent to Vietnam—I saw the orders in the works.

After that, I moved back home, and within a year we wrote *Culture Is Our Business*—we wrote it sitting side by side at the ping-pong table at home. I guess the results were mixed since our approach was like throwing darts at a target—"some hit, and some missed." That's the idea of a probe.

When I did my master's at Stevens Point (University of Wisconsin), I got from that what I consider a rhetoric degree. And I did my PhD on *Finnegans Wake* in Texas (Dallas)—the state my mother came from. And then I worked alongside my father for a fascinating fifteen-year collaboration.

*What about the role of faith in your life and in your
work? Some critics have said your father deliberately
underplayed it in his theorizing because he
recognized the waning popularity of such orthodoxy.*

When you have faith—earned through conversion—it is not a matter of hiding or showing it. It's something you live with, that imbues you with a sense of purpose and identity.

I was a "cradle Catholic," which is actually a hard road to faith. My parents both chose Catholicism and converted, which is the way it needs to be if you are serious about faith.

I was never involved in worship till my late twenties. At that point, I chose the Catholic faith.

Why did you choose to commit to Catholicism?

Let me adapt a hackneyed phrase about the importance of understanding history— not "You can't know where you are till you know where you've been" but "You can't know where you are unless you know where you are going." We humans think we are making progress. But how can we aim for forward movement if we don't know what we are progressing toward? I was a cradle Catholic who chose to reconvert to make a commitment that amounts to declaring yourself willing to grow up and take responsibilities seriously, to say I have an identity and a soul to take seriously, and work to do. Those who won't or don't want to know God simply choose to live for eternity without him. This, I guess, is a state of damnation, to be separated from goodness, from your maker, and thus from true identity and purpose, all by choice. Probably the best book to read on this is Chesterton's *Orthodoxy*—it sounds daunting but is actually a rather slim and entertaining volume.

Could you comment on a trend some refer to as the infantilism of our culture? Certainly, this was a theme your father addressed in The Mechanical Bride.

There is a reluctance to grow up, and growing up is harder now than ever. If you have access to everything, why grow up? It used to be there was division between the worlds of kids and adults. Now that is gone, and we all share entertainment and access to information about anything. Nothing is taboo. As a dad, I tried to enforce extended reading time and limited television watching time, with success I think. You see, reading is hard; watching television, easy. It takes work and time to read, while any two year old can watch television images. As a medium, television is not even amenable to text. Early broadcasting used to try to combine pictures with text, but it was soon recognized that images dominate, and text more or less disappeared from the screen. It is not content that is different but how the two arrange the senses and organize the imagination.

We are offered a choice between what is difficult and what is easy in our culture. Is it any wonder there are so many forty-year-old carcasses with childish minds?

Could you comment on Douglas Coupland's recent biography of your father?

I think it's an interesting book. Doug knows his audience, and when he took on this project he wanted to present my father in a way that would be attractive to his readers. He has built a bridge that connects my father to a new generation of readers.

I know my brother doesn't like the book. But I think Coupland wrote it with a strategy of building readership in mind. As to throwing himself into it—including parts of his book or connecting himself to dad—that's part of his strategy. His readers are interested in him and will go through him to get to my father.

Do any current misunderstandings of your father's work come to mind?

Misreadings abound in Wikipedia. They are wrong about something so basic as providing a gloss of the phrase "the medium is the message," and they refuse correctives. They have some drivel about it meaning the form is more important than the message, which is not the point at all. Instead, my father meant to open up the term "medium"—to convey that the medium is the environment or milieu. At the time when he was writing, this was a breakthrough concept. In his day, if you looked up the word *medium* in the dictionary, first in the list of definitions would be something like "someone who talks to the dead." When he used the word, he had something less usual but specific in mind. It is a pity there is no interest in accuracy, even on the basic level of what a word means.

I have written to Wikipedia to provide clarification several times, but they refuse the revisions. I know other reputable media scholars have written too, and their suggestions have been similarly bypassed. This demonstrates some of the power and dangers of the Internet.

There have been a number of celebrations
to commemorate your father's 100-year
mark. Have you been involved in these?

There have been a number of gatherings, but I have not been overly involved in any. Perhaps what many have forgotten is that the anniversary year extends till this July 2012. In most cases, commemorative activities wrapped up by the end of 2011.

Would you like to see the Coach House at the
University of Toronto (39A Queen's Park) rebuilt
or dedicated to your father's memory?

I am not a sentimental person. I would rather see something new built rather than an effort to cobble the old Coach House together. Even in my dad's time, it was small and run down. To construct a new media centre named for my father would be a significant form of recognition—there are architectural drawings by Allan Berholtz for such a media school.

During his lifetime, did your father feel well regarded
at the University of Toronto? There has been some
reference to his wading through academic jealousies.

They were jealous and found him an embarrassment because of his high profile and some of the controversies he sparked. I once actually overheard a colleague tell him directly that he was not liked by fellow department members and that they resented him for garnering all the attention when others were so much more deserving.

After his stroke, it was more of the same. The university told him they needed the space, once it was clear he wouldn't be able to work or teach. And then they used it to store band instruments.

*What about those who criticize
his difficult personality?*

Every public person is different from the person at home. The words I'd use to describe my father are *gregarious, affable, always comfortable.*

People who see him now in film clips should understand they are seeing a cultivated or dramatic persona. You have mentioned his rather overbearing manner toward Harley Parker in the short film *Picnic in Space.* I don't remember seeing that film, but you need to take into account that he was acting in a film, probably one someone else was making and directing, so he would be conscious of acting for cameras.

*Could you comment on how your father's
illnesses affected his work and thinking?*

When he had the tumour removed in 1968, it was the size of a grapefruit. Following that operation, it was like his senses had just been turned on and up. He had been labouring so long with less than full access to sensory information, so that after the operation the effect was not so much going back to "normal" as a giant amplification. While we sit here talking, we can hear the birds chirping outside the window as background noise. For him, the chirping would be four times louder, as if someone cranked up the volume. He also had new, almost boundless, energy.

Any regrets?

None. We worked together intensively for fifteen years, and it was like being enrolled in an exhilarating course, learning together. What I need now is more time so that I can bring out the ten books that still need to be written up and published.

WORKS CITED

Chesterton, G.K. *Orthodoxy.* London: John Lane, 1909. Print.

McLuhan, Marshall. *Culture Is Our Business.* New York: Ballantine, 1970. Print.

———. *The Mechanical Bride: Folklore of Industrial Man.* New York: Vanguard, 1951. Print.

McLuhan, Eric, and Wayne Constantineau. *The Human Equation: The Constant in Human Development from Pre-Literacy to Post-Literacy.* N.p.: BPS Books, 2011. Print.

McLuhan, Eric, and Marshall McLuhan. *Media and Formal Cause.* N.p.: NeoPoiesis, 2011. Print.

———. *Theories of Communication.* New York: Peter Lang, 2011. Print.

McLuhan, Marshall, Eric McLuhan, and Kathryn Hutchon. *City as Classroom: Understanding Language and Media.* Toronto: Book Society of Canada, 1977. Print.

Schafer, R. Murray. *The Tuning of the World.* New York: Knopf, 1977. Print.

DOUGLAS COUPLAND:
WRITING McLUHAN

n 2009, Douglas Coupland published the biography *Marshall McLuhan* as part of the Extraordinary Canadians series edited by John Ralston Saul, a series of "eighteen biographies of twenty key Canadians ... centred on the meaning of each of their lives" (viii). According to Ralston Saul, an interesting link among these Canadian figures is that they were young—"at the cutting edge of their day while still in their twenties, thirties, and forties"—when they exercised power that shaped national culture and imagination, "[a]ll of them except one" (viii). Checking biographical data reveals that the exceptional figure is Marshall McLuhan, born in 1911 and waiting for widespread fame until 1962. That year publication of *The Gutenberg Galaxy: The Making of Typographic Man* rocketed him to fame and captured international attention. It is this book, Coupland believes, that contains the DNA of all of McLuhan's work, his "breakthrough." McLuhan was fifty-one years old.

At the time of our interview on 26 June 2012, Coupland was fifty years old, and he was keenly aware that his own encounter with fame differed from McLuhan's because of the age at which each "entered the machine." Coupland became a household name at age thirty with the publication of *Generation X* in 1991. He mentioned writing the biography of McLuhan "coming out of my forties, actually a hideous stretch of time for me. His ship didn't come in until he was just past my age. It makes a difference." As Coupland explained it, the difference is fascinating: "I don't think he reflected on the wonder of his accomplishments or the brevity of fame with any self-conscious reckoning, along the lines of 'I'm going to remember this my whole life.' His fame came late, and I think he was oblivious to its oscillations. Being oblivious, I don't think he knew his moment was over." When I commented that this might have made his later life easier, Coupland mused without agreeing. Then he referred to another element of McLuhan's life, his Catholicism, which set McLuhan apart from Coupland: "Well, maybe time wasn't so big for him. After all, he had his daily 'convo' with eternity, so maybe his whole conception was different."

Coupland did not deny that there was something of an odd couple pairing of biographer and subject. He did not seek out the project but described it as "thrust upon me. And once I was into it, I began recognizing with horror his unknowability." My sense is that, for Coupland, McLuhan proved to be difficult to know on several levels. Not only did the density of his ideas make them difficult to translate to readers, but also troubles arose from the tracing of his personality. He was, in a word, *bombastic.* "But," Coupland added, in his relatively soft-spoken voice, and with characteristic layered reflection, "I've known people close to me like this—and when you know what to expect that's not so bad."

Perhaps the most difficult was that McLuhan is on record expressing homophobic, anti-feminist, and racist comments and displayed some "pretty offensive behaviour." I quoted Coupland to Coupland, telling him how I had ruminated over a footnote in the biography in which he wrestles with a sense of compassion and frustration at finding McLuhan "a more than orthodox child of his era" (104). In footnote 13—stretching across the bottom sections of two pages of the biography—he asks readers to remember that McLuhan lived in an era with different social norms. He examines how swiftly times change by describing his reaction to watching

Ingrid Bergman and Cary Grant in a scene from the 1946 movie *Notorious*. A police officer catches the pair driving after drinking and lets them off with a warning. Aside from the obvious shift in legal standards, what stands out for Coupland as the cultural moment most at odds with our times is that the lead characters are *"smoking."* From the recognition that the meanings of social gestures can reverse in half a century, Coupland calls for readers to remember that "any of us are at any given time guilty of countless physical and mental crimes yet to be invented and judged by future generations" (105n13) . With McLuhan's attitudes thus contextualized, however, Coupland scales back his efforts to muster a defence by conceding in the final sentence that "none of this excuses Marshall's behaviour, but yes, it does explain it a bit" (105n13).

Reading the footnote aloud to Coupland only served to emphasize how his apologia trails off at the end, how emphasis falls on the final phrase "a bit." When asked directly how difficult it was to maintain neutrality when presenting the life and accomplishments of a man with reactionary social views, Coupland offered a thoughtful answer: "In many places, I had to exercise tact. I had no urge, no desire, to spit on the grave. There are always enough detractors. Sure, there were parts of him that are unlikable. And he was a guy who had some enemies. My job was to use some tact to make him interesting to readers."

Coupland was aware that, despite exercising tact, his portrait of McLuhan is unlikely to please everyone:

> Memorials in general are strange things. Last fall, I did a memorial for Terry Fox in Vancouver—we cut the ribbon last September. Unfortunately, word was that the family wasn't pleased. The thing with a memorial is that it is never enough for the family. I learned a similar lesson about twenty years ago—when it was popular to write profiles of famous people in magazines. An editor I knew wrote a twelve-page hagiography of an individual—really praised him to the skies. Even this was met by family outcry. It's never enough.

From speaking to Coupland, I learned that he did not find this biography project easy or light work. Going into it, he knew that some people would be offended. Working on it, he was struck by the particular difficulties posed by his assigned subject, who was dense and vague intellectually and voluble, sometimes offensive, and often unknowable personally. Coupland spoke openly about his sense of struggle with the project, followed by his sense of surprise at its prominence: "I approached it with some wariness, even a bit of insecurity. To get started, it helped to remind myself that the book was to be part of a series celebrating Canadians, which implied national rather than international readership. In the end, the book turned out to have legs—I hadn't predicted it would be quite popular in Europe."

What I learned about Coupland is that he is a person who is deeply reflective and empathic and, ironically given his role as biographer, deeply respectful of privacy—the sort of dream biographer whom you would hope for if your life earned being retold. He frequently cited the limits of biography to reach through time to bring someone to life, noting that representing McLuhan posed particular obstacles, not only because his accomplishments were complexly intellectual, but also because elements of his personal life remain undocumented. Rather than digging for dirt or pigeonholing McLuhan into supposed positions, Coupland favoured the approach of using tact, exercising empathy to explore intersecting and parallel lines in their lives, and leaving alone the gaps that McLuhan appeared to have left open. Even though we live in a "global village" barraged by flows of intimate information about others, and even though the techno-savvy Coupland has been tagged "the natural child of McLuhanism" by Ralston Saul (xii), his innate belief in the need to honour personal boundaries and privacy provides a measure of reassurance that we have not abandoned human for posthuman values. I liked Coupland immensely for saying that "There were things about Marshall McLuhan that he himself never talked about. These things were not my business."

The following represents some of our conversation about McLuhan and Coupland's experience of writing his biography.

*Eric McLuhan has commented that he understands
your purpose was to appeal to a younger generation
of readers who likely have not read much McLuhan,
so you had to engage their interest "to get them to him
through you." How would you describe your purpose?*

For many, the name Marshall McLuhan is recognizable, but that's about it. So one of my first interests was to move beyond the name, to provide at least an outline of his ideas and work. It's not easy work to access, let alone translate to readers. When I read *The Gutenberg Galaxy,* it often felt like swimming in molasses—borderline opaque. By reading and in some places rereading *Gutenberg,* I was rewarded by seeing it as DNA for everything McLuhan did later—a template of sorts. But the challenge for me as biographer was how to make it appealing without reducing it too much. It would have been easier to write the life of Henry Ford or of a mountaineer. There would be a clearer line of action to work with.

Regarding the private life and man, I found he was in many areas "unknowable." Of course, this is true of all of us in some respect. When I couldn't understand him, I found myself scouring my own cranium for a comparative response. I suppose this is in line with the postmodern claim that we interpret others through a lens of subjectivity. But in this case I had no choice other than to think through myself, because of his "unknowability."

*One reviewer refers to your approach to writing
biography as "pathography"—which he defines
as "a form of biography that filters the life of the
subject through the sieve of his or her medical
history" (Linton 172). Could you respond to this?*

Let me respond in two ways. First, about reviews in general, I never read them—haven't read a review for twenty-two years. I think it's a form of vampirism, but like drinking your own blood. So, no, I don't know that review.

About the general idea of biography involving pathography, I'd agree. From Prozac onwards, we've changed the nature of life and mind. Any biographer in our generation needs to be a bit of an armchair physician, because we live in such a medicalized culture. I suppose people have always thought about the connections between feeling and thinking. Back in the day, they would have been referred to as "rheum" and "vapours," what we would now diagnose as some particular form of depression. But at this stage, we are immersed in a culture that depends on science and technology to alter feelings.

To see if it was possible to understand more about McLuhan from a medical, gene-based angle, I asked Eric for a swab of his DNA, and he generously cooperated. I wanted to take it to a lab for analysis to see what they might find or confirm. All I found was that for $199 the lab gave out very general information. For another $299, they offered to provide more detail but still pretty much in the realm of common knowledge or sense. So I guess what I found from pursuing this is that DNA testing is far from being consumer ready or friendly and is maybe even a bit of a scam.

How much did you know about Marshall
McLuhan before you wrote the biography?

Actually, not that much. He was not a figure we studied in art school, which is the area I trained in. In the biography, I talk about establishing an interest in him when I was working for Frank Stronach's magazine *Dista*, looking for interesting images to fax [see 207–09]. I travelled up north of Toronto to the gravesite by subway and bus. It was like a Siberian landscape, and once I got my bearings I had to scratch away the snow from the flat gravestone to make a rubbing of it. It was charming to find that the inscription used computer font. I think you can Google the image, at a site actually called Find a Grave.

What story about him surprises or interests you most?

Most people now don't realize the meteoric nature of his fame. He was on the cover of *Time* magazine. How many of us ever get to that? And he accomplished this celebrity after already having a long career, in his early fifties. By this time, he had already made lots of enemies. After years of being outspoken and really saying all sorts of crazy shit, there he is on the cover of *Time* magazine, unstoppable after being a maverick annoyance for years.

Can you comment on something that was essential to shaping your understanding of McLuhan?

The book that has it all—that has the DNA of everything else he went on to think and write—is *The Gutenberg Galaxy*. He wrote that just after his mother died, and it has so much energy and density, it's as if he realized he had to get serious about making his mark. It was time. By contrast, *The Mechanical Bride* was phlegmatic juvenilia, *en passant*. To read *Gutenberg Galaxy* is like swimming in molasses, with so much of it being borderline opaque. You read it, and then you have to go back and read again. If you haven't read *Gutenberg*, you haven't got a really solid platform for understanding McLuhan, because the rest of the work plays out themes and variations.

Of course, the difficulty of *Gutenberg* explains some of my difficulty as a biographer. How do you reduce someone who thinks like this to several hundred pages? Maybe the real question is how to present someone whose thinking is so fast and dense to readers who are too young to have heard of McLuhan or who are more like our parents' age but never read him.

McLuhan is no action figure but a hard thinker, and my challenge was to make him relevant and interesting to readers who probably know him as nothing more than a name.

WORKS CITED

Coupland, Douglas. *Marshall McLuhan*. Toronto: Penguin, 2009. Print.

Linton, David. Review of *Extraordinary Canadians: Marshall McLuhan, Douglas Coupland*. *Explorations in Media Ecology* 10 (1 & 2): 171-173.

McLuhan, Marshall. *The Gutenberg Galaxy: The Making of Typographic Man*. Toronto: U of Toronto P, 1962. Print.

Ralston Saul, John. Introduction to Coupland.

CONTRIBUTORS

DAVID BEARD has published in the *International Journal of Listening, Archival Science, Philosophy and Rhetoric* (for which he won the Rohrer Award with co-author William Keith), *Southern Journal of Communication,* and *Enculturation.* He also co-edited a special issue of *Enculturation* on the works of Marshall McLuhan. His most recent scholarship appears in *Clockwork Rhetoric* (University of Mississippi Press) and *A Century of Communication Studies: The Unfinished Conversation* (Taylor and Francis).

ELIZABETH BIRMINGHAM is a professor of English at North Dakota State University. Her doctorate is in rhetoric and professional communication, with a thirty-hour specialization in architectural history, theory, and criticism. Her recent published research is on gender in anime and manga, on topics ranging from incest tropes in shojo manga, to the antimodernist rhetoric of Steampunk anime, to feminist ecocriticism and the films of Hayao Miyazaki. She is married to Kevin Brooks, and they have collaborated in raising five children and writing this one article.

DOUG BRENT is a professor in the Department of Communication and Culture at the University of Calgary. His teaching and research interests centre on rhetorical history and theory, writing studies, postsecondary education, and communication history. He has published on these topics in journals such as *EJournal, First Monday,* and *College Composition and Communication.* His current research project is a study of strategies used by senior undergraduate communication studies students when writing from sources. For 2014–15, he is a visiting professor at Old Dominion University in Norfolk, Virginia.

KEVIN BROOKS is a professor of English at North Dakota State University who teaches and conducts research in the media ecology tradition largely initiated by Marshall McLuhan. With David Beard, he co-edited *McLuhan at 100: Picking through the Rag and Bone Shop of a Career,* a special issue of the online journal *Enculturation,* and he has drawn on McLuhan throughout his scholarly career.

KAREN BROWN is a professor at Dominican University (River Forest, IL) in the Graduate School of Library and Information Science and teaches foundations of the profession, collection management, and literacy and learning. Prior to joining Dominican University's faculty in 2000, she developed and coordinated continuing education programs for the Chicago Library System, one of Illinois's former regional library systems. She has also held positions focusing on management, collection development, reference, and instruction at the University of Wisconsin, University of Maryland, Columbia University, and Bard College. She holds a PhD in media ecology from New York University and master's degrees in library science and adult education from the University of Wisconsin.

KATHLEEN BUDDLE is an associate professor of anthropology specializing in media and criminal anthropologies at the University of Manitoba. Her research addresses First Nations media activism in Canada; cultural performance and politics in the production of urban Aboriginal localities; Native street gangs, the cultural production of prairie lawlessness, and the disciplining of the bodies of criminal others; and the authorizing of new social categories by Native women's organizations as they struggle to shift public debates about Native families onto more productive terrain. She has numerous scholarly journal and book chapter publications and has made several documentary films.

MARY PAT FALLON is an assistant professor at Dominican University (River Forest, IL) in the Graduate School of Library and Information Science and teaches reference and online searching, collection management, and literacy and learning. Prior to joining the faculty in 2006, she worked as the assistant director of Dominican University's library. She holds an EdD in higher education from Benedictine University, a master's degree in library and information science from Dominican University, and a master's degree in English from DePaul University.

DAVID CHARLES GORE is an associate professor in the Department of Communication at the University of Minnesota, Duluth, where he teaches courses in the history and theory of rhetoric. His research interests revolve around questions of citizenship, including the rhetoric of political economy as it relates to virtue and the rhetoric of religion as it relates to life in a secular world. His work has been published in *Philosophy and Rhetoric, Dialogue: A Journal of Mormon Thought, White House Studies,* and *KB Journal.*

CATHERINE JENKINS is a PhD candidate in Communication and Culture, a joint program at Ryerson-York Universities in Toronto. Her research explores the impact of medical imaging technologies on patient-physician communication. She teaches at the School of Professional Communication at Ryerson. "Aberrant Decoding: Dementia and the Collision of Television with Reality," was published in *The Intima: A Journal of Narrative Medicine* in 2012, and the book chapter "Life Extension, Immortality, and the Patient Voice" was published in 2014 in *The Power of Death: Perceptions of Death in the Western World* (Berghahn Books).

ADAM LAUDER is a PhD candidate at the University of Toronto. He curated the travelling exhibition *It's Alive! Bertram Brooker and Vitalism,* and he co-curated *Imaging Disaster* with Cassandra Getty. He is the editor of *H& IT ON* and the author of chapters appearing in *The Logic of Nature, The Romance of Space,* and *Byproduct: On the Excess of Embedded Art Practices.* He has contributed features to magazines, including *Border Crossings, C,* and *Canadian Art,* as well as articles to journals such as *Art Documentation, Canadian Journal of Communication, Future Anterior, Technoetic Arts, Journal of Canadian Art History, TOPIA,* and *Visual Resources.*

DAVID LINTON is a professor emeritus of communication arts at Marymount Manhattan College in New York City, where he taught a variety of media and film classes as well as served as department and division chair. His publications have included work on Shakespeare as a media theorist, the history of the Luddite movement, depictions of the reading behaviour of the Virgin Mary, and related topics. His recent scholarly focus has been on the cultural construction of menstruation, a subject that he blogs about frequently on the site re:Cycling, the blog of the Society for Menstrual Cycle Research, of which he is a board member.

JAQUELINE MCLEOD ROGERS is a professor and chair in the Department of Rhetoric, Writing, and Communications at the University of Winnipeg. In the spirit of this collection, much of her research is interdisciplinary and collaborative. She has recently published on Margaret Mead, family rhetorics, transatlantic suffrage cartoons, and local place and writing. She is currently involved in several long-term research projects, one exploring literacy opportunities for women transitioning from prison, another looking at privacy ethics for women blogging, and another at place-based rhetorics.

ALLEN MILLS teaches at the University of Winnipeg and lives two streets over from where Marshall McLuhan lived. He once tried to get a federal plaque on McLuhan's house but discovered that the federal government thought that McLuhan had more to do with Toronto than Winnipeg. His specialization is with the intellectual foundations of Canadian politics. He is currently completing a book on Pierre Trudeau.

JAMES SCOTT is a lifelong academic who divides his time among teaching, writing, and video production. Since 1962, he has been a member of the Saint Louis University Department of English, where he holds the rank of professor and directs the Film Studies Program. He also taught for four years at the University of the Ruhr, in the Federal Republic of Germany, as guest professor and later under the auspices of the Alexander von Humboldt Foundation. For the past three decades, he has been continuously involved in film and television production, scripting and producing more than twenty educational programs. His scholarly interests include film, theatre, fiction, and cultural studies, and he has published recently in *Film and History, Allegorica,* and the *International Journal of Arts in Society.* He is currently at work on a book concerning ethnic themes in the films of Woody Allen, Martin Scorsese, and Spike Lee.

CATHERINE TAYLOR is a professor of education and rhetoric in the Department of Rhetoric, Writing, and Communications at the University of Winnipeg. Her interdisciplinary approach to scholarship, combining critical discourse theory with large-scale empirical studies, reflects her doctoral focus on cultural studies and critical pedagogy. Her work on LGBTQ youth and inclusive education, conducted in partnership with Egale Canada Human Rights Trust, Manitoba Teachers' Society, has appeared in many scholarly books and peer-reviewed journals in a range of disciplines.

YONI VAN DEN EEDE is a postdoctoral fellow of the Research Foundation-Flanders affiliated with the Centre for Ethics and Humanism and the Centre for Media Sociology, both at the Vrije Universiteit Brussel (Free University of Brussels). He conducts research on the philosophy of technology, media theory, and media ecology, with an emphasis on phenomenological, cultural, and existential themes. He is the author of *Amor Technologiae: Marshall McLuhan as Philosopher of Technology* (VUBPRESS).

TRACY WHALEN is an associate professor in the Department of Rhetoric, Writing, and Communications at the University of Winnipeg. Her research interests include the affective dynamics of rhetoric, specifically moments of intensity or theatricality in literary and non-literary texts. Her most recent published work highlights the rhetorical dimensions of charisma, iconicity, and embodied performance in the public sphere. She is currently conducting an ethnographic study that explores the intersections among vernacular gesture, piety, and gender, a project that comes out of a long-standing interest in rhetorical delivery and identification.

INDEX

A

Aboriginal community radio, 116, 121–23

Aboriginal community television, 123–24, 127

Aboriginal films and videos, xxiv, 125; and cultural storytelling, 126

Aboriginal peoples: and mass media, 114, 118, 120, 123–24, 126

Aboriginal People's Television Network, 116, 125

Abstraction-Music painting, 97

acoustic space, 76, 81, 113, 126

Adams, Henry, 25

advertising, 92–98; as multisensory media, 91, 102, 104–5

Aesthetic Orientalism, 28

air transportation: and connectedness, 142

Allen, Woody, xviii, 261

American Registry of Diagnostic Medical Sonographers, 182

American Society of Tropical Medicine and Hygiene journal, 179

Amin, Ash, 135

Anatomy of Absurdity, The, 212

Ang, Ien, 128

Anglican Church, 229

Annie Hall, xviii, 233, 261

Antell, Karen, 157–58

antimodernism, 20–25, 28–29, 33–36, 39. *See also* modernism

Anti-Personnel Landmines Detection Product Development (APOPO), 179

Anton, Corey, xv

Appadurai, Arjun, 118

Aquinas, Thomas, 224; sensory philosophy of, 96

architecture, 73–74, 76; social space of, 70; and urban design, 138

Aristotle's four causes, 235. *See also* rhetoric, Aristotelian

Arnett, Ronald C., 248

Art and Illusion: A Study in the Psychology of Pictorial Representation, 68, 78–79, 81, 83

Arts and Crafts movement, 24, 31

Arts and Letters Club, Toronto, 94

Askew, Kelly, 112

Athenaeum at Goucher College, 164–65

Augé, Marc, 140

Augustine of Hippo, 225, 236–38

automobile: effect on landscape, 140–41, 143, 151

Avatar film, 34, 36–37, 39